Deconstructing Brexit Discourses

This book expands on and complements the burgeoning Brexit literature by placing the UK's vote to leave the EU in its longer historical and discursive contexts.

It examines the embedded Euroscepticism, which has dominated British political discourse on the European project, and the role of the UK within it, for at least the last three decades. Brexit was the consequence of a consistent denigration of the European integration project in the public sphere in which the terrain, and the conceptual vocabulary, of debate were set by a dominant, right-wing Eurosceptic discourse. This framed the EU as inherently heterogeneous and antagonistic to the UK. The book examines how ideas of British exceptionalism, which underpin Eurosceptic discourses, are sustained and reproduced and offers an account of their enduring, affective power amongst the British population. It is in this context that it was possible for pro-Brexit campaigners to assemble and enthuse a new coalition of voters sufficient to deliver a 'leave' majority on 23 June 2016.

This text will be of key interest to scholars and students of British, EU and European politics, the media and press, public opinion, political behaviour and nationalism studies.

Benjamin Hawkins is a Senior Research Associate at the MRC Epidemiology Unit, University of Cambridge, UK.

Critical European Studies

Series Editor: *Yannis A. Stivachtis, Virginia Tech, USA.*
Formerly co-edited with *Hartmut Behr, Newcastle University, UK.*

Lobbyists and Bureaucrats in Brussels
Capitalism's Brokers
Sylvain Laurens

Europeanization as Discursive Practice
Constructing Territoriality in Central Europe and the Western Balkans
Senka Neuman Stanivuković

The Criminalisation of Communism in the European Political Space after the Cold War
Laure Neumayer

Conditionality, EU and Turkey
From Transformation to Retrenchment
Rahime Süleymanoğlu-Kürüm

Perceptions of the European Union's Identity in International Relations
Edited by Anna Skolimowska

European Citizenship and Identity Outside of the European Union
Europe Outside Europe?
Agnieszka Weinar

Historic Power Europe
A Post-Hegelian Interpretation of European Integration
Davide Barile

Deconstructing Brexit Discourses
Embedded Euroscepticism, Fantasy Objects and the United Kingdom's Vote to Leave the European Union
Benjamin Hawkins

For more information about this series please visit: https://www.routledge.com/Critical-European-Studies/book-series/CEU

Deconstructing Brexit Discourses

Embedded Euroscepticism, Fantasy Objects and the United Kingdom's Vote to Leave the European Union

Benjamin Hawkins

LONDON AND NEW YORK

First published 2022
by Routledge
2 Park Square, Milton Park, Abingdon, Oxon OX14 4RN

and by Routledge
605 Third Avenue, New York, NY 10158

Routledge is an imprint of the Taylor & Francis Group, an informa business

© 2022 Benjamin Hawkins

The right of Benjamin Hawkins to be identified as author of this work has been asserted by him in accordance with sections 77 and 78 of the Copyright, Designs and Patents Act 1988.

All rights reserved. No part of this book may be reprinted or reproduced or utilised in any form or by any electronic, mechanical, or other means, now known or hereafter invented, including photocopying and recording, or in any information storage or retrieval system, without permission in writing from the publishers.

Trademark notice: Product or corporate names may be trademarks or registered trademarks, and are used only for identification and explanation without intent to infringe.

British Library Cataloguing-in-Publication Data
A catalogue record for this book is available from the British Library

Library of Congress Cataloging-in-Publication Data
Names: Hawkins, Benjamin, author.
Title: Deconstructing Brexit discourses : embedded Euroscepticism, fantasyobjects and the United Kingdom's vote to leave the European Union/Benjamin Hawkins.
Description: Abingdon, Oxon ; New York, NY : Routledge, 2022. | Includes bibliographical references and index.
Identifiers: LCCN 2021011844 (print) | LCCN 2021011845 (ebook) | ISBN9781138299283 (hardback) | ISBN 9781032070124 (paperback) | ISBN9781315098067 (ebook)
Subjects: LCSH: European Union--Great Britain. | Discourseanalysis--Political aspects--Great Britain. | Exceptionalism--Great Britain. | Political culture--Great Britain--History--21st century. | Great Britain--Foreign relations--European Union countries. | European Union countries--Foreign relations--Great Britain. | Great Britain--Politics and government--2007-Classification: LCC JZ1572. A54 H39 2022 (print) | LCC JZ1572. A54 (ebook)| DDC 341.242/20941--dc23
LC record available at https://lccn.loc.gov/2021011844
LC ebook record available at https://lccn.loc.gov/2021011845

ISBN: 978-1-138-29928-3 (hbk)
ISBN: 978-1-032-07012-4 (pbk)
ISBN: 978-1-315-09806-7 (ebk)

DOI: 10.4324/9781315098067

Typeset in Times New Roman
by MPS Limited, Dehradun

Printed in the United Kingdom
by Henry Ling Limited

For Sandy and all the Europeans we met along the way.

Contents

List of tables xi
Preface xii
Acknowledgements xiv
List of abbreviations xv

1 **Introduction** 1
  Delivering the referendum 5
  A critical logics approach 7
  Terminology and parameters 9
  Overview of the book 10

2 **The research context** 11
  Explaining the referendum result 11
    Turnout 14
    Social class 15
    Long-term factors 16
  The wider research context 18
    Euroscepticism 18
    The media 23
    Euroscepticism and (Anglo-British) national identity 25
    Public opinion 28
    Right-wing populism 30
  Summary 32

3 **Discourse theory, subjectivity and national identity** 34
  Conceptual framework 34
    Equivalence, difference and the limits of discourse 36
    Hegemony 36

Discourse theory, Lacan and the subject 38
  Laclau and Mouffe's conception of the subject 39
Discourse theory and nationalism 43
  The power of nationalist discourses 45
  The construction of political enemies 47
Summary 50

4 Deploying discourse theory   51
  Logics of critical explanation 51
  Media coverage of the EU treaty reform process 56

5 **Embedded Euroscepticism**   61
  The nationalist logic of European politics 62
  EU politics as a zero-sum game 63
    Britain, France and the EU 64
    Britain, Germany and the EU 64
    The Franco-German alliance 65
    The UK's special treatment 65
  Britain's European 'other' 66
    Positioning Britain and 'Europe' 67
    The EU as a colonial power 67
  The EU as economic other 68
  Europe as cultural 'other' 71
  Leaving the European Union 72
  Britain as Europe's saviour 73
  The hegemony of the Eurosceptic discourse 74
  The critical logics of the Eurosceptic discourse 75
Summary 77

6 **Social logics of the *Vote Leave* discourse**   78
  The EU as political 'other' 79
    (Anti-)democracy 80
    Ever closer control 84
    EU as foreign, colonial power 85
  The EU as economic 'other' 86
    The single market 88
    International trade 89
    The Euro as economic catastrophe 91
    The Eurozone as disciplinary control 92
  EU as a source of unlimited migration 94
    Migration and the European economy 95

Freedom of movement and asylum seekers 95
Immigration as a security threat 97
Summary 99

7 **Political logics of the *Vote Leave* discourse** 102
Constructing the remain elite 103
  The national elite 104
  The global financial elite 105
  Big business 106
Constructing the (leave) people 107
  Old-fashioned common sense 108
  Standing up to the remain bullies 108
  Voting 'leave' as a heroic act 110
Immigration as class politics 111
  Interpellating the Lexit vote 113
  Platitudes of reasonableness 116
Summary 119

8 **Fantasmatic logics of the *Vote Leave* discourse** 121
Horrific dimension: 'hard' remain 122
  The Eurozone 125
  Opening the floodgates 126
Beatific dimension: taking back control 129
  Brexit as national renewal 131
The lyin' and the unicorns: all the benefits and none of the costs 135
EU membership as humiliation 136
Summary 140

9 **Nigel Farage and Leave.EU** 142
Social logics 142
Political logics 144
  Ordinary decent people 144
  Of all parties and none 145
  War and legacy for the Brexit veterans 146
  Man of the people 147
    You are not allowed to talk about (anything except) immigration these days 149
Fantasmatic logics: the national is personal 153
Summary 155

10 Conclusions 157
Brexit as a hegemonic project 157
Brexit as populist insurgency 160
The EU as conceptual challenge 161
The EU as fantasy object 165
Contradictions and choices in the referendum and beyond 167
Beyond Brexit 169
Contribution and limitations 173
Summary 174

References 175
Index 186

Tables

4.1	Distribution of Newspapers Analysed in Chapter 5	57
4.2	Number of Articles Collected on the EU Treaty Reform Process and Examined in Chapter 5	58
4.3	Distribution of Newspapers Analysed in Chapters 6–9	58
4.4	Distribution of Newspaper Articles Analysed in Chapters 6–9	59

Preface

The outcome of the United Kingdom (UK)'s referendum on European Union (EU) membership on 23 June 2016 came as a surprise to much of the population, including, it is reported, those at the highest echelons of the UK government and the 'remain' campaign. Having spent much of my educational and professional careers studying the EU, and the rationale for European integration, the result also appeared hard to reconcile with the likely political and economic consequences of Brexit. Yet as someone who grew up in the UK and had observed anecdotally the responses of the British people to it – both internally from London and Edinburgh and externally from different vantage points across Europe – the result confirmed what I had instinctively thought would happen if the British electorate were offered a chance to vote in a simple 'in' or 'out' referendum on the UK's continuing membership of the EU. This was based more on gut feeling than on research or evidence. It reflected the conversations I had with friends, family and acquaintances; the reactions they had to the EU, their sense of what the UK is and where it belongs in the world. For many of those I spoke to, outside a relatively small circle of colleagues and classmates who were, like me, studying European integration itself, the EU was treated at best as an object of curiosity and, at worst, as something sinister and malign. It was always, though, something foreign and distant, which existed 'over there;' something external to the UK, which was not 'ours.'

My intuitions about the result of a referendum that I never expected to be called were based also on the absence of an actively engaged and coherent pro-European voice in the mainstream political arena and the wider public sphere. The latter, until recently at least, was dominated by an almost universally hostile print media, which exercised a significant agenda-setting capacity over other media such as television and radio. Even titles such as *The Guardian* and *The Mirror*, notionally in favour of the UK's membership of the EU, engaged with it in concessive, almost apologetic terms. Their political coverage of the EU occurred on a terrain of understanding, and using a conceptual vocabulary, defined by Eurosceptic voices, where they engaged with the issue at all. That is not to say that there was not a (sizeable) section of the UK population in favour of European integration and the UK's participation in it, which was evidently prepared to vote accordingly in 2016. The point is rather that their pro-Europeanism was often superficial or unconscious. A sense of European identity – alongside or, crucially, as part of British, English, Scottish, Welsh or (Northern) Irish identity – remained latent or concessive for so many in Britain, and certainly failed to impact on the contours of mainstream public discourse. Ironically, it was the result of the 2016 referendum, and the prospect of losing the status and associated rights of EU citizenship, which served as the catalyst for activating a self-conscious and explicitly articulated European identity for many previously passive (or perhaps complacent) Europeans.

During the referendum campaign, in which I was involved in a very minor way, as I read on a daily basis about the bias to the *status quo*, the cautiousness of voters and saw the great and the good of the UK and global economic and political order take their turn to warn about the consequences of a leave vote I began, at times, to question my intuition. In the early part of the campaign, handing out flyers in South-East London, and the conversations that this sometimes led to with passers-by, gave little indication of what the result would be, even if it were possible to read the country from one small, albeit diverse, corner of this global city. As the vote moved closer, though, I sensed people becoming more assertive and more willing to tell me how they planned to vote, sometimes in quite direct, Anglo-Saxon terms. On the day of the referendum itself the torrential rain in London – and the equally hostile responses of commuters stepping off their evening trains – appeared to be a harbinger of what was to come. Later that night, my fears were confirmed as it was announced that the UK had indeed voted to leave the EU.

How though did this come to happen? Why after 43 years of membership did such a sizeable percentage of the UK electorate feel that their country was so different to its neighbours that they wanted to withdraw from the most integrated transnational market and the most successful peace project in human history? This book is the culmination of three decades of personal and intellectual curiosity about precisely this issue. Why is Britain, or at least why do its people see themselves as being, different from its closest neighbours? Cod psychology and popular history point to island geography, centuries of conflict with European neighbours and the experience of Empire to explain this. But the apparent inevitability of Eurosceptic attitudes rang hollow to someone who had always felt British and European identities not only to be compatible but inseparable, and who had been taught to problematise and question the origins of essentialist, totalising narratives. Another version of Britain – one compatible with being a fully European country – could have been possible, and could be in the future. For now, though, the path of the UK to the periphery of Europe and the wider global order, outside the EU, has been set. This book aims to explain how we got here and, perhaps, to identify where the beginning of the route back may lie.

Benjamin Hawkins,
London, 11 January 2021

Acknowledgements

I would like to thank Lynn Dobson for her support in supervising the initial project from which this book ultimately emerged. Many thanks also to Anna Durrance-Bagale for her extremely diligent work in preparing and formatting the final manuscript. And finally, thank you to Sandra Gulyurtlu for allowing me to use our holiday time to work on this project and for bearing with me during the difficult moments of the writing process.

Abbreviations

CJEU	Court of Justice of the European Union
DT	Discourse Theory
EMU	Economic and Monetary Union (the Euro)
EP	European Parliament
EU	European Union
NATO	North Atlantic Treaty Organization
QMV	Qualified Majority Voting
TCA	Trade and Cooperation Agreement
TEU	Treaty on European Union (Maastricht Treaty)
ToL	Treaty of Lisbon
UK	United Kingdom of Great Britain and Northern Ireland
UKIP	United Kingdom Independence Party
USA	United States of America
WTO	World Trade Organization
WW2	World War 2

1 Introduction

The decision by voters in a referendum on 23 June 2016 that the UK should leave the EU – by a margin of 51.8% (17.4m votes) to 48.2% (16.1m votes) on a turnout of 72.2% of the eligible franchise – plunged the UK into its greatest political and economic crisis since the end of the Second World War (WW2). The referendum result was not widely predicted by those in the UK government or even the main campaign groups and sent shockwaves through the political classes in the UK, Europe and beyond. Indeed, internal polling by the official 'remain' campaign, *Britain Stronger in Europe,* and the head of the UK Statistics Authority had predicted up to a ten-point margin of victory on the day of the vote (Evans and Menon, 2017; Shipman, 2016). The result confirmed that, after 43 years, significant sections of the British electorate had still not fully reconciled themselves to the UK's position as an EU member-state. This occurred despite extensive evidence of the Europeanisation of the British state and politics over this period (Bache and Jordan, 2006), albeit in ways which may have escaped the awareness of the average voter (Hawkins, 2012).

The question which has preoccupied scholars since the referendum is why, after over four decades as a member-state, more than half of those who voted – around a third of the UK's adult population – felt their destiny lay outside this shared endeavour with their closest neighbours. As will be discussed in more detail in the following chapter, answers to this question have been sought in a variety of places: the socio-economic profile of leave voters; the immediate political context in which the referendum was called and held – most notably the austerity policies implemented since 2010 – and in terms of the key tropes, events and personalities which dominated the referendum campaign (Clarke et al., 2017). Others have thus sought longer term or comparative explanations of British Euroscepticism and the emergence of populist, nativist radical right parties across Europe and beyond (Vasilopoulou, 2018). To some degree, these were all factors in delivering the outcome of the vote. Yet any analysis of the referendum which does not place voter choices of 23 June 2016 in the wider historical and discursive context of the British 'Europe' debate is incomplete. The Brexit decision relates to questions of political and national identity which have underpinned debates

DOI: 10.4324/9781315098067-1

on European integration and the allegiances which citizens feel toward the EU. However, these political-cultural explanations of the referendum outcome must also be able to account for both the 'stickiness' and the affective force of Eurosceptic narratives which see the destiny of the UK as separate from that of its continental neighbours.

The referendum campaign demonstrated the importance of the media in shaping popular conceptions of the EU in the UK. From a short-term perspective, the official campaign period saw the condensing and consolidation of ideas and arguments about the relationship between Britain and Europe which had slowly percolated in popular discourse over the preceding half century, and with ever greater intensity over the preceding three decades. It also underlined the shift which had occurred in the media landscape, undetected by many at the time of the vote, from traditional print and broadcast media to online and social media platforms. This precipitated a shift away from the authority and journalistic norms of established news brands like the BBC to consumer-populated platforms such as Facebook, on which information of often uncertain provenance could be quickly and widely disseminated, and to which existing regulatory regimes and election financing laws, designed for the analogue age, seemed ill equipped to respond (Ruzza and Pejovic, 2019).

From a longer-term perspective, the parameters of debate in the UK about the EU had been shaped by a hostile (especially print) media environment (Anderson and Weymouth, 1999; Gavin, 2000; Ichijo, 2002; Geddes, 2003; Hawkins, 2012, 2015; Daddow, 2012, 2015; Copeland and Copsey, 2017; Moore and Ramsay, 2017; Koller et al., 2019). Fearful of the potential electoral consequences of alienating titles such as *The Sun* and *The Daily Mail*, pro-European politicians – including those less ideologically convinced who nonetheless understood the strategic and economic importance of the EU to the UK – neglected or failed to make the case for the UK's membership of the EU to the general public. They were unable (and in some cases, unwilling to try) to shift the key terms and underlying assumptions of the 'European' debate which provided the context for both the campaigns to hold, and subsequently to win, a referendum on EU membership.

Drawing on the insights of post-structuralist discourse theory (DT), this book offers an account of the Brexit referendum outcome as the result of a hegemonic discursive project which combined long-standing Eurosceptic tropes of British exceptionalism and separation from 'Europe,' with an expansive political project to associate EU membership with a wider political agenda to form a temporary electoral coalition capable of delivering a majority vote on 23 June. It argues that while short-term explanations for the referendum result are important – and a different result in such a close outcome could certainly have emerged had individuals taken different decisions or events played out in different ways – the leave vote was made possible by a decades-long process of 'softening up' by Eurosceptic voices afforded a disproportionately prominent platform within the UK public sphere, and particularly within the print media. This facilitated the emergence of predominant Eurosceptic discourse and shaped the terrain on which debates about the EU occurred, the terms in which they were couched and the conceptual lens through which they were viewed. As MacShane (2016) has commented, the embedded tropes of a decades-long denigration of the European integration project in the UK simply could not be overturned by even the most effective short campaign before the referendum.

While the outcome of the Brexit vote is not reducible to the discursive context in which the referendum was held, it was a key contextual factor which was a necessary (if not sufficient) condition for the leave vote. The pre-eminence of Eurosceptic discourses – and their centrality to ideas of Britishness and Anglo-British national identity – affected the political landscape in profound ways which led ultimately to the conditions emerging in which the proposition of leaving the EU came onto the political agenda, a referendum on this was held and 'lost.' It provided not just the conceptual vocabulary in which debates on the EU were conducted, but facilitated the emergence of a population of potential leave voters socialised into a particular understanding of the EU and its effects on the UK as seen through the lens of the predominant Eurosceptic discourse.

Opinion poll data consistently showed that EU affairs were a low salience issue for voters behind the economy and public services at least prior to 2015. Brexit was thus not the (inevitable) consequence of an actively engaged and ideologically committed anti-European electorate, but was facilitated instead by the existence of a wider population of 'latent Brexiters.' That is to say, the existence of an apparently large section of the population, particularly of England but also elsewhere in the UK, who may not be consciously engaged with questions of European integration or particularly exercised by the activities of the EU and its impact on their lives but who – when asked the question 'remain or leave?' – could be effectively mobilised to vote for the latter. In the lead up to the referendum itself, the arguments made by the various leave campaigners and campaign groups drew on, and resonated with, what the public already 'knew' – or perhaps more accurately what it had been told – about the EU and its effects on the UK in the preceding decades.

Despite its frequent characterisation as a working-class rebellion or a revolt of the 'left behind,' Brexit is fundamentally an elite political project devised and executed by a small group of ideological Eurosceptics, which consolidated on the fringes of the Conservative Party in the late 1980s and early 1990s. Inspired by the confrontational rhetoric of Margaret Thatcher on the UK's budgetary obligations and an emerging 'social Europe,' this group emerged as a more coherent unit within the parliamentary party and activist ranks through the experiences of the 'Maastricht' era; i.e. the opposition to the ratification of the Treaty on European Union (TEU) by John Major's government in 1992. Their 'defeat' on Maastricht led the rebels to commit to agitate for the UK's exit, a project they pursued with no small degree of success over the next two-and-a-half decades. By the time of the next Conservative majority government in 2015, their anti-EU views had moved from the party fringes to the mainstream, becoming the predominant position of grassroots members, activists and the parliamentary party. For many of these, like Douglas Carswell and the aptly named Mark Reckless – who resigned the Conservative whip and ultimately lost their seats as MPs over the issue of Brexit – opposition to EU membership took on an almost existential quality as the defining issue of their political lives, for which they were prepared to sacrifice their careers.

David Cameron's majority government was elected following a 2015 manifesto commitment to hold an 'in-out' referendum on the UK's membership of the EU. Yet to win the ensuing vote, leave supporters would need to reach out beyond the membership of the Conservative Party and the minority of voters identifying the EU as a high salience issue. With support from key financial interests – particularly those in the hedge fund sector and in many cases with close connections to the Conservative Party establishment – the leave elite were able to assemble a contingent coalition of voters in June 2016 that formed a small but sufficient majority of those voting to deliver their long-held objective. To do this, they had to build on the underlying assumptions and the tacit 'knowledge' of voters about 'Europe' to create an 'equivalence' between EU membership and wider social and political grievances held by potential leave voters. Perhaps most crucially, their task was not just to convince voters of their argument but to motivate them to turn out and vote for it on 23 June.

This book examines the discursive strategies employed by the most prominent leave campaigners during the 2016 referendum campaign, focusing on their intertextuality with both existing Eurosceptic discourses and wider issues of political salience with the potential leave electorate, most obviously the (post-austerity) economy and immigration. It places this in the context of longer-standing Eurosceptic discourses examined through a case study of the media coverage of the most recent EU treaty reform process. Following previous studies of Brexit (Wellings, 2019), and Euroscepticism over the longer term (Hawkins, 2012, 2015), the argument presented here is that explanations for the referendum result are to be found in England. While the aspects of Eurosceptic thought found some appeal in the Celtic nations of the UK – particularly in Wales and among the Unionist population of Northern Ireland – the referendum result was delivered by English voters who make up the overwhelming majority of the UK electorate. Moreover, what is often characterised as British Euroscepticism is, in fact, largely an Anglo-British phenomenon, drawing on an explicitly English conception of Britishness and the associated tropes of identity and nationhood. Opposition to the EU, it is argued, is an effect of emergent English nationalism, albeit one articulated in the terms of Britain and the protection of British sovereignty and statehood (Wellings, 2019). Consequently, the focus of the analysis presented in this volume is on English voices, speaking of Britain for an English audience.

The argument developed below employs key concepts derived from post-structuralist DT through which it is possible to understand and explain the path to Brexit. The critical logics approach set out below analyses not only the structure of Eurosceptic discourses (social logics) – the assumptions they make and the positions they put forward – but also the transient political coalitions which formed the 'leave people' (political logics) and, crucially, the emotive force of the leave offering, which was able to drive turnout (even among previous non-voters) to deliver the referendum result (fantasmatic logics) (Glynos and Howarth, 2007). This 'affective grip' of Eurosceptic ideology over such a significant percentage of the population is key to explaining the referendum outcome.

Delivering the referendum

The decision by former Prime Minister, David Cameron, to hold a referendum on the UK's membership of the EU, and the subsequent vote for 'leave,' represents the culmination of the slowly shifting, and increasingly hostile, terrain on which British debates surrounding the EU have been conducted since at least the negotiation of the TEU, culminating in 1992. The referendum was designed to assuage Eurosceptic backbench MPs and others in the Conservative Party, who had engaged in a decades-long campaign to agitate against the UK's EU membership and to seek a referendum on its departure. Even more moderate conservatives saw their failure to win an outright majority at the 2010 election, and the rising popularity of the United Kingdom Independence Party (UKIP), as a result of Mr Cameron's failure to take a more robust stance on core Conservative policy issues, including the EU. Cameron's decision to hold the referendum can be seen as the most robust in a long line of attempts by UK Prime Ministers to demonstrate their Eurosceptic credentials to what they perceived as a Eurosceptic audience in their political party and the wider country (Daddow and Gaskarth, 2011; Daddow, 2015; Gifford, 2010, 2014, 2016). The emergence of UKIP as a dislocatory force in British politics is indicative of a wider trend in European politics: the increasing popularity of right-wing populist parties critical of the EU (Wodak et al., 2013; Mudde, 2004; Wodak, 2020; Clarke et al., 2017). More specifically, the success of the party at the 2009 elections, and the widespread predictions that they would improve upon this in 2014 – following the failure of Cameron's moderate agenda to deliver a majority at the 2010 UK general elections – meant the Prime Minister was under considerable pressure to shift back onto more traditional Conservative terrain and 'Europe' was a touchstone issue for those in his party putting forward such arguments.

A related factor in the delivery of the referendum was the emergence of Nigel Farage as a formidable political campaigner and perhaps the most effective communicator in British politics. While it was leadership of the initially single-issue UKIP which elevated Farage to national prominence, he has developed a personal profile and individual brand which transcends the political parties he has built around himself. The ascent of UKIP under Farage's leadership in the years preceding the 2014 European elections, and its decline to irrelevance since Farage stepped down as leader for the final time, is testimony to this. Similarly, the achievement of Farage's Brexit Party in winning the 2019 European elections with slightly over 30% of the vote only weeks after it was formed as a vehicle for Farage to contest the elections, reflects his ability to speak to and animate certain sections of the electorate.

During the 2016 referendum, *Leave.EU* provided the institutional platform from which Farage campaigned. The group was formed by Arron Banks in July 2015 (under its original name, *The Know*) with financial support from businessmen Jim Mellon and Richard Tice. Following its relaunch under its new moniker in September 2016, the group received an endorsement from Nigel Farage at the 2015 UKIP party conference. From the very outset tensions emerged between *Vote Leave* and *Leave.EU*, with overtures from Banks that the two groups should merge rebuffed by the *Vote Leave* leadership in late 2015. Both parties sought the designation as the official leave campaign amid rising concerns, articulated by Farage, that the failure of the leave side to speak with a single voice could undermine their side's chances of victory in the coming vote. Following the Electoral Commission's decision for *Vote Leave* in April 2016, *Leave.EU* announced that it would continue to campaign as an independent, unofficial leave group.

The differences between the campaigns were both personal and substantive, with *Vote Leave* drawing on the support of what can be termed the Tory leave establishment – or more colourfully the 'paleosceptics' – the group of MPs such as Bernard Jenkin and Bill Cash and others who trace their opposition to the UK's membership of the EU and the agitation against this back at least to the ratification of the Maastricht treaty. While *Vote Leave* reached out across party lines – with Labour MPs Gisela Stuart and Graham Stringer serving as its chairperson and on its campaign committee, respectively – the majority of the politicians endorsing the campaign were drawn from the Conservative Party. Aside from Farage, the leading figures in *Leave.EU*, such as Banks, were little known to the public and had limited profiles even among those who follow UK politics closely. The idea of *Leave.EU* as interlopers to the political establishment was reflected in their reported exclusion from both the Conservative Party and Trades Union Congress conferences in 2015. Moreover, they were seen by some in *Vote Leave* circles as being outside of the Eurosceptic mainstream as defined by those whose engagement with the issue predated the emergence of UKIP or who sought to frame opposition to EU membership in liberal-internationalist terms.

In terms of substance, the approach of *Vote Leave* to the referendum question, and the content and framing of its messaging, at least at the outset of the campaign differed from those of *Leave.EU. Vote Leave* sought to pitch its campaign to moderate, small 'c' conservative voters. Its aim was to detoxify the idea of leaving the EU, presenting this as a mainstream position, finding support with voters across the political spectrum. *Leave.EU*, meanwhile, was prepared to push the boundaries of mainstream opinion far further, adopting both a more assertive, shriller tone and focusing from the outset on immigration as a key issue of concern to voters. This reflects a strategy designed not to win over the political centre, but to convince those who felt alienated by the mainstream parties, and perhaps by politics in general, that this campaign is somehow different and the outcome could bring about potentially radical change to an unsatisfactory *status quo*. There also appears to be a class and demographic component to this differentiation between the two campaigns' target audiences. While *Vote Leave* attempted to appeal to more affluent, (upper) middle class, working-age voters who traditionally vote Conservative, but may also have voted for New Labour, *Leave.EU* appealed to working class and older voters in lower socio-economic groupings who would have traditionally voted Labour but may, in recent years, have moved toward UKIP or abstained from voting. This is reflected in the outlets in which their interventions tended to appear. While the conservative publication, *The Daily Telegraph,* became the key outlet for *Vote Leave* articles, especially via its columnist Boris Johnson, Farage's articles were placed most frequently in the mid-range *Daily Express* (Chapter 4).

The dominance of Farage within *Leave.EU*, as a figure transcending his campaign group, is another point of divergence with *Vote Leave*, and its deployment of multiple senior figures beyond the central Johnson-Gove axis. While *Vote Leave* resembled a classic political party machine (at least one in election mode), underlining its credentials as a mainstream, common-sense position, *Leave.EU*, and Nigel Farage, presented themselves as an insurgent movement fighting against the political establishment. For this reason, the decision was taken to analyse the *Vote Leave* and *Leave. EU* interventions in the referendum campaign separately and, in the case of the latter, to focus solely on the contributions of Farage who, alongside Johnson, was by far the most frequent voice in the print media's referendum coverage.

A critical logics approach

The analysis presented in this volume draws on post-structuralist DT (Laclau and Mouffe, 1985; Howarth, 2000) and the critical logics approach to social and political explanation derived from this (Glynos and Howarth, 2007). Glynos and Howarth (2007) provide those working within the field of post-structuralist DT with a clear conceptual framework for the conduct of systematic empirical research into specific questions of importance to the social sciences. The logics of critical explanation they develop enable discourse theorists to describe, explain and critique the emergence, maintenance and dissolution of structures of meaning, rules and practices in the social world (Glynos and Howarth, 2007). Logics of critical explanation are intended to account not only for the specific characteristics of a given social order (its established norms and institutions) but also for the political practices through which it emerged, is maintained and can (potentially) be dissolved and replaced by an alternative regime of practices.

The process of explanation consists in the mobilisation of three separate yet interrelated logics – social logics, political logics and fantasmatic logics – which build on and supplement the conceptual architecture developed by Laclau and Mouffe (1985). Social logics are concerned with the rules of formation of a specific social structure or discursive formation and allow us to describe its internal architecture. Laclau (2000: 76) refers to social logics as a 'grammar' or 'cluster of rules' which govern the emergence of identities within an order of discourse. It is, therefore, useful to think of social logics as 'the rules of the game,' which exist within any sedimented social structure and dictate the relationship between specific identity positions within it. If social logics refer to the internal structure of a discursive formation, political logics refer to the practices involved in the 'constitution, contestation and sedimentation' of a particular discursive formation or political movement (Glynos and Howarth, 2007: 142). The logics of equivalence and difference describe the processes of association and differentiation through which political contestation and coalition formation take place (Laclau and Mouffe, 1985; Laclau, 2005).

In order to fully explain any given issue, consideration must be given to the fantasmatic support structures which underlie existing social structures or the emerging discursive projects which challenge the *status quo* (Glynos and Howarth, 2007). Fantasmatic logics explain why a particular, hegemonic articulation of the social is able to maintain its 'grip' over the subjects (Glynos and Howarth, 2007: 145). They explain the ability (or inability) of a particular discursive formation to attain pre-eminence, or to resist change, by successfully *interpellating* subjects within that discourse and maintaining its hold on their loyalty (Glynos and Howarth, 2007). They identify two principal forms of narrative in which the ideological and affective functions of fantasy are played out, which they term the 'beatific' and the 'horrific' dimensions of fantasy. The former is structured around the idea of 'a fullness-to-come' once a specific obstacle to this fullness is overcome; the latter, meanwhile, tells of the impending disaster which will prevail if the obstacle in question is not surmounted (Glynos and Howarth, 2007: 147). While the specific beatific and horrific aspects of fantasy may take various forms in different contexts, they are often associated with images of 'omnipotence or of total control' in the case of beatific narratives or of 'impotence and victimhood' in the case of horrific narratives (Glynos and Howarth, 2007: 147). As will be argued later, the Eurosceptic discourse is characterised by precisely these fantasmatic constructions of the EU and the threat it poses to the UK.

Terminology and parameters

A brief explanatory note is needed on the terminology employed in the current book since certain concepts are used in specific ways which, in some cases, may differ from their more generic, everyday uses. Firstly, the book uses the term 'UK' in preference to Britain. In part, this reflects the fact that it is the UK (versus Britain) which was formally the EU member-state. However, it also reflects the important distinction between Great Britain (excluding Northern Ireland) and the UK within the context of the negotiations on the terms of the UK's withdrawal from the EU and, in particular, the implementation of the Ireland/Northern Ireland protocol. The preference for 'UK' is also an attempt to differentiate the analysis for the discourses on the UK and the EU from the content of those discourses themselves which are almost always cast in terms of (Great) Britain. 'The UK' is used in this analysis as a more neutral term detached from the ideological investment of the term Britain in Eurosceptic and pro-Brexit discourses.

The analysis presented here draws also on the concept of 'Anglo-Britain' which is discussed in greater detail in the following chapter, i.e. a specifically English concept of Britain, used by and for an English audience in which the boundaries between Englishness and Britishness are blurred. This reflects that while the analysis in this book focuses on claims about the 'UK's' position inside the EU, couched in terms of Britain and British interests, this relates to a specifically English question. The term 'EUropean' is used at times to indicate the conflation of the EU with the wider idea of Europe. It is used to refer both to the EU as the political and institutional embodiment of Europe more generally and also the use of 'Europe' to refer to the more specific concept of the EU.

A distinction is made in the book between Eurosceptic and pro-Brexit discourses. The term Eurosceptic discourse is used as a wider umbrella term for the longer-term opposition to the UK's membership of the EU. The term, as it is used here, refers to a specifically right-wing variant of opposition to the EU which emerged historically in the 1980s within the Conservative Party and the traditionally Conservative-supporting sections of the print media. This is examined principally in Chapter 5. The term 'pro-Brexit discourse,' meanwhile, is used to refer to the specific sub-discourse which emerged during the 2016 referendum campaign and is analysed in Chapters 6–9. At times, the analysis differentiates between the *Vote Leave* (Chapters 6–8) and the *Leave.EU* or 'Faragist' (Chapter 9) components of the pro-Brexit discourse which are analysed separately later. While there are strong familial resemblances between these two variations of the pro-Brexit discourse, and they draw on a common set of assumptions about the nature of politics and the EU, they differ in terms of emphasis and tone in ways which are noteworthy for the argument presented here, and which were important in constructing the disparate coalition of 'leave' voters which constituted their eventual majority.

Overview of the book

This book examines the contributions of key political actors in the referendum campaign via an analysis of their interventions in the print media. It identifies the ways in which these actors were able to draw on highly established Eurosceptic tropes and deeply sedimented, 'common-sense' assumptions about the nature of Britain and 'Europe' in constructing their argument for the UK to leave the EU. At the same time, we identify ways in which pro-Brexit discourses (i.e. those evident in the short campaign leading up to the referendum) diverge from established, long-standing Eurosceptic discourses (Hawkins, 2012, 2015). This, it will be argued, was essential to expand the political constituency of the Brexit vote beyond its relatively small core of elites and true believers into a popular movement capable of mobilising support and gaining a majority of votes cast. Through the application of the critical logics approach to examine the discursive context in which the UK's vote to leave the EU occurred, we are able to understand not just the structure and political dynamics of the pro-Brexit and Eurosceptic discourses, but their affective power over large sections of the population.

The following chapter places the current study within the context of the wider research literature on the 2016 referendum and the longer-term analysis of the relationship between the position of the UK within the EU, public opinion on European integration and media coverage of EU affairs, as well as comparative analyses of political Euroscepticism and right-wing populism across the continent. Chapter 3 introduces the key ontological and epistemological assumptions of post-structuralism DT and the conceptual vocabulary which this provides for analysing social and political phenomena such as Brexit. In particular, this focuses on discourse-theoretical accounts of nationalism which facilitate the analysis of Brexit as a nationalist project in Anglo-Britain. Chapter 4 introduces the critical logics approach derived from the broader post-structuralist-discourse-theoretical tradition in greater detail and sets out the research design of the studies from which the empirical analysis in this book emerges. Chapter 5 presents the contours of long-standing Eurosceptic discourses in the UK through an analysis of the media coverage of the EU treaty reform process which culminated in the Treaty of Lisbon (ToL).

Chapters 6–9 focus on the pro-Brexit discourses evident in the build-up to the 2016 referendum through an analysis of interventions by Brexit supporters in the print media. Chapters 6–8 analyse, respectively, the social, political and fantasmatic logics evident in the contributions of the main *Vote Leave* campaigners, while Chapter 9 examines those from Nigel Farage, as the epicentre of the *Leave.EU* campaign. Chapter 10 draws together the key themes and findings of the study and discusses the contribution in light of the existing literature and subsequent developments since the referendum result became known. It offers final reflections on the potential future trajectory of UK–EU relations in light of the Brexit debate and longer-term embeddedness of Euroscepticism in the UK.

2 The research context

This chapter situates the fundamental problem addressed in this volume – the factors underlying and explaining the 'leave' victory in the 2016 referendum on the UK's membership of the EU – and the approach taken to explaining this event within the context of the existing research on this topic. This necessitates engagement with a range of different literatures. The chapter begins by reviewing the 'proximate explanations' for the referendum result which seek to explain voter choices in terms of key demographic and socio-economic factors identifiable among leave voters. However, as was explained in the Introduction, the referendum result needs to be understood in terms of the specific historical and political conditions in which it was held. This requires engagement with the long-term contextual factors creating the conditions of possibility for, and shaping the outcome of, the vote such as the deeply sedimented Euroscepticism evident in the UK's media and the wider political culture. Finally, we place British Euroscepticism within the context of the literature on right-wing populism with which anti-EU sentiments are generally associated across Europe. The chapter concludes by recapitulating the key arguments of the book in the context of these studies.

Explaining the referendum result

The question of why the UK voted to leave the EU, and who voted for Brexit, has already received significant scholarly attention. Perhaps most obviously, the Brexit vote was divided by geography and nationality. While England (53.4%) and Wales (52.5%) voted in favour of leaving the EU, voters in both Scotland (62%) and Northern Ireland (55.8%) firmly rejected this proposition. Within England, there was a clear divide between London and other large metropolitan areas such as Manchester (60.4%), Liverpool (58.2%), Newcastle (50.7%) and Leeds (50.3%), which voted to remain, and Middle England which voted to leave. Aside from London, though, eight of nine English regions had a leave majority. Even in London, the overall remain majority (60%) hid some stark divisions between the 28 boroughs that voted remain and the five (outer) boroughs – Barking and Dagenham

(62.4%), Bexley (63%), Havering (70%), Hillingdon (56.36%) and Sutton (53.68%) – which had strong leave majorities. These results contrast dramatically with the most pro-remain areas of the capital such as Lambeth (79%), Hackney (78%) and Haringey (76%).

In terms of explanations for the vote, a consensus has largely emerged among scholars that age and education levels were closely associated with voting outcomes, with older, less educated voters voting overwhelmingly for leave while younger voters with higher levels of educational attainment voted largely to remain (Curtice, 2016; Goodwin and Heath, 2016a; Goodwin and Heath, 2016b; Harris and Charlton, 2016; Hobolt, 2016; Arnorsson and Zoega, 2016; Manley et al., 2017; Hearne et al., 2019). However, Beecham et al. (2018) find that education level alone, and particularly attainment of a university degree, was the strongest predictor of voting behaviours in the referendum, describing it as a 'global variable' whose effect remains consistent across geographical locations (Beecham et al., 2018). Manley et al. (2017) meanwhile argue that a combination of age and education is key to explaining voter choices in the referendum at local authority level. To some extent these factors are hard to disaggregate since younger people are far more likely to have higher educational qualifications and university degrees than older voters. In contrast to this, Park and Kim (2018) found that skill level (as a proxy for economic insecurity) was more important than age, education, gender or political alignment in explaining leave voting.

Closely linked to the issue of education is that of social class and deprivation. Goodwin and Heath (2016a: 328–9) found that the leave vote tended to be highest 'in communities that tend to be more economically disadvantaged than average, where average levels of education are low and the local population is heavily white' and that these areas 'contrast very sharply with those that gave Remain its strongest support.' Carreras (2019) argues that economically disadvantaged voters' propensity to support Brexit emerged from a sense that they had little to lose from the *status quo* and thus believed that any (economic) changes precipitated by Brexit would likely be for the better. This is supported by Watson (2018) who argues that leave voters constitute a class of 'let down' voters who felt a profound sense of disconnect between the overall (national) economy and their own lived reality and economic circumstances. These 'left behind' voters (Ford and Goodwin, 2014) – older, white, working class, (predominantly) male voters whose skillsets are ill suited to the requirement of a post-industrial, increasingly globalised economy – had previously been identified as forming the basis of UKIP's core support on policy issues (Evans and Mellon, 2016; Goodwin and Milazzo, 2016). Importantly, this analysis had a cultural as well as an economic component. As mainstream political parties shifted toward a new 'liberal' consensus on both economic and socio-cultural issues, voters in these demographic groups felt that their (socially conservative) ideas and values were out of step with the modern world and believed themselves ignored and denigrated by politicians and those whose votes they now courted (Ford and Goodwin, 2014). The focus on identity and conservative, often authoritarian, social attitudes as a key factor driving support for leave among these sub-populations is supported by Kaufmann (2016). Sobolewska and Ford (2020), meanwhile, identify age and educational level as key drivers of leave voting in the context of wider, emerging cleavages in UK politics between these ethno-centric, socially conservatives voters and younger, urban socially liberal which has structured voter choice after 2016 too. In addition, they highlight the sense of distrust and antipathy which has emerged between these groups of voters which is associated with an observable polarisation in British political discourse in recent years.

The economic inequalities and cultural marginalisation felt by these groups began to crystallise in response to the apparent consensus among mainstream political parties on social and economic issues and gave rise to a perception that they had been abandoned by a privileged and out of touch elite (Curtice, 2016; Hobolt, 2016). Iakhnis et al. (2018) suggest however that anti-elitist sentiments only influenced the Brexit vote among those with high nativist (ie anti-immigrant) sentiments. Weaker evidence has been identified that the size of the Brexit vote correlates with the size of the non-white population (Goodwin and Heath, 2016a, 2016b). Hobolt (2016) similarly found that the economic concerns of economically vulnerable populations translated into concerns about immigration, which in turn fuelled support for Brexit.

Unsurprisingly, prior support for UKIP was also found to be one of the strongest predictors of voting leave in the referendum (Goodwin and Heath, 2016a). Clarke et al. (2017a) found that positive perceptions of leading 'leave' campaigners, particularly Boris Johnson and Nigel Farage, were also closely associated with voting leave. Cues from party leaders, such as David Cameron and Jeremy Corbyn, about voting intentions, and to a lesser extent parties, were also factors influencing the electorate (Clarke et al., 2017b). Political parties were particularly influential where they were united on the Brexit issue (Alaimo and Solivetti, 2019) while leadership cues were most impactful among undecided voters and those with mixed views on European integration (Johnston et al., 2020). These studies make the fact that most Labour voters were unclear about the party's position on the referendum, and the very low profile of Labour leader, Jeremy Corbyn, particularly relevant (Hobolt, 2016).

Clarke et al. (2017b) identified that opposition toward immigration was associated with voting leave (see also Hearne et al., 2019; Iakhnis et al., 2018; Hutchings and Sullivan, 2019). This reflects previous studies associating opposition to the EU with hostility to different cultures, minorities and national outgroups (McLaren, 2002; de Vreese and Boomgaarden,

2005; Hobolt et al., 2011). For remain voters, meanwhile it was economic stability and security, as opposed to the openness of the UK's borders to new arrivals that was the key issue (Hobolt, 2016; Evans and Menon, 2017).

In keeping with the 'left behind' thesis (Arnorsson and Zoega, 2016) found that leave support tended to be highest in previously affluent areas such as Lincolnshire and Yorkshire (which both voted 65% leave) which had benefitted from technological advances during the industrial revolution, but had experienced significant decline in the second half of the twentieth century with the shift in manufacturing and heavy industry overseas. Dorling (2016), meanwhile, has argued that austerity, and the economic hardship experienced by the inhabitants of many leave voting areas as a result of these policies since 2010, explains their decision to vote leave. Carl et al. (2018), however, challenge the idea that inequality and fiscal policy were determining factors for leave voters from a comparative perspective, arguing that these are not correlated with opposition to EU membership across member-states.

Turnout

A key issue in the referendum was turnout and the relative willingness of those who (notionally at least) supported the leave and remain sides to actually cast their vote. Goodwin and Heath (2016a) find that turnout was higher in areas which voted overall for leave versus remain (and was highest in those areas that had supported UKIP in the 2014 European elections), suggesting that those opposed to EU membership were perhaps more motivated to turn out and vote or that the leave campaign was more effective in converting latent support for their side into ballots in the box. This finding is supported by Rudolph (2020) who found that among occasional voters there was a greater mobilisation of those leaning toward leave than remain to actually turn out and vote, meaning the higher turnout among low-propensity voters in the referendum favoured the leave camp.

Dorling and Tomlinson (2020) concur that the leave vote was 'got out' more effectively than the remain vote, identifying that it was London and Scotland, the areas which voted most overwhelmingly for remain, which saw the lowest turnout, possibly reflecting the (we now know false) sense among voters there (surrounded by likeminded remainers) that the result was a foregone conclusion, or perhaps a more general complacency among 'life's winners.' The low turnout in London may also reflect the transient and precarious nature of the capital's property markets in which people (particularly the young adults most likely to vote remain) tend to move house more frequently, and so may not be registered to vote. In contrast, the South East region (excluding London) which voted 52% for Brexit had the highest overall turnout.

While turnout for the referendum overall was 72.2%, this hides significant demographic as well as regional variations with turnout among the over 65s (most likely to vote leave) at 90% versus 27% for 18 to 24 year olds (most likely to vote remain) (Becker et al., 2017). However, given the underlying demographics (ie that there are more older than younger voters), and propensity to vote leave by all but the youngest eligible age bracket, it would have taken turnout approaching 100% among the youngest voters to overturn the referendum result (Becker et al., 2017). Consequently, while arguments that young people enabled Brexit to happen by failing to come out and vote for their interests have some validity, this needs to be seen in the context of wider voting patterns (Evans and Menon, 2017).

Social class

Similar caution needs to be exercised with claims that Brexit was driven primarily by working class voters or what some have termed the 'left behind.' As Beecham et al. (2018) argue, given the sheer number of people voting for 'leave' (a majority of those voting!) it is impossible to explain this solely in terms of 'left behind' populations. Instead, a much larger and diverse coalition (in socio-economic terms) made up the leave vote. Carl et al. (2018) question the explanatory power of the left behind thesis for Brexit from a comparative perspective arguing that these populations are found in greater numbers in other member-states that have not seen any sustained moves to leave the EU or public sentiment in favour of this.

Dorling (2016) highlights that while a higher percentage of voters in the 'working class' voted leave than in other socio-economic groups, the majority of leave voters, in absolute terms, were from the 'middle classes,' since the latter represent a larger subsection of the overall electorate. Similarly, the idea that Brexit was delivered primarily by working class voters in the North of England (ie traditional Labour voters in what came to be more widely known as the 'red wall' seats at the 2019 general election) does not stand up to scrutiny. In fact, because of the population distribution and differential rates of turnout a majority of leave voters in absolute numbers lived in the South of England (Dorling, 2016). As Dorling and Tomlinson (2020: 28) summarise:

> because of the different levels of turnout and numbers of registered voters, most people who voted leave – by absolute numbers – lived in Southern England. Furthermore, of all those who voted leave 59% were middle class (often labelled A, B or C1) and only 41% were working class (labelled C2, D or E). The proportion of leave voters who were of the two lowest social classes (D and E) was just 24%.

The same authors argue that constituency level income data demonstrate that, while the highest level of support for remain came from the richest decile of the country, support for leave was highest among deciles 4–7: 'literally "Middle England"' (Dorling and Tomlinson, 2020: 299). Furthermore, when mapped onto the results of the 2017 general election three-quarters of these leave constituencies voted in Conservative MPs. According to Dorling and Tomlinson (2020: 302):

> In short, then, Tory England voted Britain out. These were areas that had often loyally voted Conservative for decades, but economically were not doing anything like as well as other Tory areas which cannot have seemed right to many people living there. Adults in the least deprived tenth of England areas, all but three being overwhelmingly Tory, had almost all voted to remain, but people (especially older people, who are more often Tory voters) in less well-off Conservative constituencies overwhelmingly voted leave. People in much more deprived areas were less likely to vote leave, much less likely to vote Conservative, but also less likely to vote at all in either elections or referenda.

As opposed to actual deprivation, the left behind thesis may instead apply more strongly to the voters' *perceptions* of their (relative) economic circumstances in the context of a highly unequal UK society and the gap which existed between these, what they saw others had and what they felt they deserved. Rather than seeing the leave vote as being made up predominantly of those left behind at the bottom of the social scale or on the margins of society, we must think of it instead as a forgotten middle, discontented with their relative lot. Fortunately for those in power then and now they placed their blame for the *status quo* not at the door of the Conservative governments which they continued to elect, but on the EU and, as will be discussed below, migrants to the UK who were continuously invoked (as opposed to endemic under-investment) as the cause of pressure on jobs, wages and public services.

Long-term factors

Becker et al. (2017) argue that the extent to which fundamental demographic and socio-economic factors (age, education, income and class) eclipse exposure to the EU – ie the effects of EU policies and activities themselves – is striking in explaining voter choice in the 2016 referendum. The exception to this appears to be immigration, with areas experiencing high levels of immigration from the 12 mainly central and Eastern European countries which acceded to the EU in 2004 linked to vote leave share (Becker et al., 2017) and previous support for UKIP (Becker and Fetzer, 2016). This suggests strongly that the Brexit vote cannot be explained simply as a rational calculation by voters of the costs and benefits of EU membership but relates instead to wider political and economic factors. Studies also show that the leave side may have led throughout the campaign (Clarke et al., 2017a; Evans and Menon, 2017), and opinion may not have shifted considerably in the preceding two years (Evans and Prosser, 2016). However, this is not to say the campaign was without consequence. Maintaining the *status quo* against your (numerous and well resourced) opponents' arguments, and preventing any meaningful shift toward remain – as occurred in the 1975 campaign – is itself a creditable result. Moreover, while the short campaign may not have changed minds to its cause in the aggregate, it may have fired bellies by motivating potential leave voters – some of whom had previously been politically disengaged and/or vote abstainers – to turn out and cast their ballots. This suggests that explanations for the leave vote must be sought in longer-term factors, rather than just proximal factors during the referendum campaign itself.

Carl et al. (2018) argue that the population of the UK has been consistently the least supportive of EU membership among member-states, with associated low levels of identification with the EU and high levels of exclusively national identity among British citizens (see also Hooghe and Marks, 2005; Hooghe and Marks, 2009; Hawkins, 2012; Hawkins, 2015). Hobolt (2016), meanwhile, identifies strong national (English) identity as being a key driver of opposition to the EU and thus voting leave. Moreover, this sense of detachment from the EU has been exacerbated by political events in the EU since the early 1990s: the withdrawal of the UK from the exchange rate mechanism in 1992 (black Wednesday); the increasing pace of European political integration; the Eurozone debt crisis; and immigration from Eastern Europe (Carl et al., 2018). Frosini and Gilbert (2020) agree that deepening integration under the Maastricht and Lisbon Treaties, and the apparently associated loss of freedom and independence, allied to increasing levels of immigration, lay behind the Brexit vote.

This is in keeping with previous studies that found that attitudes toward the EU are intimately tied to political identities, with Eurosceptic sentiments closely correlated with exclusively national identities (ie those which eschew any identification with 'Europe') (Hooghe and Marks, 2009; Wellings, 2012; Hawkins, 2012). Political identities, and the fact that so few Britons identified as being 'European' in any form at all, are thus key factors in explaining the 2016 referendum result and the deeply sedimented Euroscepticism which underpins this. This is linked in turn to the wider socio-political context in which these identities are formed and maintained and the form and content of predominant political discourses on the UK and the EU.

***

Several clear themes and trends emerge from the literature on the Brexit referendum. Firstly, it must be pointed out that leave voters were not monolithic and that, by definition, a broad coalition of voters had to be formed to deliver a majority for this side of the campaign. Yet while scholars disagree to an extent about the relative explanatory power of different individual characteristics, clearly identifiable sub-populations of 'archetypal' leave voters seem to emerge. In terms of demographics, older voters (especially men) tended to favour leave while the young favoured remain; from a socio-economic perspective, those with lower levels of education and skills tended to vote leave while those with university degrees favoured remain; those holding socially conservative views and those opposed to immigration (or with a wider scepticism about other cultures) also, unsurprisingly, voted to leave.

While the 'left behind' thesis holds some weight in explaining the Brexit vote, the leave victory was therefore carried as much by (relatively) wealthy (small c and often also big C) voters in 'Middle England' and the South as by the economically and politically marginalised or northern, working class voters. The 'permanence' of the explanatory characteristics of voting intention suggest this is likely to have changed little during the campaign and the emerging research literature seems to support this assumption. Where the campaign may have been crucial, however, is in motivating less politically engaged or less strident potential leave 'supporters' – who may usually abstain – to go out and actually vote, while encouraging lukewarm remain voters to do the opposite.

The wider research context

In addition to the proximate explanations of the Brexit vote, the previous section underlined that it is necessary to look to longer-term factors which may explain the referendum result, most notably the consistently high levels of antipathy toward the EU evident over decades, and to place the analysis of Brexit in the context of the wider research literature on opposition to the EU in the UK and beyond. Furthermore, it supports the analysis above that issues of identity, versus 'rational' economic calculations, are key determinants of attitudes toward the EU and voting behaviour. Four areas of scholarship were thus identified as being of particular relevance to the subject matter of this book. The first is the comparative political science literature on Euroscepticism across the EU at both party and population levels; the second is a more focused set of studies which examine the phenomenon in the UK specifically, often in the context of debates around emerging English or Anglo-British national identity; the third places the Euroscepticism in the context of wider political trends in Europe in recent decades, particularly the emergence and consolidation of right-wing populist movements; the fourth examines the discursive arena in which debates about the EU are conducted and the role of media in framing debates about the EU in the UK and across member-states.

Euroscepticism

While the term Euroscepticism has since its inception had a distinctively British flavour – emerging from British press reporting on European integration in the 1980s (Spiering, 2004) – it has come to be used to capture a more general sense of unease about, and antipathy toward the emergence and consolidation of European-level institutions and policies across its member-states (see Taggart, 1998). Opposition to the European integration process has been a more or less constant feature since its inception (Vasilopoulou, 2018), leading scholars to describe Euroscepticism as a deeply 'embedded' and 'persistent' phenomenon at both the national and European levels (Usherwood and Startin, 2013). Vasilopoulou (2013) has identified three distinct phases of Euroscepticism. The first phase covers the years leading up to and following the creation of the European communities in the 1950s, in which opposition to European integration remained an elite-level phenomenon. The start of the second phase, coinciding with the negotiation and ratification of the TEU in 1992, saw the emergence of the EU as an object of public debate and political contestation. The significant deepening of integration which this entailed and the incursion of the EU into both politically and symbolically important areas of public policy – such as Economic and Monetary Union (EMU) and citizens' rights – marked a shift from permissive consensus to a constraining dissensus on further Europeanisation symbolised by the rejections of the treaty in national referenda (Hooghe, 2007; Hooghe and Marks, 2005; Hooghe and Marks, 2007; Hooghe and Marks, 2009). The third phase emerged in the aftermath of the Eurozone crisis – and the perceived failure of EU institutions to respond to social and economic crises resulting at least partly from its policies – and is characterised by widespread public and political mobilisation against the EU by both political parties and civil society groups.

From a British perspective, it is the second phase – or more precisely the negotiation of the 'Maastricht' treaty – which represents a decisive juncture in the formation of the modern Eurosceptic movement with veteran Conservative MP William Cash and prominent Eurosceptic members of the Prime Minister John Major's cabinet opposing its ratification. The effects of this were not only the emergence of an anti-integrationist parliamentary bloc but the radicalisation of a new generation of Eurosceptic activists such as future Conservative (and later) UKIP MP Mark Reckless and Conservative MEP Daniel Hannan who, following Maastricht, resolved to campaign for and win a referendum on the UK's membership of the EU. It is, therefore, this phase in which the form and character of British Euroscepticism can be traced while the more radical forms of popular, civil society-based opposition to the politics of the Eurozone, which characterised the most recent phase were far less prominent in the UK than in countries such as Greece. More recently Usherwood (2018) has identified a specifically British fourth phase of Euroscepticism in the post-Brexit era in which the key focus will be the different paths open to Eurosceptic groups now their objective of the UK ceding from the Union has been achieved.

The literature on Euroscepticism can be divided into two distinct yet related strands, focusing on Eurosceptic political parties, which is discussed immediately below, and on public opinion, addressed in the following section. The literature on media coverage and the effects on public opinion is treated separately below. The tendency toward greater public scepticism about the EU since the early 1990s, and its associated emergence as a party-political issue, has resulted in increasing electoral success for Eurosceptic parties at both national and European elections. This has been mirrored in the increasing shift of such parties, and the issues they promote, from the periphery (Taggart, 1998) to the mainstream, resulting in their entry into government in multiple EU member-states (Taggart and Szczerbiak, 2013) and their increasingly important presence within the European Parliament (EP). This shift has been most obvious on the (far) right of the political spectrum with Euroscepticism being associated principally (although not exclusively) with right-wing populist parties. Halikiopoulou et al. (2012) have identified nationalism – often associated with the political right – as a common denominator of right- and left-wing Eurosceptic parties.

Beyond their underlying nationalism and a generalised hostility to political organisation at the supra-national level, right-wing Eurosceptic parties differ in terms of the degree and specific focus of their opposition to the EU (see Vasilopoulou, 2018). This has led to the development of a number of attempts to categorise such parties. Taggart and Szczerbiak (2001, 2004) distinguish between 'hard' (opposed to the very principle of European integration) and 'soft' (opposed to the specific manifestation of Europeanisation in its current form) variants, while Flood (2002), Conti (2003), Mudde (2007) and Vasilopoulou (2018) have developed more differentiated typologies. Harmsen and Spiering (2004: 17) argue that different manifestations of Euroscepticism must be understood within the particular national context from which they emerge, including the different 'political traditions and experiences of European integration' which frame debates about the EU.

In keeping with this, a now sizeable literature has emerged on the specific case of British Euroscepticism, manifested both in both government policy (and thus party positions) and public opinion (Baker et al., 1993; Baker et al., 1994; Baker et al., 2002; George, 1998; Diez, 1999; Aspinwall, 2000; Aspinwall, 2004; Forster, 2002; Usherwood, 2002; Gifford, 2006; Gifford, 2010; Gifford, 2014; Gifford, 2016; Hawkins, 2012; Hawkins, 2015; Wellings, 2010; Wellings, 2012; Wellings, 2019; Wellings, 2008; Wellings and Baxendale, 2015; Gifford and Tournier-Sol, 2015), as well as comparative studies acknowledging the key explanatory role of national political cultures in the UK and elsewhere (Diez-Medrano, 2003).

However, there are at least two ways in which a specifically British variant of Euroscepticism differs from its manifestations elsewhere in Europe. The first is that the British version is Eurosceptic not just in the sense of being opposed to the institutionalisation of political decision making at the European level, in either its 'hard' or 'soft' variants, but in a more radical sense. That is to say it is sceptical about whether the UK is European at all.

This differentiates the British right-wing Eurosceptic from populist anti-EU parties and movements elsewhere in Europe, particularly those which define their identity in opposition to extra-European immigration and emphasise European culture and values in opposition to what they perceive as the malign influence of Islam on European society (see (Vasilopoulou, 2018). For example, the German PEGIDA (*Patriotische Europäer gegen die Islamisierung des Abendlands*) movement defines itself by – and takes its name from the acronym describing – its opposition to the Islamification of 'the West,' of which it sees Germany as an integral part. This reflects the fundamental embeddedness of German identities in European identity in a way which would make Ger-exit an existential threat to the EU in a way which Brexit is not. While it is perfectly possible to imagine an EU (and an underlying conception of Europe) to which 'Britain' is peripheral, neither of these make sense without Germany (as well as France and certain other member-states) at its core. The UK, within the predominant Eurosceptic discourse, occupies a position adrift in the North Atlantic, apart from Europe in perfect isolation or yearning to reconnect with its post-imperial 'kith and kin' in the Commonwealth.

The second key feature of British Euroscepticism is the central position which it occupies within the Westminster polity and the wider political culture which surrounds it (Gifford, 2006; Gifford, 2014; Hawkins, 2012; Startin, 2015). While Eurosceptic forces are evident in most EU member-states, these positions have been championed principally by insurgent parties outside the political mainstream and by actors outside the main mass political parties. While, as noted above, Eurosceptic parties have in recent years entered into government in coalition with mainstream, usually centre-right, parties of government (and their brands and ideas may have been 'mainstreamed' as a result of this), they remain junior partners in government and are identifiable outliers on the political spectrum.

In the UK by contrast, Euroscepticism emerged as a political phenomenon within what has been dubbed the 'natural party of government.' The very term Eurosceptic – at least in the British context in which it was first coined – is synonymous with a particularly Conservative form of opposition to the EU. While this may have emerged in the period of deepening European integration from the mid-1980s as a niche position among a certain faction on the right of the parliamentary party, they were able to exercise significant pressure on successive governments and the position of the party in opposition since the time of John Major. What is more, opposition to the EU, and the UK's membership of it, has moved from the periphery over the last two decades to be the mainstream position of Conservative parliamentarians with successive elections seeing the election of an ever more Eurosceptic cohort of MPs in ways which reflect the almost exclusively Europhobic disposition of the party membership (see Gifford, 2014). Party members have consistently chosen party leaders on the basis of their Eurosceptic credentials and, on occasions (eg in the case of William Hague and Iain Duncan Smith), at the expense of their electability.

In part, this reflects the consequences of the Westminster first-past-the-post electoral system which tends toward the emergence of a small number of mass political parties capable of winning power and, in extremis, the development of the two party system (Aspinwall, 2000; Gifford, 2014; Taggart and Szczerbiak, 2001; Taggart and Szczerbiak, 2004; Duverger, 1954). The effect of this is that dominant parties become the key focus of politically ambitious individuals and movements seeking policy change. Whereas in proportional voting systems it makes sense to form political parties and compete for votes, with the potential to enter into power via coalition governments, in majoritarian systems the route to power electorally runs exclusively through the main parties. These must then accommodate a wide range of political opinions internally, with the effect that 'coalition formation' takes place between different factions within parties as opposed to between parties in government. This was evident in the ongoing debates in the Labour Party between 'Blairite' (ie centre-left) and Corbynite (ie radical-left) tendencies within the Labour Party for control of its policy agenda.

The experience of both main UK parties demonstrates how political groups on the extremes of the spectrum may come to dominate the main parties and as a result the government. In the case of the Conservatives, Euroscepticism had emerged as the dominant ideological position of the party and, following their majority at the 2015 General Election, the UK government in a way which would be unthinkable in any other large EU member-state. In more recent times the UK has perhaps fallen into line with its continental neighbours with the emergence of a radical-right populist Eurosceptic party on the margins of the political spectrum in the form of UKIP. Similarly, Euroscepticism has edged into the mainstream in other member-states (Taggart and Szczerbiak, 2013). This should not detract from the extent to which Euroscepticism has established itself firmly as the mainstream position within the most electorally successful political party in the UK, the long-standing nature of this phenomenon and the wider structuring effects this has had on the political system and wider societal debates.

It would be misplaced to see Euroscepticism purely in terms of the internal politics of the Conservative Party, notwithstanding the disruptive influence of the recent UKIP insurgency since the systemic influence of Euroscepticism extends beyond this. As Gifford (2006) argues it should be seen instead as an endemic feature of the British party system which has become a key mode of legitimation for political parties across the spectrum in post-imperial Britain (see also Gifford, 2014). Equivocation and at times even outright hostility toward the EU was evident also under the 'New' Labour administrations of Tony Blair and Gordon Brown. Notwithstanding the pro-European credentials of the former at least it was seen to be a key aspect of party management and appeal to the electorate to continue the approach of previous Conservative governments in positioning the UK in opposition to the institutions of the EU and its other most powerful member-states (Gifford, 2006; Gifford, 2010; Daddow and Gaskarth, 2011; Hawkins, 2012). At other times, governments of both stripes have sought to manage 'Europe' as a political issue by playing down its significance or confining it to the margins of political discourse and, in so doing, precluding the space for the development of alternative conceptualisations of the UK's position within the EU or to challenge the accepted (sceptical) norms of British EU policy (Gifford, 2014).

The media

The mainstream position of Euroscepticism is evident also in the coverage of EU affairs in the British media and the print media in particular (Anderson and Weymouth, 1999; Gavin, 2000; Ichijo, 2002; Carey and Burton, 2004; Geddes, 2003; Hawkins, 2012; Hawkins, 2015; Daddow, 2012; Daddow, 2015; Copeland and Copsey, 2017; Moore and Ramsay, 2017). UK newspapers are dominated by Eurosceptic discourses which set the terms of public debate pertaining to the EU (Hawkins, 2012). The UK newspaper sector is characterised by high levels of competition between a residually large number of daily and Sunday titles, and often sensationalist reporting, facilitated by some of the world's most liberal libel laws (Richardson, 2006). These traits are most notable in its (in)famous 'tabloid' sector (ie *The Sun, The Mirror* and *The Star*; the so-called 'red-tops' because of their shared title livery), but is evident also in 'mid-range' quasi-tabloids (ie *The Mail* and *The Express*). As far as coverage of the EU is concerned, however, the sensationalism and caricatures extend into the more high-brow 'broadsheets', at least on the right of the political spectrum (ie *The Telegraph* and *The Times*).

Having been sacked from *The Times* for falsifying quotes in a story, the current British Prime Minister sought to rehabilitate his career as the Brussels correspondent for the *Telegraph* in which his rather ambiguous relationship with the truth created an entire new genre of political reportage focusing on the apparently unending capacity of 'Brussels bureaucrats' for pointless forms of regulation and intervening in the lives of British citizens. While much hilarity ensued, in certain quarters at least, the apparent desire of a 'foreign entity' to control the mundanities of British life provided the lens through which many came to view the EU in a country with enduringly low levels of knowledge about, or interest in, the EU; a country which Andrew Geddes (2003) dubbed 'the don't know, don't care' capital of the EU. In such a context, media coverage has great power to shape the way in which people view an entity such as the EU, whose relevance to their daily lives may not be immediately obvious in their lived experience in the way in which a missed bin collection may shape perceptions of a local council more readily than a local newspaper.

Within the right-wing media there is a consistent and predominant Eurosceptic discourse evident which frames the way the position of the UK within the EU was viewed by the media and the wider public more generally (Hawkins, 2012; Hawkins, 2015). This discourse is informed by an underlying nationalism which sees the nation as the principal, or perhaps even the only, legitimate political community and thus the nation state as the only legitimate form of political organisation. Not only does this disregard the existence of sub-state (English, Irish, Scottish and Welsh) nationalities within the UK, it can make sense of the EU only as a forum for international bargaining (between the UK, France, Germany and other member-states) or as an emerging 'super-state' in its own right (Hawkins, 2012). The key tropes of this discourse are that there is a radical separation between the UK and the EU in terms of politics, economics and culture which means that the UK is fundamentally incompatible with EU membership. Indeed, the EU functions as the 'other' against which the very idea of Britishness is defined. Crucially, however, it is not a benign 'other' but looms over the UK as a hostile, quasi-imperial power seeking to gain ever greater control over the UK through the political ambition of the European Commission and the expansionist rulings of the Court of Justice of the European Union (CJEU). The EU functions for the benefit of its core member-states (ie France and Germany) and an undefined collection of actors identified metonymically as 'Europe' or 'Brussels.' The UK experiences this as humiliating subjugation in which its interests are explicitly undermined by the collective policy making while it is expected to fund its own demise through its apparently oversized budget contributions (Hawkins, 2015).

The effects of this discourse are not limited to the right-wing newspapers in which it is most clearly and overtly articulated but has wider structuring effects over the entire discursive space (Hawkins, 2012). Even in left-of-centre, formally pro-EU newspapers, pro-European arguments are framed in concessive terms having to position themselves against the default Euroscepticism which frames the debate. Key concepts, assumptions, tropes and motifs which characterise the debate preclude the articulation of a more positive form of pro-Europeanism which positions Britain as an integral part of the EU and the EU as a mechanism for the delivery of mutually beneficial policy and geo-political outcomes. In addition, the 'out-of-sight-out-of-mind' approach taken by UK governments when confronted by apparent schisms between their policy preferences and the views of their key constituents (ie voters), seems also to be followed by certain newspaper editors concerned that a pro-EU stance may alienate their readership. This approach reflects also the findings of studies of the UK media's re-presentation of EU affairs, which demonstrate significantly higher levels of coverage of these issues in right-wing, Eurosceptic titles versus left-wing, at least formally, pro-EU publications with this effect most clearly evident in the tabloid sector (ie *The Sun* versus the *Daily Mirror*) (Hawkins, 2012).

More recently, scholars working in the field of linguistics (for an overview see Koller et al., 2019) have examined the discursive 'drivers' of the Brexit referendum decision and the post-referendum debates on the negotiation of the UK's terms of departure from the EU (Zappettini, 2019; Hansson, 2019; Musolff, 2019), as well as the connections between the two (Lutzky and Kehoe, 2019), placing these in their longer-term discursive-historical context (Buckledee, 2018). These studies focus on both popular (Bouko and Garcia, 2019) and elite (Bennett, 2019; Wenzl, 2019; Demata, 2019) discourses, including those on the EU 'side.' They analyse a range of data sources and media, including traditional media (eg TV, see Bennett, 2019), social media and online fora (Zappavigna, 2019; Kopf, 2019; Bouko and Garcia, 2019) as well as political speeches (Cap, 2019; Demata, 2019). These studies examine both the content and function of different outlets within debates. For example, while Cap (2019) analyses the content of Nigel Farage's speeches in a way that resembles the approach taken in the current volume, Zappavigna (2019) examines how twitter networks sought to amplify and extend the reach of Brexit-related interventions by Michael Gove. Others have analysed the effects which Brexit has had on language and the evolution of a new metaphorical vocabulary (eg of cakes and cakeism) (see Charteris-Black, 2019; Lalić-Krstin and Silaški, 2019; Musolff, 2019).

These studies identify a range of themes examined in the current volume, and in the studies cited above, in the pre-referendum period from a micro-linguistic perspective, for example the construction of in-groups and out-groups through the use of the pronoun 'we' (Wenzl, 2019); the identification of democracy as a key fault line between the UK and the EU (Wenzl, 2019); the contrast between apparently EU and UK values (Bennett, 2019); immigration (Cap, 2019); and 'global Britain' (Zappettini, 2019). In addition, these studies extend beyond the ambitions of the present book by examining the post-referendum period and offering comparative analyses with 'EU' discourses. At the same time, the argument developed here complements these previous studies by offering a detailed, book-length treatment of the pre-referendum debate, from the perspective of critical social and political theory. The focus here is thus on the discursive *politics* of Brexit, with the emphasis on the latter. Through an engagement with post-structuralist DT (Laclau and Mouffe, 1985) and the associated critical logics approach (Glynos and Howarth, 2007), it shifts the emphasis of the study toward the 'politics' end of this discursive-political continuum compared with those cited immediately above. Through the application of the concept of *fantasmatic logics*, discussed in a later chapter, the study seeks to explain the affective power of these discourses as well as their linguistic structure and the socio-political relationships which they seek to constitute.

Euroscepticism and (Anglo-British) national identity

Perhaps most fundamentally, Euroscepticism is at the heart of conceptions about the very meaning of what 'Britain' is. It has been argued elsewhere that Britain is defined in opposition to an idea of Europe which finds its institutional and political manifestation in the EU (Gifford, 2006; Hawkins, 2012; Wellings, 2012; Vines, 2014). As Gifford (2006: 862) comments:

> In a context of imperial decline, the nation has had to be persistently regenerated and there has been a need for an 'other' against which a 'new' Britain can be redefined. [...] Euroscepticism emerged as the guardian of powerful national myths and drew on assumptions about British political identity that appeared to further the process of post-imperial decline.

The question of EU membership in the context of national identity has been brought into sharper relief, and given greater urgency, by internal constitutional developments within the UK over the last two decades. Scottish and Welsh devolution, and the newly assertive forms of national consciousness that have accompanied the devolution of governance arrangements, have made explicit tensions within the UK and ambiguities around national identities which could previously be ignored or elided from debate. Most obviously this relates to questions of English national identity. Perhaps the most striking consequence of the political development described above is the absence of a self-conscious, political English nationalism – at least one framed explicitly in those terms – in response to developments in Cardiff and Edinburgh. As Ben Wellings (2019) has argued, the very nature of the UK as a political project, and the predominance of England within this (in terms of its size and the locus of political power) required the foregrounding of Britishness at the expense of political Englishness in order to forge the UK as a political entity and to guarantee its survival into the present day. At the same time, the focus on Britishness reflects the centrality of empire in the formation of Britain. In the same way that the idea of Britain emerged to elide out the dominance of England (demographically, economically and culturally) within the UK, conferring British identity and forms of citizenship on the subjects of empire served as a way of justifying colonialism and the reproduction of an expansionist concept of Britain as a global political entity whose contours extended beyond just the North-Atlantic archipelago. The denial of Englishness within the British-imperial political project led to the formation of an overwhelmingly English conception of Britishness as the founding ideology of the new state and its dominions. In keeping with this, emergent nationalism in post-imperial, post-devolution England has manifested itself in the form of a newly assertive form of British – or Anglo-British – nationalism, eschewing references to England as a distinct political community (Wellings, 2019).

Moreover, the specific form which this has taken, and the terms in which Anglo-Britishness has been defined, are in keeping with the identification of Britain as a post-imperial society (Wellings, 2002; Wellings, 2012). Firstly, the focus on the British constitutional tradition, defined by crown-in-parliament sovereignty, manifested in the idea that the defence of sovereignty reflects not only the difference between the British (common law) and continental legal systems, but the foundational role of the ideology of British constitutionalism in the formation of the UK. As such, the defence of sovereignty plays an existential role in ideologies of Anglo-British nationalism which extends beyond concerns for national self-determination evident in other Eurosceptic movements. This occurs in the context in which the foundational myths of Anglo-British imaginary are disproportionately focused on the historical experience of conflict with Europe, most obviously in WW2 as 'Britain's finest hour.' English nationalism has thus been articulated most vociferously as call to reassert British sovereignty in the context of the threat of depending European integration.

Secondly, the predominance of England within the UK means that English (Anglo-British) nationalism cannot manifest itself as an independence movement from 'Britain' as have Scottish nationalists. In fact, to the extent that Anglo-British nationalism implies the continuation of the UK as a political entity in the face of challenges from sub-state Celtic nationalisms it must explicitly deny such a possibility. As such, Anglo-Britishness requires a different 'other' against which to define itself and its struggle for national self-determination. The EU has offered itself as a discursive object which facilitates the reproduction of the UK as an internally coherent political entity through its radical heterogeneity from its European other (Hawkins, 2015).

Thirdly, as suggested above the legacy of empire, and the expansionist conception of Britain which this implied, provides an alternative narrative of national destiny for the UK in the same way that EU membership outside the UK functions in discourses of Scottish nationalism. Since its inception, the UK has been an explicitly trans-national project; both through the subsumption of the four 'home' nations in a single constitutional structure and through the pursuance of trans-continental empire which provided a motivation for the 1707 Act of Union though which it came into being. The remnants of empire – present in pro-Brexit discourses through the concept of the 'Anglosphere' – offered itself as an alternative context in which 'Britain' could exist outside the EU. English nationalism, therefore, coalesces around the contention that Anglo-Britain is tied to the wrong trans-national entity; that it can leave Europe and return to its true home among its post-imperial 'kith and kin' drawn together by a common language, legal and constitutional tradition (Wellings, 2019). From this perspective, Euroscepticism functions as the founding ideology of a slowly fermenting English nationalism which precludes its own expression but was a key driving force for the 2016 referendum result.

Public opinion

The literature on public opinion on European integration can be divided into three broad categories which seek to explain voter positions in terms of utilitarian calculations, domestic cues/benchmarks (ie deriving opinions about the EU from proxy issues in national politics) and identity (for an overview see Hobolt and de Vries, 2016). It is the latter which is of most relevance to the argument developed in the current volume. Recent studies argue that anti-EU sentiments are the manifestation of a general hostility toward other cultures and those perceived as outsiders (McLaren, 2002; Azrout et al., 2011). Those who are less open or less positively disposed toward other cultures also oppose European integration. In keeping with this, anti-immigrant attitudes are a powerful predictor of opposition to the EU (McLaren, 2002; de Vreese and Boomgaarden, 2005; de Vreese et al., 2008; Hobolt et al., 2011). These attitudes are found to solidify where there is a perceived threat to the national in-group from such outsiders (McLaren, 2006; McLaren, 2002; Boomgaarden et al., 2011).

Sean Carey (2002) found that those individuals who demonstrated a strong attachment to their nation, and who expressed high levels of national pride, were also likely to oppose integration (Carey, 2002). However, national identity would appear to have different effects on support for the EU in different national contexts. While Christin and Trechsel (2002) found a correlation between attachment to the nation and opposition to EU membership among Swiss citizens, Haesly (2001) found that, in the case of Scottish and Welsh respondents, strong national identities were actually associated with *higher* levels of support for European integrations. This would seem to be reflected in the support for EU integration expressed by both Scottish and Welsh nationalist parties in recent years.

Hooghe and Marks (2005) take the theorisation of the effects of national identity a step further, distinguishing between those who define their identity in purely (exclusive) national terms and those who define themselves as possessing a multi-layered (inclusive) identity consisting of both national and European components. In an evaluation of several competing explanatory models of European integration they found that exclusive national identity was among the most powerful explanatory factors in their analysis (Hooghe and Marks, 2005). Where national elites were divided on the question of Europe, exclusive national identity was found to have an *even greater* negative effect on levels of support than in member-states where there was a general consensus on the European project among elites. Interestingly, however, while there was a clear divide in terms of their level of support for European integration between those possessing exclusive and inclusive identities, there appeared to be no discernible difference in attitudes toward integration between those whose inclusive identity was defined in primarily national or European terms, ie between those who considered themselves French and European versus those who considered themselves to be European and French (Hooghe and Marks, 2005).

These findings would seem to be borne out in the case of the UK, which Eurobarometer surveys have consistently identified as having both one of the lowest levels of support among its citizenry for European integration, and the highest percentage of citizens who define their political identity in purely national terms. Moreover, significant divisions exist both between and within the main British political parties on the question of Europe, perhaps most obviously visible during the referendum campaign when the Conservative cabinet was divided between the '*Vote Leave*' and '*Better Together*' campaigns effectively led by a (then) future and current Prime Minister respectively. While the major political parties support British membership of the EU, they vary greatly in the strength of their support. Meanwhile the Liberal Democrats who between 2010 and 2015 were coalition partners with the largely Eurosceptic Conservative Party have been consistently strong advocates of a maximalist approach to Britain's participation in the European integration project. While the decades-long policy of the Labour Party was to remain in the EU and Labour MPs, like the party's membership and (albeit to a slightly lesser degree) their core electorate, were overwhelmingly pro-European, the equivocal and lukewarm support given to the remain campaign by the leader, Jeremy Corbyn, meant the party's position in the referendum remained unclear even to many voters. The vociferous support for the leave campaign by prominent Labour MPs such as Kate Hoey and Frank Field may also have contributed to the impression of a party divided on the issue of the day, at least in the short-term build up to the 2016 vote.

While the studies set out above offer an insight into the factors which cause antipathy toward the EU, they do not offer an account of how and why citizens, such as those in the UK, come to construct their identities in these narrow, exclusionary terms. To understand such processes it is necessary to examine the impact of social context and broader societal discourses on the formation of national identity. Some scholars have attempted to do just this from a comparative perspective. Diez-Medrano (2003) attempts to explain variations in identity constructions between states in terms of differing national histories, arguing that British, Spanish and German attitudes to the EU must be understood in terms of the specific sociocultural frames through which they are viewed. While for Spaniards and Germans, European integration symbolises emancipation from an inglorious past, for the British EU membership is the institutional embodiment of Britain's loss of status and influence in the world and serves only as a reminder of its decline as a nation. Britain is constructed in terms which are inherently antithetical to the rest of Europe, and the central reference points of British identity are rooted in the twentieth century and its history of European conflict.

While this study makes an important contribution to understanding the sociological factors underpinning identity and thus public opinions, it fails to problematise the predominant historical narratives which it identifies as the key explanation of the national dispositions toward the EU. There is an underlying, essentialist assumption that official national histories are objective facts which necessarily determine the way in which citizens view the interests and mission of their country in the world. In contrast to this objectivist conception, we should instead view official national histories as the result of hegemonic political projects which are contestable and, consequently, must constantly be reproduced in popular culture to ensure their survival. From this perspective, the version of Britain's history which Diez-Medrano puts forward to explain the cultural identity of Britain is thus only one version among many potential and conflicting narratives. As such, his account offers only a partial explanation for British Euroscepticism. To move beyond this, it is necessary to explain the underlying assumptions of this account of British exceptionalism and separation from Europe and how they inform debates about Britain and the EU.

Right-wing populism

The literature on right-wing populism is also of relevance to the study of the Brexit vote and the discourses of Euroscepticism which underpinned it (see Wodak et al., 2013; Bustikova, 2009; Mudde, 2004; Mudde, 2007; Mudde, 2010; Mudde, 2018; Hainsworth, 2008; Bar-On, 2008; Ignazi, 2006; Betz, 1994). In his seminal article, Mudde (2004) defines populism as an approach to politics and society which seeks to divide the latter into two distinct and dichotomous camps: a corrupt and self-interested elite and 'the people' they seek to exploit for their own ends. Right-wing populist discourses are overtly nationalist and are structured around the identification of an 'other' against which the 'nation' is defined (Pelinka, 2013; Wodak, 2013). Consequently, the anti-elitism of populist discourses may have both internal and external components, identify elements within a society (ie governing elites and institutions) as well as external enemies (eg neighbouring countries, international organisations or more amorphous global forces) working against the interests of 'the people' with the two tropes often coexisting (Pelinka, 2013; Wodak, 2013). An entity such as the EU easily lends itself to populists looking to construct foreign enemies with which national political elites are allegedly complicit. More recently, Wodak (2020) has charted the normalisation and mainstreaming in right-wing populist discourses, in part through the promotion of these by charismatic leaders, in ways which reflect the migration of Euroscepticism, associated at times with authoritarian forms of anti-immigrant rhetoric, to the 'reasonable' centre ground of UK politics by the figureheads of the 'leave' campaign.

This literature is of relevance to understanding both the contours of the Brexit referendum campaign and the longer trajectory of Euroscepticism in the UK. Both the internal and external components of populist discourses are relevant in different ways. In the subsequent chapters it will be argued that the inherent nationalism of British Eurosceptic discourses depends on a process of 'othering' the EU in which Britain is defined in opposition to a radically heterogeneous EUropean other (Hawkins, 2012) and Euroscepticism becomes the defining feature of Anglo-British nationalism. Gifford (2006: 883) has argued that the politics of national identity in the UK has led to the 'structural susceptibility of the British post-imperial order to the politics of populism.'

While there is an underlying anti-elitism evident in Eurosceptic discourse analysed in Chapter 5, this is confined largely to the European level. The interim period leading up to the Brexit referendum saw the emergence of a party of the populist radical right in the form of UKIP, which enjoyed increasing electoral success at the European level and in the devolved assembly in Wales (if excluded from Westminster by the first past the post voting system), and high levels of visibility in the media. Partly as a consequence of this – and the centrality of UKIP leader Nigel Farage and his *Leave.EU* vehicle in the referendum campaign – but also as a result of the need for leave campaigners to construct a broader electoral coalition to win the referendum analysed in Chapters 6-9 of the book, the debates preceding 23 June are characterised by a radical populism which seeks to link leaving the EU to a range of issues of greater salience to potential leave voters. This involved a focus on the sociological and economic consequences of immigration, but also a persistent anti-elitism which positioned the interests of the pro-remain establishment (and their friends and allies in the EU and beyond) in stark opposition to those of 'the people.'

It will be noted that the post-structuralist DT of Laclau and Mouffe, which provides the theoretical underpinning for this book, has been deployed to analyse the phenomenon of populism (Laclau, 2005). However, the concept of populism developed in his later work differs from that employed here in important ways. For Laclau, populism is an emancipatory political force associated with the construction of popular-democratic movements under the unifying rubric of 'the people.' This positions populism as a phenomenon of the political left whereby popular uprising becomes synonymous with the struggle for social justice via the construction of a hegemonic equivalential chain in which subaltern class interests become synonymous with those of 'the people.' While the current volume shares Laclau's analysis that the conceptual vocabulary of DT provides an insightful analytical toolkit with which to examine emerging political movements, it is sceptical about the democratic or emancipatory credentials of populist movements. That is not to say that these are impossible ontologically, but that the empirical evidence (at the ontic level) suggests that contemporary populist movements in Europe and elsewhere cleave to the right.

Whereas Laclau sees the emancipatory potential of populism to exist in the possibility of forming solidarity between the interests of the marginalised and the general population (via their shared rejection of an exploitative elite and the political system which serves its interests), contemporary populist movements present the interests of the people as synonymous with those of the ruling elite via the stigmatisation of marginalised and vulnerable groups and the construction of imaged political enemies. This serves as a means of constructing legitimacy for highly inequitable regimes in which the people are exploited alongside the very 'others' they are taught to scapegoat and blame for their circumstances. As such, both perspectives share a common focus on the function of hegemonic discursive practices in the maintenance and dislocation of reactionary political regimes. The focus of the current volume is on the ideological practices which sustained the Brexit movement through the articulation of the interest of a narrow elite. It stops short though of identifying the counter-hegemonic movement which would be able to challenge the entrenching power of the Brexit elite though counter-hegemonic discursive practice and the construction of a pro-European political movement.

Summary

The existing literature suggests that the outcome of the Brexit referendum can only be explained through a combination of long- and short-term factors; and in terms of both proximate concerns directly associated with the EU (eg about sovereignty and national self-determination) and a wider set of issues (most notably immigration), which came to be associated with EU membership through the discursive production of the EU as a political object in the context of the referendum debates. The referendum campaign took place in an overwhelmingly hostile media environment and a political culture shaped by a decades-long diet of negative stories and misinformation about 'Europe' in which a radical heterogeneity was constructed between 'Britain' and the hostile European 'other' against which it was defined. This related also to emerging, and politically conscious, forms of English (or rather Anglo-British) national identity which began to assert itself in the context of both deepening European integration and Celtic devolution. This created the conditions of possibility for the construction of temporary coalitions of interests which could be mobilised on referendum day to achieve a majority leave vote on an issue of previously low salience to most voters.

The key question which emerges is how and why the 'European question' became the vehicle for the mobilisation of far wider socio-economic discontent when the reasons for the economic and political marginalisation felt by voters lie far closer to home in the austerity policies of the UK government; the unresponsive (though widely lionised) Westminster political and voting systems; and the policy offering of mainstream parties whose economic and, perhaps more crucially, social outlook had come to alienate significant sections of the electorate. Moreover, how was this anti-Europeanism as political rebellion able to strike such a chord with voters that they turned out to vote for this leap into the unknown in higher numbers than those opting for the *status quo*, or voting in previous national elections?

The answer, it is argued here, can be found by examining Brexit, and the longer Eurosceptic movement from which it emerged, as a hegemonic political project using the conceptual architecture and analytical vocabulary provided by post-structuralist DT. This provides us with an analytical toolkit able to understand the structure of pro-Brexit discourses, the assumptions they make about the relationship between the UK and the EU, while placing campaign messages in the context of long-standing and deeply sedimented Eurosceptic discourses which frame British political discourse and our understanding of the UK as a political entity. In addition, it allows us to understand the political moves employed by campaigners to construct Brexit as a majoritarian political project through the suturing together of different constituencies of voters into a winning coalition. Finally, it is able to explain the affective hold of this project over voters and its success in motivating even those more apathetic and disengaged to turn out and vote for Brexit. The next chapter introduces post-structuralist DT and its key concepts and sets out how this was employed to analyse the Brexit referendum campaign.

3 Discourse theory, subjectivity and national identity

The post-structuralist DT that emerged from the work of Ernesto Laclau and Chantal Mouffe (1985) presents a comprehensive ontology of the social world and develops an at times complex set of concepts and logics which are deployed in this study to examine the structure and political effect of British Eurosceptic discourses (Laclau and Mouffe, 1985). Any discussion of this body of theory necessitates some familiarity with the highly specialised vocabulary which Laclau and Mouffe develop within their work. Consequently, the first part of the chapter is dedicated to introducing the main ontological assumptions of DT and outlining the concepts and logics which they developed. The second part of the chapter focuses on the discourse theoretical account of the subject and sets out the relationship which is seen to exist between subjective identities and broader social structures. The third part of the chapter examines the discourse theoretical account of nationhood and nationalism, which will be used in the following chapters to analyse the construction of Anglo-British nationalism within Eurosceptic discourses.

Conceptual framework

Laclau and Mouffe's 1985 post-structuralist DT has its intellectual foundations in the structuralist linguistics of Ferdinand de Saussure (1974), the post-structuralism of Derrida (1978) and the Marxist concept of ideology as developed in the writing of Antonio Gramsci (1971). In addition, it draws also on the insights of Michel Foucault's (1972) theory of discourse and the post-structuralist psychoanalytic theory of Jacques Lacan (1977). In Laclau's later works (1990, 1996, 2005), the influence of Lacan comes increasingly to the fore and is central to subsequent attempts to refine and operationalise the central tenets of DT in the 'critical logics' approach developed by Jason Glynos and David Howarth (Laclau, 1990; Laclau, 1996; Laclau, 2005; Glynos and Howarth, 2007).

The underlying assumption of DT is that 'all objects and actions are inherently meaningful and that their meaning is conferred by particular systems of significant difference' (Howarth, 2000: 101; see also Howarth and

Stavrakakis, 2000: 2). Consequently, the object of study for discourse theorists is the emergence, reproduction and contestation of systems of meaning known as discourses in which the identity of social objects is conferred by the differential position they occupy within that discourse (Howarth, 2000: 131). This builds on the insights of Saussure that it is not anything intrinsic to the signifier 'C-A-T' that ties it to the concept of a cat that it represents, but its difference from other related signifiers such as 'dog' or 'bird.'

True to its roots in post-structuralism, DT rejects the idea that there is a transcendental organising principle that dictates the structure of society. For discourse theorists, the social order is not a given, objective reality but is, instead, a contingent and historically specific articulation of the social (Laclau and Mouffe, 1985; Howarth, 2000). DT can be understood, therefore, as an attempt to theorise the emergence and maintenance of social orders – what Laclau and Mouffe term 'objectivities' or 'society effects' – in the conditions of ultimate indeterminacy (Laclau, 2005; Laclau and Mouffe, 1985).

For Laclau and Mouffe (1985) *discourses* are relational systems of meaning which confer identities on social objects and actors as a result of the differential position they occupy in relation to one another and within the overarching system of meaning. Discourses function then as semi-permanent structures (or *quasi*-structures) which bring order to a particular social context (see Glynos and Howarth, 2007). They are, as David Howarth (2000: 104) comments, the 'publicly available and essentially incomplete frameworks of meaning which enable social life to be conducted.' The concept of discourse needs to be understood alongside the related concept of *the discursive* (or the *field of discursivity*) as it is sometimes described. The latter represents the (ontological) conditions of possibility, or the wider discursive space, in which multiple (ontic) discourses can emerge and compete for pre-eminence or hegemony (see below).

Discourses are inherently unstable and radically incomplete (Torfing, 1999). That is to say, no discourse is ever able to articulate society in its entirety, domesticating all potential identity positions within a single discursive formation. Consequently, the possibility remains that any discursive formation may be undermined and subverted by those identity positions it excludes (Torfing, 1999: 85–6). Certain discourses may achieve a high level of sedimentation and with this the appearance of necessity or permanence (eg democracy as a political system or the national as a political community). However, competing discourses can always emerge to challenge even the most firmly sedimented discursive formations. It is this radical contingency that differentiates a discourse – as a partial and semi-permanent fixation of meaning – from a transcendental structure. Discourses then can be seen as the result of a complex dialectic relationship between the logics of contingency and necessity, in which the structuring force of a discourse is able to subvert the contingency of the social by introducing a semi-permanent order to the social (Laclau, 1996: 22ff; Howarth, 2000: 103).

Equivalence, difference and the limits of discourse

All discourses are relational and radically incomplete, meaning there are certain identity positions that cannot be domesticated within them. This incompleteness has an existential function in discourses for it is only in terms of that which is excluded from a discourse – or remains external to it – that its organisational logic become evident. The shared identity of the different components (which Laclau and Mouffe term 'moments') of a discourse – what binds them together as a common entity – is their shared heterogeneity from the (excluded) 'other.' For example, the identity position of 'the monarch' cannot be subsumed within republican discourses and it is the shared rejection of monarchy that identifies (otherwise different objects and actors) as republican.

The emergence of discourses is thus the result of a complex interplay of the *logics of equivalence* and *difference* (Laclau, 2005: 77ff). On the one hand, the *logic of difference* dictates the relational identity of moments within a discourse by highlighting the ways in which they differ from one another; on the other hand, *logic of equivalence* subverts this system of differences by creating chains of equivalence among these otherwise disparate elements (Laclau and Mouffe, 1985). The formation of chains of equivalence results in the emergence of discourses as coherent and identifiable entities that can structure the identity of those social elements articulated as moments of that discourse. Similarly, by subverting the system of differences that exists between the moments of a discourse, the logic of equivalence creates a strict distinction between a discourse and its discursive exterior. The logic of equivalence also highlights the crucial importance of 'nodal points' in the formation of discourses.

The commonality between different components of a discourse is explained through the concept of the *nodal point*. The latter exists as a common thread running through a particular discourse but which functions as the symbolic representation or the positive manifestation of the negation of the other within that discourse. Since the logic of equivalence is constructed in opposition to those identities which it excludes, the nodal point can be thought of as an empty signifier that symbolises the negation of all that is excluded from the discourse and its structures. This in turn explains the central importance of the category of antagonism in Laclau and Mouffe's social ontology. The production of a discourse structured around an empty signifier requires the simultaneous production of an antagonistic and incompatible *equivalential chain* offering an alternative articulation of society (Laclau, 2005: 83–4).

Hegemony

Laclau and Mouffe (1985) account for the nature of political struggle between rival discourses with reference to the concepts of hegemony and hegemonic practices, which they adapt from the work of Antonio Gramsci (1971). Hegemonic practices involve 'the linking together of different identities and political forces into a common project, and the creation of new social orders from a variety of dispersed elements' (Howarth, 2000: 109). A successful hegemonic project, therefore, is one that is able to domesticate a whole variety of disparate identity positions into a single discursive formation and provide a *surface of inscription* for a wide array of competing demands (Torfing, 1999: 101). In so doing, it can achieve a position of discursive predominance in which it comes to determine what it is and is not possible to say within a certain discursive context.

A hegemonic discourse, therefore, is one whose values, assumptions and language take on the appearance of self-evidence and of permanence. It becomes the 'common-sense' that governs the way people talk and think about the world around them and becomes generally accepted as the undeniable or unquestioned 'truth' about the world. For this reason, the construction of hegemonic projects has been equated by Laclau and Mouffe (1985) with the construction of competing *objectivities*.

As will be argued below, the signifier which most readily lends itself to performing this hegemonic function in modern democratic societies is the empty signifier 'nation.' Consequently, rival discursive projects compete to 'hegemonise' the signifier of the nation, filling it out with a specific ontic content. In so doing, a political project is able to present its narrow, sectional demands as synonymous with those of the nation or the demands of the nation in general. As Laclau (1996: 43) comments:

> A class or group is considered to be hegemonic when it is not closed in a narrow corporatist perspective, but presents itself as realising the broader aims either of emancipating or ensuring order for wider masses of the population.

Successful hegemonic discourses, which are able to maintain their position of pre-eminence, can become deeply *sedimented* to the extent that they are treated as objective 'truths' about the social world. Consequently, the ability of competing discourses to challenge them, and ultimately to dislodge them from their position of pre-eminence by bringing about a rearticulation of the prevailing social order, can appear virtually impossible. The hegemony of neo-liberal discourses, for instance, has led to the assumption among many politicians and scholars that there is simply 'no other way' than the neo-liberal agenda and that society must inevitably be restructured to meet the demands of this economic model.

However, the sedimentation of discourses should not be confused with their necessity or permanence. The potential always exists within the ontological framework of DT for the radical re-articulation of even the most successful and highly sedimented discourses. The existence of competing, dissenting voices such as, for instance, those in the anti-globalisation and anti-capitalist protest movements, highlight the inability of the neo-liberal discourse to fully articulate the social. There are certain identities that simply cannot be articulated within this hegemonic discourse and which are instead articulated into the rival discourses.

The existence of a plurality of competing discourses in the social means that the possibility of a shift in the existing *status quo* can never be completely closed off. No matter how sedimented the hegemonic discourse becomes, its ultimate contingency is unavoidable. It is reliant solely upon the constant rearticulation of its hegemony. Despite their longevity and their apparent self-evidence, discourses are always capable of rearticulation and dissolution. For example, the hegemonic discourse of communism in Eastern Europe appeared during the mid to late 1980s to have reached such a level of sedimentation that its (permanent) survival was assumed and its sudden collapse totally unforeseen in the East, as well as in the West. Yet, by the end of the decade, the discourses of communism had collapsed more spectacularly than anyone could have predicted. They were replaced throughout the Eastern Bloc by the discourse of liberal democracy. This demonstrates the possibility of substantive rearticulation of social elements regardless of their level of sedimentation.

Discourse theory, Lacan and the subject

It is this common grounding in post-structuralism that creates the link between Lacanian psychoanalysis and Laclau and Mouffe's DT. Lacan differentiates the category of the subject not only from the Freudian ego but also from the essentialist conceptions of subjectivity found within the western philosophical tradition. The development of the Lacanian subject marks a clear departure from the Cartesian notion of an autonomous, self-transparent consciousness, or *cogito,* to which Lacan makes extensive reference throughout his career (Evans, 1996: 195–6). Rather than a positively given consciousness with a fully-constituted identity, the Lacanian subject is characterised by its radical incompleteness and its alienation from itself (Fink, 1995).

It is hard to do justice to the complexity and inherent ambiguity of Lacan's conceptual vocabulary in the context of the current volume. Nevertheless, some understanding of Lacan's theory of psychological development is necessary to fully appreciate the discourse theoretical conception of the subject and the broader theory of the social world it proposes. For Lacan, the concept of the split ego (*Ich-Spaltung*) – the radical alienation of the subject from its own essential being through its integration into the world of language – is constitutive of subjectivity itself (Laclau, 1995: 268). Human psychological development is driven by the attempt to overcome this split, alienated form of subjectivity and to achieve a stable and fully reconciled identity. Lacan introduces three main concepts, or registers, which he employs throughout his writing, to articulate the process of human psychological development: the Real, the symbolic and the imaginary.

The Lacanian *Real* refers to a place at the centre of our being that eludes signification. It is the location of a primal, pre-symbolic enjoyment (or *jouissance* in Lacan's terms). It is the realm of a mythical unity before the alienation brought about by entry into the *imaginary* and *symbolic* phases of development. With the advent of language, the child is thrown into the realm of the symbolic and it is at this stage that the subject fully emerges. In the symbolic identity is sought in language through a process of identification with the 'socially *available* discursive constructions such as ideologies' which are capable of providing an identity (Stavrakakis, 1999: 36, emphasis in original).

Although the experience of the Real is beyond symbolisation, its traces linger within the subject as the desire to return to this primal state of unity before the split and to experience again the *jouissance* of the Real. To do so, the subject attempts to construct a fully-constituted identity for itself through identification with the symbolic world. Identification with the object, however, is unable to produce a stable or fully-constituted identity for the subject (Stavrakakis, 1999: 20) since, from a post-structuralist perspective, the social objects with which the subject identifies are themselves lacking, and so cannot offer the stable identity the subject seeks. The object in which identity is sought is then characterised by the same constitutive lack we find in the subject, and cannot provide the latter stable, fully-constituted identity (Evans, 1996).

The construction of a fully-constituted subjective identity through identification with social objects is then ultimately impossible and cannot bring about the reconciliation of the subject with itself. In other words, it will never be able to overcome the fundamental alienation experienced by the loss of the Real. However, the subject's desires to experience again the primal enjoyment of the Real through symbolic identification leads to the fantasmatic investment in certain signifiers (objects to obtain or subject positions to occupy) which come to represent the primal *jouissance* of the Real. Fantasy, in the Lacanian conceptual architecture signals the possibility to the subjects that the lost unity of the Real can somehow be recovered in the symbolic, and the 'lack' at the core of their being may be filled (Stavrakakis, 1999: 36–7). However, the object of desire, once realised, is never able to satisfy the subject's yearning, being only a pale imitation of what was lost and can never be recovered.

Laclau and Mouffe's conception of the subject

Discourse theory gives rise to two related, yet ultimately distinct, concepts which deal with the category of the subject: *subject positions* and *political subjectivity*. In *Hegemony and Socialist Strategy* (1985: 115 ff), only the former is evident and the term subject appears to be synonymous with the subject positions occupied within a discursive formation. A subject position is a differential identity within a specific discursive formation whose identity, like that of social objects, is defined in relation to all other identities articulated within that discursive formation (the logic of difference) and the overarching system of meaning which constitutes the unifying principle of that discourse (the logic of equivalence). The subject for Laclau and Mouffe at this stage of their thinking, therefore, cannot be the origin of social relations, but is instead an effect of hegemonic articulatory practice. It is the subject of the structure.

A variety of different subject positions are articulated within each discursive framework, which confer certain identities on the individuals who identify with them. Subjects then achieve their identity from occupying these positions and assuming the role defined for them by these differential identities. Individuals may occupy several subject positions simultaneously within competing discursive formations (Howarth, 2000; Howarth and Stavrakakis, 2000). Similarly, it is equally possible for an individual to occupy multiple subject positions within the same discourse. Within competing discourses the subject positions occupied by an individual will be (at least potentially) contradictory and incompatible with one another. However, the multiple subject positions occupied by the same individual within a particular discursive formation will be complementary to the extent that they are able to be subsumed within a single system of differences and in reference to the same nodal point.

The notion of the subject as subject position is, however, a very static and passive concept, which hollows out to a large extent the concept of articulation. The subject appears to be reduced to a function of the structure and is stripped of any form of agency. If subjectivity is governed exclusively by the structural position into which that subject is articulated, then it is impossible for the subject to become a political agent (in the sense in which Laclau and Mouffe use the term) and to subvert the prevailing social structure. Consequently, the possibility of a re-articulation of the prevailing discursive structure subsides. The structure begins to appear highly sedimented and resistant to change and the subject as subject position becomes indistinguishable from the structure (Laclau, 1990: 60–1). They are one and the same since the identity of the subject is determined by the structure, and the structure is not open to subversion by the subject.

This type of sedimentation means it becomes impossible to distinguish the concept of a discourse, from that of a structure in the fullest sense of the term. DT is then confronted with the same criticisms to which structuralist theory is open; that while it is able to theorise the *status quo*, it is unable to conceptualise social change or the role of political agency in subverting social structures. Such a rigidly structuralist conception of the subject is clearly out of keeping with the post-structuralism espoused by Laclau and Mouffe. While they maintain that some form of structuration is essential if any form of social order is to be possible, they insist that hegemonic discursive structures are inherently unstable and open to change. It is the contingency of discursive formations which differentiates them from the concept of structure.

One possible response to this is that, although the subject positions internal to a given structure are dictated purely by the differential identity constructed within that discursive formation, no discourse is able to structure the social in its entirety. There will always be certain identities that are mutually exclusive and cannot coexist within a single system of differences because they fundamentally contradict one another. Those identities which are excluded from a given discourse form its constitutive exterior, which is both its condition of possibility and, at the same time, a source of instability. It could be argued, therefore, that this radical exterior is the point from which critique, and ultimately social change, is possible. In other words, while critique from within a given discourse is impossible it can come from without.

On the surface, this seems a plausible account of potential social change and one which is clearly in keeping with Laclau and Mouffe's conception of social relations as inherently antagonistic. Hegemonic discourses are undermined from without by those elements unable to achieve an identity within them. Through the logics of equivalence and difference, these elements are able to form rival, competing discursive formations which offer a different conception of society and challenge the predominant discursive formation. However, a radical rearticulation of the prevailing social order involves not simply the assertion of those identities excluded from the hegemonic discourse, but also the *re*articulation of those internal to the hegemonic discourse by bringing about a dislocation in its signifying chains. Identities within the existing social structure – the moments of the hegemonic discourse – must be converted into floating signifiers and rearticulated in terms of the emerging, rival hegemonic order.

Some identity positions internal to the old hegemonic discourse will be excluded from the new order, but many will be rearticulated – with their identity altered to varying degrees – as moments of the new discourse, in which they will occupy a new differential position dependent upon the organisational logic of that discourse. In Saussurean terms, the identity achieved by signifiers in the new hegemonic discourse will be different from those connoted by the same signifier within the previous hegemonic discourse. This is as equally true of social objects and practices as it is of subject positions.

What appears to be missing from the account then is an understanding of how such a rearticulation of the hegemonic discourse comes about and how the rearticulation of subject identities is involved in this process. Such an account is found in Laclau's later work (Laclau, 1990; Laclau, 1996; Laclau and Zac, 1994) in which he develops the concept of 'political subjectivity' to account for the role of human agents in the process of social change. Laclau's engagement with Lacan is evident in his consideration of the effects of contingency on the category of the subject. How are we to think about the subject when confronted with the ultimate indeterminacy of the object/structure? The conception of subject as subject position present in *Hegemony and Socialist Strategy* is supplemented by a more substantive theorisation of the subject as a political agent.

Given the failure of discourses to structure society in its entirety and thus to permanently fix all social identities, the subject must act to construct an identity by identifying itself with certain political projects or ideologies (Howarth, 2000: 109; see also Laclau, 1990). Moreover, the subject, in constructing its identity through an active process of identification, also subverts and alters the structure within which it is situated. The subject then is not simply the effect of the structure, consigned to occupy certain subject positions, but is also its (partial) cause. It is this active form of agency – the subject of identification rather than structured identity – that Laclau calls political subjectivity (Laclau, 1990: 60–1). The subject thus understood is the locus of a decision to identify itself with certain discursively constructed identity positions (Laclau, 1990: 60).

That is not to say, however, that the decision is purely voluntaristic, or that an infinite array of potential identities is open to the subject. While the structure may be lacking or unstable, it is not absent. The decision, the process of identification, always takes place within a specific context, within a discursive formation which places constraints on the agency of the subject. There are some decisions which are simply not open to the subject or which it is unable to make. The extent to which a radical rearticulation of identity is possible will depend on the stability and sedimentation of the hegemonic discursive formation. For this reason, the decision, the moment of the subject as political agent is inextricably linked to the category of dislocation.

The antagonistic nature of social relations means that the structuring discursive formation is always susceptible to dislocatory events: phenomena which cannot be subsumed by or domesticated within a particular discursive formation (Torfing, 1999: 148). Dislocation is the embodiment of the lack in the structure, the very point at which the structure's contingency becomes visible (Laclau, 1990: 60). It is in times of dislocation in the discursive order that the subject is called upon to construct its identity in relation to one of the available discursive formations competing for hegemony. Since this decision requires the subject to choose a certain option, this automatically implies the rejection of other equally possible alternatives that it could have taken. Since such decisions will ultimately decide the form of the reconstituted social order, this act of exclusion is an exercise of power which is constitutive of society (Laclau, 1990: 60).

It is only in the context of a radical structural undecidability that a decision, in the true sense of the word, is possible. If all identity were positively given by the structure, there would be no room left for the decision, for the outcome would be predetermined either by the material conditions in which the nominal decision takes place (as in Marx) or as a result of the unfolding logic of ultimate rationality present in the world (as in the Hegelian dialectic). In either case, the position of the subject within the emerging social order would have been already decided (Laclau, 1996). The possibility of the decision, by contrast, implies that there is a need for the decision as a constitutive act brought about by the lack of any such determinism in the structure (Laclau, 1990: 60). The decision then is the trace of the contingent within the social, the point at which the failure of the hegemonic discursive formation to fully determine social relations becomes apparent (Laclau, 1990: 39–41; 60–1). Since the moment of decision is the moment in which political subjectivity comes alive, the subject is nothing other than the 'pure form of the structure's dislocation,' the ultimate undecidability of the structure (Laclau, 1990: 60). It is the subject of lack in the fullest sense.

In summary, the subject, in the sense of political subjectivity, is best understood as the trace of contingency within the prevailing social objectivity. It is the moment of dislocation and decision which is both partially determined by, and constitutive of, discursive structures. The greater the dislocated within the structure, the more the field of decision, and thus the field of the subject, will expand (Laclau, 1990: 39–40). The effect of the decision is to redefine not only the identity of the subject, but of the structure too. Each assertion of identity by the subject necessarily leads to a rearticulation of its relationship with the discursive structures in which it obtains its identity. In times of great social sedimentation, however, when the contingency of the structure is most hidden and the myth of permanence and objectivity is at its strongest, the subject is reduced to subject position: the collection of partially fixed identity positions which it occupies. In light of these conclusions about the nature of subjectivity within the ontology of DT, we are now able to assess the significance this has for our understanding of society and politics in general and the phenomenon of Euroscepticism in particular.

Discourse theory and nationalism

Jacob Torfing (1999: 192) argues that, for discourse theorists, the concept of nationalism refers to:

> a certain articulation of the empty signifier of the nation, which itself becomes the nodal point in the political discourse of modern democracy and generally functions as a way of symbolising an absent communitarian fullness.

To claim that the nation functions as the nodal point in the discourse of modern democracy is to attribute to it a crucial function in structuring social relations in western democratic societies. The nation becomes the central reference point around which competing political projects are structured and in terms of which political demands are articulated. The call for a certain type of healthcare or economic policy, for example, will be made in terms of the national interest or the good of the nation.

From a discourse-theoretical perspective, therefore, the function of that nation is not only to structure social relations, but to provide a source of political legitimacy for the exercise of power. This echoes Billig's (1995) argument that 'banal' nationalism is the ideology underlying all western democratic societies. According to Billig, modern societies are constructed as national societies and claims to political legitimacy are made in reference to the concept of 'the nation' and 'the national interest.' Ben Wellings (2008) goes even further in seeing the legitimation of power as the defining feature of nationalism in the modern world.

Torfing (1999: 192) explains the function of the nation in modern political communities with reference to the work of Claude Lefort. Lefort (1988: 16–7) argues that power in pre-democratic feudal societies is embodied in the person of the prince, who legitimates the exercise of this power with reference to some form of divine ordinance. It is beholden to the prince to mediate between the god and the citizenry. Following what Lefort terms the 'Democratic Revolution' (Torfing 1999: 192), the concentration of power in a single figure is no longer possible. With the dissolution of an external authority provided by god, the unity and stability of society begins to disintegrate. However, the image of unity and completeness is necessary if social order is to be maintained. It is essential, therefore, for competing political projects to suture the emerging divisions and to offer an articulation of society as a stable and fully-constituted entity around a central nodal point such as the nation. In modern democratic societies, therefore, the nation has replaced god as the ultimate source of political authority.

Laclau's (1990; 1996) concept of the empty signifier is crucial to understanding the function of the nation in contemporary political discourses. The empty signifier is at once a moment in the hegemonic discursive formation and at the same time the signifier of the fundamental lack in the social structure. That is to say the emergence of nationalist discourses involves defining the nation and attributing to it certain values and characteristics. However, the signifier 'nation' also assumes the ontological function of providing the conditions of possibility for the emergence of social order through the promise of an absent communitarian fullness.

There are a plurality of competing articulations of the national mission, which attempt to hegemonise the empty signifier 'nation' and to speak in the name of society writ large (Torfing, 1999: 192; cf Billig, 1995: 87). These political projects seek to establish 'an expansive hegemony' which is able to garner widespread adherence and to legitimise its authority with reference to 'the nation' and 'the people' (Torfing 1999: 193). Consequently, the latter function as *surfaces of inscription* for the various (disparate) social demands which are articulated as moments of the hegemonic discourse (Torfing, 1999: 193).

The power of nationalist discourses

Nationalist discourses function by presenting an account of the social world in which 'society' is equated with 'nation.' The strength of this discourse, and its ability to structure the social world, depends on this account of the social world assuming the appearance of necessity or 'common sense' in the way described above. As Billig (1995) argues, the logic of nationalism is also able to present itself as a universal theory of the political which situates the nation in a world of similar nations. Nations are, therefore, presented as natural, universally present political communities. Any alternative articulations of political community, which subvert the principle of nationalism in any way are denounced as false constructions, which go against universal principles of human nature represented by nationalism.

For the discourse theorists, however, there is no such thing as a natural or necessary political community, only contingent semi-permanent articulations of the social world, which must be constantly reproduced through ideological practices. While nationalist discourses have reached an extremely high level of sedimentation and may take on the appearance of necessity, they remain discourses nonetheless and remain open to the possibility of a radical rearticulation of the social world. Another nodal point may come to replace the nation as the term around which all other political discourses are structured. It is necessary, therefore, for the discourse theorists to account for the continued force of nationalist discourses.

The argument presented here is that the affective power of nationalist discourses can be understood in terms of the Lacanian conception of the subject and the three orders of the Real, the imaginary and the symbolic. Zizek argues that Lacanian theory provides a conceptual architecture with which to analyse the emergence and maintenance of the affective ties between subject and nation. It is inadequate, he claims, to explain the prevalence and force of nationalist discourse as a 'pure discursive effect,' since such an account lacks sufficient 'substance' to account for the strength of feeling generated by nationalism, and the enduring loyalty felt by individuals to the national cause (Zizek, 1993: 202; cf. Anderson, 1991: 141; Jenkins and Sofos, 1996: 11; Billig, 1995: 18). The missing 'substance' that Zizek sees in purely discursive accounts of nationalism is the primordial, pre-symbolic enjoyment which Lacan terms *jouissance*; it is only in terms of *jouissance* that we are fully able to understand the power of nationalist discourses.

Following Zizek, Stavrakakis, (2005: 76) also argues that the discursive construction of the nation as a nodal point within a particular discourse is, in and of itself, insufficient to explain the prevalence and the strength of nationalist sentiment and must be supported by 'an affective investment' with the nation. 'Nationalism,' he continues, 'works through people's hearts, nerves and gut' (Stavrakakis, 2005: 76). Consequently, it is necessary to supplement the discourse theoretical account of the emergence and structure of nationalist discourses with a theory capable of explaining the affective 'pull' of these discourses on national subjects and the emotional investment of the latter in these discourses. By adding the additional layer of psychoanalytic theory to our analysis we are able to comprehend nationalism as a deeper, psychological need for a unified and harmonious society (Stavrakakis, 2005; Butler et al., 2000; Laclau, 1996).

It described above how the Lacanian subject is characterised by a constitutive lack. On its entry into the symbolic order – the realm of the word and the signifier – the lacking subject becomes alienated from its own identity. It is compelled to construct an identity for itself through a process of identification with the various subject positions available for it in the discursive context in which it is situated. This lack in the subject manifests itself in a yearning for lost *jouissance* and the desire to recapture the absent fullness of the Real. As Stavrakakis (1999: 42) comments, the subject experiences 'a lack of *jouissance*, the lack of a pre-symbolic, Real enjoyment which is always posited as something lost, as a lost fullness.'

Identification, however, is never able to provide the subject with a fully-constituted identity (Stavrakakis, 2005: 71). The social order in which an identity *qua* identification is sought – the big Other in Lacan's terms – is also lacking and is, therefore, unable to provide the subject with the identity for which it yearns. At this stage, the relationship between the alienated, lacking subject and the broader social structure becomes clear. The attempt to reconstruct society as a unified and self-reconciled entity is inextricably linked to the desire of the subject for a fully-constituted identity. For only in a fully-constituted society in which all social antagonism is eradicated, and in which all identity positions can find articulation in an exhaustive and unified relational totality, is identity (as opposed to identification) possible.

The subject then is faced with the impossibility of achieving a fully-constituted identity and, in so doing, recapturing the lost *jouissance* of the Real. It is in this light that the full significance of the concept of fantasy in Lacan's theory becomes apparent. Fantasy is the means by which the impossibility of society and thus of identity is masked over and, at the same time, the process of identification is driven on. Since the ultimate impossibility of a fully-constituted identity is obscured, the desire to seek our identity through a process of identification with the prevailing social order persists. As Stavrakakis (1999: 46) comments:

> If the human condition is marked by a quest for a lost/ impossible enjoyment, fantasy 'offers the promise of an encounter with this precious *jouissance*, an encounter which is fantasised as covering over the lack in the Other and, consequently, as filling the lack in the subject.'

At the root of fantasy, therefore, is the desire for closure and stability in the symbolic (or discursive) order. The image of a fully-constituted society is an enduring and frequently recurring motif in fantasmatic construction of the social, which provides the underpinning for numerous political projects. To quote Stavrakakis (1999: 52) once more:

> From millenarianism to the *Communist Manifesto* and up to the Green ideology, we know that every political promise is supported by a reference to a lost state of harmony, unity and fullness, a reference to a pre-symbolic real which most political projects aspires to bring back.

Different political projects attempt to construct a harmonious and fully-constituted social objectivity, but in differing terms and centred around different nodal points (see Laclau, 2005). Nationalism, it is argued here, represents another attempt to mask the lack in the 'big Other' – and in so doing the lack in the subject – with reference to a mythical communitarian fullness organised around the signifiers of 'the nation' and 'the people.' In the following section it will be argued that the construction of nationalist discourses requires the construction of political enemies, who function not only as the 'other' against which the national in-group is defined, but form a crucial part of the fantasy structures which support them.

The construction of political enemies

In the previous section it was argued that nationalist discourses function, in both discourse theoretical and psychoanalytical terms, to provide an account of society as a unified, harmonious and stable totality. In presenting society *qua* nation in this way, it becomes a potential object of identification for the subject, capable of providing stable identity constructions (or subject positions) with which it can align itself. However, the appearance of completeness and permanence on which the nationalist discourse depends is the result of ideological practices which mask the ultimate contingency and instability of all discursive formations.

Like all discourses, the nationalist discourse is partial and incomplete and depends for its very existence on those elements which it excludes, or which cannot be articulated within its chain of equivalence. As Torfing (1999: 193) comments:

> in the final instance the homogenization and substantialization of the nation can only be obtained in and through the discursive construction of "enemies of the nation," which are simultaneously outside and inside the nation....

Consequently, the construction of the nation requires the simultaneous construction of an alternative chain of equivalence in which certain enemies combine to conspire against the nation. The conspiracy against the nation can involve external actors, or as a fifth column, an enemy within (see Laclau, 2005: 86-7). Similarly, it may depict both threats as acting in collaboration with one another against the national interest.

The importance of these enemies of the nation is again evident from both a discourse theoretical and a psychoanalytical perspective. The importance of the excluded 'other' within the ontology of DT was discussed above. However, Lacanian theory allows us to theorise the specific function of the enemy within nationalist discourses. The argument here draws on the discussion of racism and nationalism in the work of Zizek (1989, 1993) in which he accounts for the prevalence of racist and exclusionary nationalist discourses in terms of the Lacanian categories of fantasy, desire and *jouissance*. In *Tarrying with the Negative* (1993: 201), Zizek presents nationalist discourses as being primarily concerned with the maintenance and protection of a mythical essence of nationhood (the national 'Thing'), no matter how ephemeral and elusive the definition of this 'Thing' may be:

> National identification is by definition sustained by a relationship toward the Nation qua Thing. This Nation-Thing is determined by a series of contradictory properties. It appears to us as 'our Thing' [...], as something accessible only to us, as something 'they,' the others, cannot grasp; nonetheless it is something constantly menaced by 'them.' [...] If we are asked how we can recognise the presence of this Thing, the only consistent answer is that the Thing is present in that elusive entity called 'our way of life.'

In a later passage, Zizek (1993: 202) clarifies his position that the national Thing must be understood in terms of the Lacanian category of enjoyment (or *jouissance*). 'A nation exists,' Zizek (1993: 202) argues, 'so long as its specific *enjoyment* continues to be materialized in a set of social practices and transmitted through national myths that structure these practices' (cf. Bracher, 1996: 5). The construction of the national Thing *qua* enjoyment, however, only makes sense in contrast to 'others' who organise their enjoyment in different ways. There is a uniqueness attributed to the national Thing, which differentiates it from any other. What makes it unique is its inaccessibility to the outsider; it is 'our' national Thing and, as such, is inaccessible and incomprehensible to 'them' (Zizek, 1993: 201).

The idea of a unique, closed-off national essence is buttressed by the idea that 'our' enjoyment is somehow threatened by the presence of these outsiders. To quote Zizek once more (1993: 204):

> Every nationality has built its own mythology narrating how other nations deprive it of a vital part of enjoyment the possession of which would allow it to live fully.

The construction of the 'other,' therefore, positions them not just as different from 'us,' but as hostile to our way of life; as something which is both radically heterogeneous and which threatens the existence of our national community.

At the basis of our constructions of the other is the inability to discern among them a clear set of motives and desires. It is impossible, in other words, to know with any degree of certainty what it is the 'other' wants from us, a dilemma Zizek (1989) summarises under the rubric '*che vuoi?*' ('what do you want?'). Consequently, the aims and objectives of the other become the basis of our own fantasy constructions in which we impute to them a myriad of plans and designs which remain concealed beneath the surface (Myers, 2003: 94). These hidden agendas, it is argued, pose a threat to the nation and so must be brought to light and stopped, before they can be realised further.

The threat posed by the other usually manifests itself, according to Zizek (1993: 203), in terms of their incomprehensible and excessive enjoyment:

> We always impute to the "other" an excessive enjoyment: he wants to steal our enjoyment (by ruining our way of life) and/or he has access to some secret, perverse enjoyment. In short, what really bothers us about the "other" is the peculiar way he organises his enjoyment, precisely the surplus, the "excess" that pertains to this way: the smell of "their" food, "their" noisy songs and dances, "their" strange manners, "their" strange attitude to work. To the racist, the "other" is either a workaholic stealing our jobs or an idler living on our labor, and it is quite amusing to notice the haste with which one passes from reproaching the other with a refusal to work to reproaching him for the theft of work.

That the 'other' comes to represent what are ultimately contradictory and mutually exclusive characteristics is evidence that racist discourses are not based in a rational assessment of socio-political reality, but centre in the fantasmatic construction of the 'other' as *threat* (Zizek, 1993: 205). A clear distinction must be made between the actual members of a particular ethnic or national grouping and the construction of the outsider as an object of fantasy often articulated as nouns ('the Jew' or 'the Serb' in Zizek's examples) as a moment of discourse supported by the theft-of-enjoyment fantasy.

It is insufficient to explain the passion which nationalist fantasies are able to engender in their adherents simply in terms of a threat to our national identity, and their potential 'theft of our enjoyment' runs deeper than this; to the very core of our beings in the symbolic order. As Zizek (1993: 203, emphasis in original) argues:

> What we conceal by imputing to the Other the theft of our enjoyment is the traumatic fact that *we never possessed what was allegedly stolen from us*: the lack ("castration") is originary, enjoyment constitutes itself as "stolen".

In other words, the potential 'theft' of our enjoyment reminds us that the *jouissance* we experience acts only to mask the fundamental loss which occurs with the passage into the symbolic order and the very impossibility of a complete, fully-reconciled subjectivity. It is in the figure of the 'other' that we experience the return of the Real and are reminded again of the fundamental lack which is at the heart of being. As Zizek (1993: 206) comments:

> the fascinating image of the Other gives a body to our innermost split, to what is "in us more than ourselves" and thus prevents us from achieving full identity with ourselves.

For this reason, our hatred of the 'other' is really hatred of our own excessive enjoyment, being as it is a pale imitation of the lost primal *jouissance*. It brings us face to face with the ultimate instability of our own identity and the impossibility of experiencing again the self-reconciliation of the Real.

Summary

In this chapter, it was argued that DT and Lacanian psychoanalysis provide us with a set of tools that can be employed to study the construction of the nation as a form of political community and the interpellation of individuals as national subjects. From a discourse theoretical perspective the concept of the nation functions as a nodal point in relation to which an account of society as a national community is produced, and the meaning and identity of social objects are constructed. Similarly, the post-structuralist account of the subject, with its roots also in Lacanian psychoanalytic theory, is able to account for the emergence of the individual *qua* national subject. The Lacanian subject is characterised by a fundamental lack of identity and must, therefore, construct an identity for itself through a process of identification with the surrounding social structure. Nationalist discourses provide precisely such an account of society with which subjects can identify and fill out this constitutive void. By introducing the Lacanian concepts of *jouissance* and fantasy which are integral to the post-structuralist account of political subjectivity, it is possible to account not only for the structure of nationalist discourses, but also their strength and longevity. The fantasmatic support structures which underpin nationalist discourses, it is argued, are the means through which they are able to maintain their effective hold over the national community. Having examined the main concepts and logics of DT above, the following chapter sets out how these can be operationalised to study the construction of Britain and the EU in Eurosceptic discourses.

4 Deploying discourse theory

This chapter will set out the way in which post-structuralist DT, introduced in the previous chapter, can be applied to the question of British Euroscepticism. It aims to link the theoretical discussions in the previous chapter with the actual process of conducting discourse theoretically inspired research. The first section introduces the work of Glynos and Howarth (2007) on *Logics of Critical Explanation in the Social Sciences,* in which the authors investigate the epistemological consequences of deploying DT and Lacanian theory to examine questions of social and political importance. In so doing, they assess the type of knowledge claims discourse theorists are able to make from within the ontological framework in which they operate. The remainder of the chapter sets out the time frame, and the choice of materials to be examined during the current project.

Logics of critical explanation

Having set out the underlying social ontology of discourse in the previous chapter, we are now in a position to consider in greater detail the epistemological and methodological considerations involved in deploying DT to the question of British Euroscepticism. A detailed discussion of these issues has been reserved until now since any evaluation of the logics of critical explanation requires a high level of familiarity with both the concepts and logics of post-structuralist DT and the Lacanian concepts of fantasy and *jouissance*.

The aim of discourse theorists is to make sense of processes and actions through the lens of a new conceptual architecture based around a distinctive social ontology. In this sense, their goal is to understand their object of study more fully through a process of rearticulating the issue in question using the concepts and logics which constitute the discourse theoretical account of the social world. Any attempt to understand social phenomena in this way is synonymous with the process of explanation (Howarth, 2000: 130–2). Equally, this process of explanation and understanding is inseparable from the process of rearticulation described previously. By rearticulating an object of study using the conceptual

DOI: 10.4324/9781315098067-4

architecture of DT, we are at the same time providing an account of its emergence and maintenance as a meaningful social object.

The process of description, understanding and explanation in which discourse theorists are engaged is, therefore, not a linear and sequential process encompassing three separate phases in the process of conducting research. Rather, these are three dimensions of a single, unified process. For this reason, discourse theoretical research can be seen to follow a retroductive logic of enquiry. It aims to transcend the narrow models of testing and explanation which characterise much of mainstream social science, and which depend on an untenable distinction between facts and theory (Glynos and Howarth, 2007: 18 ff). Glynos and Howarth (2007: 133) develop the idea of logics of critical explanation, which they argue enable the discourse theorist to describe, explain and critique the emergence, maintenance and dissolution of structures of meaning, rules and practices in the social world. The contribution of Glynos and Howarth is to provide a clear conceptual framework through which to conduct research on specific empirical cases in which the various dimensions of the constitution of the social are addressed.

To talk about the logic of a particular practice or regime of practices is to 'seek to capture those aspects which make it tick' (Glynos and Howarth, 2007: 135). The logic of a particular practice, however, refers not only to the rules of formation of a particular social order but also to its historical conditions of possibility. As Glynos and Howarth (2007: 136) comment 'the logic of a practice comprises the rules or grammar of the practice, as well as the conditions which make the practice both possible and vulnerable.' Logics of explanation then are intended to account not only for the specific characteristics of a given social order but also to the political practices through which it emerges, is maintained and, potentially, can be dissolved and replaced by an alternative regime of practices.

The process of explanation consists in the mobilisation of three separate yet interrelated logics – social logics, political logics and fantasmatic logics – which build on and supplement the conceptual architecture developed by Laclau and Mouffe (1985). *Social logics* are concerned with the rules of formation of a specific social structure or discursive formation, and allow us to describe the internal architecture of a particular social order. It is perhaps useful to think of social logics as 'the rules of the game' which exist within any sedimented social structure and dictate the relationship between specific identity positions within it. Laclau (2000: 76) refers to social logics as a 'grammar' or 'cluster of rules' which govern the emergence of identities within an order of discourse.

If social logics refer to the internal structure of a discursive formation, *political logics* refer to the practices involved in the 'constitution, contestation and sedimentation' of a particular discursive formation (Glynos and Howarth, 2007: 142). They account for the political actions by which a particular articulation of the social is able to achieve and maintain hegemony. Conversely, the same logics account for the process of political contestation through which existing, sedimented discourses can be challenged by rival discursive projects, which aim to bring about a dislocation in the hegemonic discourse leading to a rearticulation of existing social relations.

In his most recent works, Laclau (2005: 117) too appears to distinguish between social and political logics in this way, arguing that '[w]hile social logics refer to rule following, political logics are related to the institution of the social.' However, the existence of what Glynos and Howarth term political logics can be traced back to his earlier work with Chantal Mouffe. As was detailed in Chapter 3, Laclau and Mouffe (1985) develop the logics of equivalence and difference to explain the emergence, maintenance and dissolution of discursive formations. Glynos and Howarth (2007: 141–5) identify these logics of equivalence and difference as specifically political logics in the sense that they refer specifically to the processes through which political contestation takes place. Political movements seek to achieve hegemony for their world views through the construction of equivalential chains around central nodal points which offer a surface of inscription for different social demands (Laclau and Mouffe, 1985; Laclau, 2005).

It will be recalled from the discussion in the previous chapter that the *logic of equivalence* functions by uniting disparate identity positions which are linked together in a single discursive formation through their shared rejection of a common enemy or antithetical identity structure. The *logic of difference*, meanwhile, accounts for the system of differential identities which persist within a discursive formation, despite the equivalence which is constructed between the various moments of that discourse. Together the logics of equivalence and difference enable us to examine and explain the process through which rival political projects construct competing social objectivities.

For Glynos and Howarth (2007), mapping the rules of formation of a hegemonic discursive formation and explaining its emergence, maintenance and/or dissolution in terms of the logics of equivalence and difference does not fully exhaust the process of critical explanation in which discourse theorists are engaged. The applications of social and political logics must be supplemented with a further consideration of the fantasmatic support structures which underlie existing social structures. Therefore, Glynos and Howarth (2007) introduce what they term fantasmatic logics, which completes their analytical toolkit.

While social logics account for the system of social relations in a given discursive terrain, and political logics explain how a particular set of social relations or regime came into being, is maintained or is being contested, *fantasmatic logics* explain why a particular, hegemonic articulation of the social is able to maintain its 'grip' over the subjects (Glynos and Howarth, 2007: 145). Fantasmatic logics aim to explain the ability (or inability) of a particular discursive formation to attain pre-eminence or to resist change

(Glynos and Howarth, 2007: 145). As such, they are of crucial importance to the current study, which is concerned with the deeply sedimented discourses of British national identity.

The prominence given to the fantasmatic dimension of social relations marks the increasing influence of Lacanian theory in the field of DT (Stavrakakis, 1999; Butler et al., 2000; Laclau, 2005). In particular, Laclau's (2005: 110 ff) work on populism has highlighted the crucial importance to discourse theorists of this affective dimension of political relations, and the indebtedness of their insights in this context to Lacan.

As was argued in the previous chapter, the concept of the subject developed by discourse theorists (Laclau, 1990, 1996) owes much to Lacanian psychoanalysis and to the application of Lacanian concepts in the work of Zizek (1989, 1993); on Zizek's dialogue with Laclau, see Butler et al. (2000). Glynos and Howarth (2007) too draw on Lacan's analysis of fantasy and *jouissance* to develop their concept of fantasmatic logics. Fantasy and affective investment in particular discourses such as nationalist discourses, they argue, are of crucial importance in explaining the outcome of discursive conflicts and the success of certain discursive projects over others.

Fantasmatic logics function essentially to mask the radical incompleteness and indeterminacy of the social. The role of fantasy is to cover over 'the fundamental lack in reality' and, in so doing, suppress the emergence of the Real in the symbolic structures we live by (Glynos and Howarth, 2007: 146). Furthermore, by masking the fundamental incompleteness of the hegemonic social structures (what, in Lacanian terms, is referred to as the lack in the 'big Other'), the function of fantasy is to mask over the lack in the subject itself (Glynos and Howarth, 2007: 146). In this respect, the fantasmatic dimension plays a crucial role in the sedimentation of existing social formations, and their construction as the natural and necessary forms of social and political organisation. The process of masking over the traces of the contingency of the prevailing social order results from what Laclau and Mouffe (1985) term ideological practices. In this sense, we can refer to the processes described here as the ideological function of fantasy (Glynos and Howarth, 2007).

In addition to this ideological function, fantasy structures play a crucial role in determining the specific content of a discursive formation, or what Glynos and Howarth (2007: 147) term the specific 'vector' of political forces within a given social environment. As we saw in Chapter 3, the notion of fantasy is derived from the Lacanian concept of the lacking subject, which desires the lost fullness and primal *jouissance* of its pre-symbolic Real existence. Consequently, (Stavrakakis, 2005: 73) has argued that it is the 'promise of recapturing our lost/impossible enjoyment which provokes the fantasy support for many of our political projects and choices.' This desire for an absent fullness has been termed the 'enjoyment of closure' by Glynos and Howarth (2007: 151). The promise that a particular form of social organisation, articulated within a given discursive project, can provide us with a stable fully-constituted identity leads to the affective investment of the subject in a political project, and helps to explain the vehemence with which the goals of these projects are pursued. For analytical purposes, we can refer to this function of fantasy structures in these instances as the affective function of fantasy.

Glynos and Howarth (2007: 147) identify two principal forms of narrative in which the ideological and affective functions of fantasy are played out, which they term the 'beatific' and the 'horrific' dimensions of fantasy. The former is structured around the idea of 'a fullness-to-come' once specific obstacles to this fullness is overcome; the latter, meanwhile, tells of the impending disaster which will prevail if the obstacle in question is not surmounted (Glynos and Howarth, 2007: 147). While the specific beatific and horrific aspects of fantasy take many forms in different contexts, they are often associated with images of 'omnipotence or of total control' in the case of beatific narratives or of 'impotence and victimhood' in the case of horrific narratives (Glynos and Howarth, 2007: 147).

Having set out the function of the three related logics of enquiry in analysing specific research questions, it is necessary to say something at this point about the ontological status of these logics, or rather their relationship to the 'ontical/ontological distinction' (Glynos and Howarth, 2007: 153). One question which arises in particular at this stage concerns the apparent overlap between the concept of discourse in the works of Laclau and Mouffe (1985) and the concept of social logics set out here. While the category of political logic can be seen as an umbrella term which refers collectively to Laclau and Mouffe's logics of equivalence and difference – and, in so doing, highlights the symbiotic relationship which exists between the two in the political constitution of social reality – the concept of a social logic appears more or less indistinguishable from the concept of a discourse *qua* semi-permanent social structure.

Glynos and Howarth (2007: 153) indeed appear to differentiate the ontological status of social logics, on the one hand, from political and fantasmatic logics on the other. They argue that:

> whereas social logics are substantive, in the sense that their identity is virtually coterminous with the social practices and contexts they inform and make possible, political logics have a formal aspect, enabling us to specify them with some precision independently of the fields of meaning in which they operate. And the same is true of fantasmatic logics because we can separate out the ontological from the ontical aspects in a more robust way than is possible in the case of social logics.

Political and fantasmatic logics, therefore, can be seen as ontological categories, which are filled out or substantiated with a specific ontic content in different social contexts. They are categories which enable us to account for both the general (ontological) conditions of the possibility of a given discursive formation, and its specific (ontic) content as the product of political contestation and fantastic investment (Glynos and Howarth, 2007: 153). Social logics, by contrast, appear to lack this ontological dimension and are concerned instead with the ontic content of a particular discursive formation (Glynos and Howarth, 2007: 154).

Within this study, the concepts of social, political and fantasmatic logics set out above will be employed to explain the structure and the potency of the Eurosceptic and pro-Brexit discourses. Having identified the representation of Britain and the EU present within long-standing Eurosceptic discourses of British national identity in Chapter 5, the focus shifts to the related but distinct pro-Brexit discourses evident in the 2016 referendum campaign. Chapters 6–9 will analyse the different aspects of these discourses in terms of their social logics and through the logics of equivalence, difference and fantasy in order to account for their constitution, sedimentation and emotive force.

Media coverage of the EU treaty reform process

Chapter 5 of this book examines long-standing Eurosceptic discourses through an analysis of the coverage of the EU treaty reform process which culminated in the entry into force of the ToL in 2009 in five British daily newspapers and their Sunday equivalents. By examining these sources, it was possible to identify and analyse the key assumptions of British Eurosceptic discourse within the public sphere focusing on the construction of political identities within this. The decision to focus on newspaper articles versus other media (e.g. television, radio and online) was partly a response to existing studies on the representation of the EU in Britain, which focus overwhelmingly on this medium (Anderson and Weymouth, 1999; Ichijo, 2002). In addition, newspapers are often agenda setters in the British media (Anderson and Weymouth, 1999). There are obvious practical reasons for focusing on newspapers within a study of this size and magnitude. Although discourse theorists take a wide variety of sources as examples of discourse (Torfing, 1999; Howarth, 2000), the process of conducting discourse analysis requires in the first instance that all materials collected be converted to a form of text (Taylor, 2001; Jørgensen and Phillips, 2002). The period analysed also predates the subsequent expansion in the consumption of news online and the importance of social media evident in the Brexit referendum debates.

Newspapers, like all institutions and actors, are thus a product of the specific discursive environment in which they exist. At the same time, they play a crucial role in the reproduction and subversion of hegemonic discourses. It is impossible, therefore, to see newspapers as simply the cause or the effect of public opinion toward the EU (Hansen, 2006). Instead, there is a dynamic and mutually constitutive relationship between the two. Like the subject themselves, newspapers are simultaneously both the product and the cause of the discursive environment in which they are situated. Consequently, newspapers provide the researcher with a highly useful and practical object of study, which can be viewed as windows into a particular discursive environment (and ongoing political process) at a specific moment in time.

The articles examined were taken from the English editions of the highest selling newspapers (in bold), in each sector of the British print media in terms of political alignment and genre (Table 4.1). Since there is no mid-range left-of-centre publication available for analysis, this breakdown gave five distinct sections of the UK print media market. No analytical distinction was made between articles published in daily and Sunday newspapers and so titles are referred to by the generic version of the name (i.e. *The Mail* versus the *Daily Mail* or *Mail on Sunday*). This reflects the growing synergies in production and editorial processes between sister titles by the time of the study, most notably through the housing of both titles on shared websites through which newspapers were increasingly consumed. The only exceptions to this were the *Observer* and the *News of the World* which had distinct brand names, making the elision between daily and Sunday editions potentially misleading. The *Financial Times*, with a large international readership and limited domestic circulation, was also excluded from the study on the grounds that it did not reflect the dominant national conversation on the EU. This is despite (or perhaps because of) the fact it offers the most serious in-depth coverage of European integration in the UK media.

Articles from these newspapers were searched for and collected from the Lexis-Nexis database using the following keyword search: *European Constitution* or *EU Constitution* or *EU Treaty* or *Reform Treaty*. The terms *Lisbon Treaty* and *Treaty of Lisbon* were not used as search terms as this treaty came into existence only at the very end of the time period analysed.

Articles published over a seven-day period straddling each key event in the treaty reforms were collected. Downloaded articles were reviewed for relevance and false returns discarded. This process yielded a total of 1,346 articles. The events in the treaty reform analysed, the precise dates to be covered and the number of articles collected for each time period are shown in Table 4.2.

Chapters 6–9 draw on an analysis of byline articles published by key figures in the *Vote Leave* campaign (Boris Johnson, Michael Gove, Liam Fox, Iain Duncan Smith, Jacob Rees Mogg, Priti Patel and David Davis)

Table 4.1 Distribution of Newspapers Analysed in Chapter 5

	Left	*Right*
Quality/Broadsheet	*The Guardian/ Observer*	*The Daily Telegraph*
Mid-range		*The Daily Mail*
Tabloid	*The Daily Mirror*	*The Sun/News of the World*

58 *Deploying discourse theory*

and by Nigel Farage as the sole figurehead of the *Leave.EU* campaign in any daily national newspaper (the five titles detailed earlier plus the *Daily Express, Daily Star, The Times* and *The Independent* in the period from 1 January until 23 June 2016 (Table 4.3). The wider scope of the analysis reflects both the shorter time frame under analysis and the differing research objective of capturing pro-Brexit voices as opposed to attempting to identify Eurosceptic discourses within the wider media landscape which had informed the study from which Chapter 5 is derived.

Articles were again identified using a keyword search of the Lexis-Nexis database for each title using the author's name and 'Brexit' (e.g. 'Boris Johnson' AND 'Brexit'). Articles were then screened and reviewed for relevance. Once duplicates were removed, this yielded a total of 52 articles to be analysed across all titles. The number of articles included in the study for each author is included in Table 4.4. It should be noted that one article was

Table 4.2 Number of Articles Collected on the EU Treaty Reform Process and Examined in Chapter 5

Event	The Sun/ NOTW	The Mirror	The Mail	The Telegraph	Guardian/ Observer
Draft Constitution 20 July 2003	53	22	63	40	24
European Council 16–17 June 2004	36	12	43	48	45
Signing of Constitution 29 October 2004	29	6	32	38	24
Fr/ Dutch Referenda 29 May/1 June 2005	35	7	39	58	65
European Council 16–17 June 2005	46	17	37	89	64
European Council 15–16 June 2006	9	0	5	11	5
European Council 21–22 June 2007	45	10	31	53	32
European Council 18–19 October 2007	42	13	38	56	24

Table 4.3 Distribution of Newspapers Analysed in Chapters 6–9

	Left	Right
Quality/Broadsheet	*The Guardian/Observer* *The Independent*	*The Daily Telegraph* *The Times*
Mid-range	*The I*	*The Daily Mail* *The Daily Express*
Tabloid	*The Daily Mirror* *The Sunday People*	*The Sun/News of the World* *The Daily Star*

Deploying discourse theory 59

Table 4.4 Distribution of Newspaper Articles Analysed in Chapters 6–9

	Telegraph	Times	Guardian/ Observer	I'dent/The I	Mail	Express	Sun	Mirror/ People	Total
Boris Johnson	11	–	–	1	–	1	1	1	15
Michael Gove	1*	1	–	–	1	–	–	–	3
Iain D. Smith	1	1	–	–	1	1	–	–	4
Liam Fox	1	–	–	–	1	–	1	–	3
Priti Patel	1	–	–	–	1	–	1	–	3
Jacob R. Mogg	–	–	–	–	1	2	–	2	5
David Davis	–	–	–	–	–	–	–	1	1
Nigel Farage	4	–	–	1	–	11	–	1	17
Total	19	2	–	2	5	15	3	5	51

Note
* Gove also co-authored a further article with Johnson, which is included only in Johnson's totals.

co-authored by Michael Gove and Boris Johnson meaning the total number of discrete articles examined was 51. In addition, one of the articles attributed to Iain Duncan Smith in the table below was co-authored with three other Tory grandees and vocal Brexit supporters: Michael Howard, Norman Lamont and Nigel Lawson who, having stepped back from front-line politics sometime before the referendum campaign, were not included in the search strategy. Similarly, Nigel Farage co-authored one of his articles with two other MPs: Tom Pursglove and Kate Hoey. The lower number of articles here reflects the more circumscribed focus and shorter timeframe for analysis compared to the study from which Chapter 5 is derived.

It will be noted that no articles were identified in the main broadsheet left-of-centre titles, *The Guardian* and *The Observer*, although the left-of-centre tabloids (*The Mirror* and *The Sunday People*) feature articles by leave campaigners. At the other end of the spectrum the highest number of articles was found in *The Telegraph* (n = 19 of which 11 came from Boris Johnson) and *The Express* (n = 15, of which 11 were by Nigel Farage). The two most prolific contributors by far were Nigel Farage (n = 17) and Boris Johnson (n = 15), reflecting the strong national profiles of each, even before the referendum and the focus of the *Leave.EU* and *Vote Leave* campaigns respectively on their activities. The frequency of Johnson's bylines in *The Telegraph* reflects his prior relationship with that newspaper as a paid columnist, but is also indicative of the target demographics of the *Vote Leave* campaign. Similarly, the focus of Farage on *The Express* reflects the different audience to which he sought to appeal which will be discussed in the following chapters. In both studies, the included articles were subjected to manual thematic coding (Braun and Clarke, 2006) to identify key themes and tropes. Key passages from each of the articles were extracted using a data extraction tool and tabulated according to theme. The organisation of material in these tables formed the basis for the analysis presented in Chapters 5–9.

5 Embedded Euroscepticism

A key argument presented in this book is that it is impossible to understand the structure and impact of pro-Brexit discourses – and with this, the outcome of the 2016 vote – without examining the deeply sedimented conceptual vocabulary in terms of which debates about the EU were conducted before this and which informed the referendum campaign. This builds on Usherwood and Startin's (2013) understanding of Euroscepticism as an 'embedded and persistent' phenomenon at both the national and European levels. The current chapter focuses on longstanding Eurosceptic discourses in the UK which provide the hinterland to the Brexit referendum debate analysed in subsequent chapters. The existence of these discourses was a key contextual factor for the short campaign analysed in subsequent chapters. These provided an available pool of meanings and assumptions that could be drawn on, and employed to make sense of, often complex, opaque and seemingly distant political processes and institutions within the EU.

The chapter examines the Eurosceptic discourses evident in the coverage of the EU treaty reform process culminating in the ToL examined elsewhere (Hawkins, 2012; Hawkins, 2015). It identifies how 'Britain' and 'Europe' emerge as fundamentally heterogeneous and separate entities in Eurosceptic discourses. These discourses are informed by an underlying logic of nationalism in which the only legitimate political unit is the nation. The EU is viewed exclusively through the conceptual prism of the nation: as both an international bargaining forum skewed against the UK's interests (and toward those of a 'core' Franco-German alliance) and, at the same time, an emerging super-state. In both its manifestations, European integration is identified as the 'other' against which 'Britain' is defined. In keeping with discourse theoretical accounts of nationalism discussed in previous chapters, the EU is identified as an existential threat to the UK – in terms of its political freedom and economic prosperity – which must be resisted at all costs. This discourse depends not just on these social and political logics but on fantasies of subjugation that sustain their emotive force and the persistent hold of this thinking over significant sections of the public.

DOI: 10.4324/9781315098067-5

The nationalist logic of European politics

Within the Eurosceptic discourse, nations are assumed to be primordial entities, and nationality is identified as the predominant (if not the only genuine) form of political identity. Consequently, the 'nation-state' is seen as being the natural, and only legitimate, form of political organisation (see Billig, 1995). In contrast, the EU, as a supra-national body, is seen as an artificial political construction that runs counter to the natural order and which lacks the sense of common identity required for collective action, and democratic government via shared institutions. Conservative MEP Daniel Hannan, for example, argues that 'European democracy fails because there is no demos – no community with which we identify when we use the word "We" – only the kratos of a system that must compel obedience through force of law, not loyalty' (Hannan, *Telegraph*, 13 June 2004). The idea that the EU could emerge as a source of common identity associated with a self-conscious European political community is simply impossible within this conceptual framework.

The EU is consistently equated with historical attempts to control and dominate the UK through unflattering parallels drawn with previous attempts at trans-national government in Europe and beyond. Elsewhere, Hannan argues that 'supra-nationalism […] has never yet found a way to co-exist with democracy (Hannan, *Telegraph*, 14 May 2005). In the same article, Hannan cites the 'Habsburgs and the Ottomans, the Yugoslavs and the Soviets' as previous failed attempts to construct a supra-national state, although he fails to include the British empire and the struggles for independence fought by the peoples of countries subsumed within this. All these empires failed, Hannan argues, for 'as soon as their peoples were given the vote, they opted for self-determination.' From this perspective, the process of European political integration is simply the latest in a long line of unsuccessful, and inevitably futile, attempts to usurp or disregard national identities and the nation-state.

The apparently artificial and inorganic nature of the EU means that the goal of European integration is constructed as a utopian ideal that fails to take account of the fundamental political realities of the world in which it exists. 'Europhiles' are described variously as 'EU dreamers' (Kavanagh, *Sun*, 26 May 2005), as 'true believers' (Rennie, *Telegraph*, 26 May 2005), or as 'Euro-fanatics' (see also Phillips, *Mail*, 30 May 2005). Britain's Minister for Europe, Dennis MacShane, is described as 'insanely federalist' (Cecil, *Sun*, 1 December 2004), while Prime Minister Tony Blair is accused of being a 'blazing zealot' on the question of 'Europe' (Phillips, *Mail*, 21 June 2004). The idea that one can be a 'true-believer' in the EU invests the European integration project with quasi-religious or cult-like qualities. It is presented as something which, like the scriptures, must be accepted as an article of faith and which inspires boundless and unquestioning devotion in its adherents. The EU is thus described using language very different from that employed to describe the nations and nationalism. Nowhere are those who oppose the expansion of powers toward the EU described as 'idealistically nationalist,' since nations are the fabric of the natural political order.

The nationalist logic of the Eurosceptic discourse is evident also in the way in which the EU is represented in these discourses. The nation-state provides the conceptual lens through which European integration is viewed. The 'reductionist' version of this sees the EU simply as an inter-state bargaining forum or as an emerging state in its own right, while the 'maximalist' claims to identify an emerging European super-state which will usurp and provincialise its constituent member-states. Both strands of this discourse have given a particularly 'British' flavour through the tropes and images employed to describe the EU in each guise.

EU politics as a zero-sum game

Within the Eurosceptic discourse, certain commentators account for the existence of the EU as a forum for an inter-state between member-states. From this perspective, EU politics is a zero-sum game played by competing member-states with clear winners and losers from each new regulation or treaty revision. There is no sense of mutual gain or of common European interests emerging from the process of European integration. Almost invariably, the states which are seen to benefit are France, Germany and a changing coalition of allies, while this comes at the expense of the UK.

There are repeated references to both sport and war to describe European level negotiations; arenas in which the distinction between winning and losing is clear cut and in which the UK has historically been, or continues to be, brought into direct conflict with its neighbours. Reporting on European Council negotiations in 2005, Patrick Hennessy uses an extended military metaphor to explain both the conduct and outcome of the proceedings (Hennessy, *Telegraph*, 19 June 2005):

> By attracting a small but sufficient number of allies, and refusing to bow before French-led demands [...], the Prime Minister can claim that he at least avoided defeat in Brussels. The principal peril facing him, of course, as countless European campaigns have proved down the centuries, is that surviving a battle does not necessarily mean that you will win the war. [...] In contrast to the historic encounter between Wellington and Napoleon, there was no direct engagement. But the war of words between the two nations was as ferocious as any veteran observer of European Union summits could remember.

This plays on the idea that the European Council is simply warfare by other means. Whereas in the 19th-century international conflict was fought out bloodily on the battlefield, modern-day conflicts play out behind closed doors in the Justus Lipsius building in Brussels.

64 *Embedded Euroscepticism*

Since EU level politics is seen as a competition for advantage among rival member-states, the role of national governments is simply to defend the 'national interest' defined in purely negative and defensive terms. Collective action at EU level is never viewed in terms of mutually beneficial solutions to common problems, or an opportunity to achieve British national objectives, but as a threat which must be resisted. Constructive engagement with the EU in and of itself runs counter to the national interest. The *Telegraph,* for example, urges Prime Minister Tony Blair to 'stop fretting about his communautaire credentials and concentrate on protecting the national interest' (Hennessy, *Telegraph,* 19 June 2005).

Britain, France and the EU

The costs and benefits of EU membership are seen to reflect the relative power and influence wielded by these states within the EU machinery. The EU is seen as a French invention designed to serve its interests and maximise its power while undermining those of the UK. As Peter Hitchens (*Mail,* 15 May 2005) comments:

> The nation whose icy-brained bureaucrats devised the original European system was in the best position to make sure that it did well out of the rules. Charles de Gaulle kept Britain out of the Common Market in the Sixties mainly because he wanted to rig farming subsidies in France's favour for all time, and feared that British membership would get in the way of his plan. By the time we joined the deal was done, and it has stayed that way for more than 30 years.

This narrative, however, appears to ignore the fact that it was the UK government which declined to participate in the process of European integration at its outset, thereby foregoing the chance to set the rules of the game which Hitchens, and other Eurosceptic commentators, complain were shaped by France and others.

Britain, Germany and the EU

At other times it is Germany, not France, which is seen to be in control of the pace and direction of the treaty reform process. Germany is described by the *Mail* as the 'architect' of the EU project (Chapman, *Mail,* 18 October 2007). Similarly, it is argued that the ToL would consolidate Germany's position of dominance in the EU since '[t]he new voting system enthrones Germany as the EU's dominant power, reflecting its 82 million population' (*Telegraph,* 21 June 2004). More provocatively, it is claimed that the EU is just the latest manifestation of an inherent German desire to control Europe in its entirety through explicit references to WW2. As Tom Utley (*Telegraph,* 13 May 2005) baldly states:

one of the most powerful factors stopping us [from adopting the *Treaty Establishing a Constitution for Europe*] is our knowledge of how the Germans behaved between Hitler's election in 1933 and his suicide in 1945. We know that the last man who tried to impose supra-national authority on Europe was Adolf.

This is not an isolated example. An almost identical point is made by Melanie Phillips (*Mail,* 12 May 2003) who claims that 'what Hitler failed to do, Europe is now proposing to bring about by edict – this time with the connivance of the British Government.' Germany, in other words, is attempting to dominate and control Europe via the legalistic mechanism of the EU in the same way in which it attempted to do this through military conquest in the first half of the 20th century.

The Franco-German alliance

Within the Eurosceptic discourse, there is an equivalence created between the interests of France and Germany which set a shared agenda for the EU, which runs counter to UK interests. As David Rennie comments (Rennie, *Telegraph*, 3 June 2005):

> It is one of the grandest traditions of the European project: on the eve of any EU summit, the leaders of France and Germany meet to thrash out a joint approach, before descending, like gods from Olympus, to tell the other nations what they have agreed.

The UK is locked in battle with the Franco-German alliance, and a varying constellation of other allies, over different aspects of EU policy. In terms clearly evocative of the First World War, Helm and Evans-Pritchard (*Telegraph,* 7 November 2004), state that 'France, Spain and Germany launched a '"triple axis" […] aimed at taking charge of EU foreign policy and limiting Tony Blair's influence in Europe.'

The effect of the Franco-German alliance is to position the UK on the margins of the EU in which power is wielded by an alliance of France and Germany. This is evident also in the idea of a 'core' Europe – an inner circle of countries, under Franco-German leadership that occupy a privileged position within the EU – which emerges within the Eurosceptic discourses. The UK, by contrast, is confined to the margins of the EU decision-making process and is unable to wield the political influence enjoyed by core member-states.

The UK's special treatment

Within the Eurosceptic discourse, there is an almost complete failure to recognise that the apparent marginalisation of the UK within the EU discussed above may be, in part at least, the result of the UK's recalcitrance and defensiveness toward common European action. The significant benefits which the UK receives from EU membership and the special treatment that it has been afforded by its European partners over the past four decades are ignored. This includes a range of opt-outs and derogations from unfavoured policies such as the EMU, common action in the area of justice and home affairs and, initially at least, the 'social chapter' of the TEU as well as its highly controversial rebate on budget contributions. The very fact that the UK has been able to secure such concessions should be seen as evidence of the UK's strong bargaining position and its ability to secure its interests within the EU.

While there is righteous indignation about the perceived advantages enjoyed by other member-states such as France, it is taken for granted that the UK should be able to pick and choose the parts of the European integration project in which it wishes to participate so as to maximise its interests and minimise any potentially negative externalities. Years before the idea of 'cherry picking' entered the lexicon of the Brexit negotiations, David Trimble and Martin Howe QC suggested that the UK should pursue precisely such a strategy, taking the good things from 'Europe' while abandoning those aspects not in its interest (see Trimble, *Telegraph,* 20 October 2007, Howe, *Telegraph,* 19 October 2007). The concerns of other member-states, and the duties that Britain may have to them and the EU more generally as a result of its membership of the organisation, are simply not considered. This sense of entitlement is evidence of the exceptionalist logic that characterises Eurosceptic approaches to the EU.

Discussion about the costs and benefits of EU membership for the UK presents the EU as a club run by France and Germany to pursue their own interests and undermine those of the UK. At the same time, the preferential treatment received by the UK is downplayed or taken for granted, conferring upon the UK a special status in the minds of many commentators in which it ought to be able to dictate its own terms of membership to the rest of the EU.

Britain's European 'other'

The second dimension of the Eurosceptic discourse constructs the EU not as a bargaining forum but as a unitary political actor; an external entity, entirely separate from the UK and more analogous to a neighbouring state than an international organisation of which the UK is a member-state. Through the construction of antagonistic equivalential chains, Britain and the EU are constructed in radical opposition to one another. Each is presented as being a unified and internally homogenous entity in which internal differences and conflicts are downplayed, and the heterogeneity of each from the other is brought to the fore. In this context, the terminology and the concepts employed to discuss EU-level politics again reflect the underlying nationalist assumptions of the Eurosceptic discourse as the EU is depicted as an emerging 'super-state.'

Positioning Britain and 'Europe'

As Laclau (2005) has argued, the act of naming plays a crucial role in the emergence of an equivalential chain. Within Eurosceptic discourses, the EU is constructed as an internally homogenous actor through its metonymic representation by the terms 'Europe' and 'Brussels.' This creates the impression that the EU is a single entity able to speak with one voice on any given issue rather than a disparate collection of institutions and actors combining in different constellations across policy areas. The internal differences which may exist between different EU-level institutions, member-states or regions are played down at the expense of their common identity as 'European.' The characteristic that links these different identity positions together is their radical heterogeneity from the idea of 'Britishness.'

The separation constructed between Britain and the EU (or its metonymic representations) means that the signifiers 'Europe' and 'the EU' are employed to refer not to the EU in its entirety, but to a rump EU, which excludes the UK. Frequent reference is made to 'Britain's relationship *with* Europe (*Telegraph*, 15 June 2004, emphasis added) and to transfers of powers '*to* the European Union' (*Telegraph*, 25 June 2006, emphasis added). Similarly, there is talk of 'more powers being transferred *from* Westminster *to* Brussels' (*Mail*, 22 June 2003) and a 'transfer of sovereignty from Westminster to Brussels' (Helm, *Telegraph*, 2 October 2007). The fact that powers can be transferred to the EU from the UK assumes that a dichotomy exists between the two entities and that the latter is excluded from, and thus exercises no influence within, the former.

The EU as a colonial power

The EU is identified within the Eurosceptic discourse as 'a foreign power' attempting to assume control over certain aspects of British life in which it has no business interfering. This suggests that the UK is not part of the EU, but engaged in bilateral relations *with* the latter as with a neighbouring state. Furthermore, the EU is not identified as an ally, but as a hostile, quasi-imperial power plotting to control and exploit the UK by any means possible. This creates the impression of a piecemeal, yet coordinated, attempt by the EU to assume control of the UK one policy at a time. The ultimate objective of the European integration process is a 'secret agenda' to construct a European super-state that will usurp its constituent member-states.

Consequently, the deepening of European integration in any form is seen as a threat from which the UK must be defended. Great emphasis is placed on the ability of the British government to resist any further deepening integration process and, where this is not possible, to seek opt-outs from any common action. The key political priority is the maintenance of unanimity-based decision making and to avoid the 'loss' or 'surrender' of the UK's veto within the Council of Ministers as a way of curtailing further integration. Qualified Majority Voting (QMV) is viewed as a potential threat to the British national interest through which regulation could be forced on the UK against its interests, but there is no consideration of the fact that QMV may allow the UK to pass measures that are in its interest and which may otherwise be blocked. It is, therefore, an overwhelmingly negative mindset that provides the framework through which EU level politics is evaluated. The EU is something which is done to the UK; something to be feared and approached with trepidation rather than a means to achieving desirable policy outcomes.

This highly defensive position toward the EU is captured by former Chancellor of the Exchequer Gordon Brown on the subject of the EU and the European Constitution (*Mail,* 17 May 2005). In ways which would foreshadow the strategy of the 'remain' campaign in the 2016 referendum, it revealed that Brown believed a mooted referendum in the UK on the aforementioned 'Constitution' was potentially winnable if the argument in favour of the Constitution were to be made 'from a position that was robustly critical of the EU.' Thus, even in one of those rare moments in which a senior British politician is speaking in favour of Britain's positive engagement with the EU, it is tempered by a highly negative account of the EU itself. No positive argument is made for Britain's membership of the EU, highlighting the benefits Britain receives from this. It is easy to understand why the British public has shown so little enthusiasm for the EU when the organisation is presented in such negative terms by political leaders: as a threat which must be guarded against and a flawed institution in need of reform.

The EU as economic other

Within the Eurosceptic discourse, Britain is constructed as an economic power, committed to free-trade and liberalised markets, faced with a heterogeneous (inferior and outdated) European economic model, which both the supra-national institutions (ie the Commission and the CJEU) and a hostile coalition of 'core' EU member-states seek to impose on it. Within this discourse, the Eurozone functions as a central reference point for the construction of the UK as an economic actor. Questions about the economic performance of member-state economies and the viability of the Euro – and indeed whether the UK should adopt the Euro – provided the backdrop to the EU treaty reform process between 2003 and 2007. The relatively poor performance of the Eurozone economy compared with that of the UK is continually highlighted. Furthermore, the strong performance of the UK economy is attributed in large part to the UK government's decision not to adopt the Euro. However, even outside the Euro, Britain was not immune from its effects with the UK's economic performance allegedly being undermined by the close integration of the UK with the Eurozone. Within the Eurosceptic discourse, therefore, a certain paradox emerges in which the UK is presented as being both economically powerful compared with the Eurozone and at the same time vulnerable to its effects.

The separation of the UK from the EU was not confined to the issue of membership of the Euro, but involves a wider set of characteristics that typify the UK and 'European' economic models. The UK is presented as a modern, flexible, dynamic economy that is well placed to benefit from the new economic realities such as the emergence of China and India. The UK, it is argued, favours free-trade, liberal markets and a minimal role for the state in managing the economy. The 'European' economy, by contrast, is seen to be protectionist, overregulated, inflexible and overburdened by the costs of social security provisions, which renders it unfit to meet the challenges of an increasingly globalised economy. As Roger Bootle (*Telegraph*, 22 October 2007) comments:

> they have stopped their labour markets from functioning effectively, presided over huge public debts which threaten to become unsustainable under the weight of unfunded pension policies, and are in thrall to aggressive, depredatory trade unions.

Consequently, the British economy 'has become the envy of Europe by limiting the powers of unions and boosting flexibility in the workplace' to turn itself 'into a thriving low-tax economy' (Pascoe-Watson, *Sun*, 20 June 2003).

The Eurosceptic discourse is characterised by an almost paranoid concern that the EU institutions and its core member-states (ie France and Germany) are plotting to undermine the UK's economic success. At times, it is claimed that the UK could be forced to adopt the Euro in order to undermine the comparative advantage it has outside the single currency. UK membership of the Euro, it is implied, would be advantageous to the existing members of the Eurozone as it would place the same monetary and fiscal constraints on the UK as existing Eurozone members. The UK would, therefore, be 'dragged down' to continental European levels of economic output and unemployment. As Simon Heffer (*Mail*, 13 May 2005) argues:

> The fact is that, outside the Euro, and less regulated than our neighbours, Britain is simply too economically successful for some of its partners, and so handicaps must be shackled on to us.

This would allow existing member-states to continue their project of 'building Europe', shielded from the competition posed by the UK's alternative economic model.

David Hughes argues that the proposed EU 'constitution' would be 'a giant ball and chain on the British economy' (Hughes, *Mail*, 29 October 2004). Of particular concern in the context of the treaty reform process is the proposal to include in this a Charter of Fundamental Rights which would restrict current UK employment practices and, it is argued, undermine its current flexibility and efficiency. Sarah Oliver argues that the Constitutional Treaty, enshrining a French-inspired economic model on the EU, could mean a return for Britain to the industrial disputes of the past (Oliver, *Mail*, 15 June 2003):

> To those who remember the industrial strife of the Seventies, the power and extremism of the trade unions in France will be horribly familiar and a grim warning of what life could be like under Giscard d'Estaing's federal European constitution.

The implication is that the political leaders in continental Europe are unwilling to reform their own failing economies and see the liberalised British economy as a threat to their existing form of economic management. Consequently, their aim is to undermine the British economy and the competitive advantage it is seen to enjoy over its neighbours.

Peter Hitchens argues that the reluctance to reform the French economy is based on a deep-seated fear of individual responsibility and an over-reliance on the protection of the state which is evident throughout French society. Despite its post-war prosperity, Hitchens argues, France is a country surprisingly reminiscent of East Germany in which 'even the conservatives are socialists' by UK standards and there is a pervasive fear of independence and competition (Hitchens, *Mail*, 15 May 2005). In the same article, he refers to France as 'a nation of mummy's boys, suspicious of independence and the cold winds of competition.' Britain represents the antithesis of this, a manly acceptance of the harsh realities of the world and the value of self-sufficiency and independence. As an agreement was reached on the final text of the ToL, the apparent attempts by the French government to remove a specific reference to an internal market of 'free and undistorted' competition from the stated aims of the EU received a great deal of attention within the British media. The unwillingness of certain EU member-states to reform their apparently outdated labour markets or to embrace competition within the single market is seen as evidence of the underlying insularity of the EU.

The EU and other member-states are accused of protecting the inefficient European economies from competition from more dynamic economies, such as those of the United States of America (USA) and China. They are criticised for attempting to create a highly-regulated internal market rather than attempting to open Europe up to the rest of the world. As David Trimble argues: 'too many of our EU partners are stuck in the reactionary mindset of seeking to use the EU as a means of hiding from the rest of the world' (Trimble, *Telegraph* 20 October 2007). The UK, by contrast, is seen to be more outward-looking and internationalist in its orientation by virtue of its maritime and colonial past. It is, therefore, uniquely placed to exploit the economic and geo-political realities of the interconnected world of the 21st century. An 'independent' UK, he goes on to argue, could act as an advocate for free trade in global forums such as the World Trade Organization (WTO). While other member-states have no alternative but to seek their place in the world via the EU, the UK has a genuine alternative due to the post-colonial legacy of the Commonwealth and its apparently 'special relationship' with the USA, which represent more natural alliances for the UK than the EU. The Telegraph (22 November 2004) argues, for example, that 'our true strategic interests – and, in particular, our alliances with other free, English speaking nations – are being tossed aside for the sake of Euro-dogma.'

Europe as cultural 'other'

Within the right-wing press, the significance of the EU treaty reform process is not limited to the political sphere, but is felt also in the broader cultural sphere. For example, Melanie Phillips (*Mail,* 12 May 2003, emphasis added) argues that, as a result of the Charter of Fundamental Rights, which formed part of the Constitutional Treaty:

> We will lose our freedom to make *moral* choices. We will be bound by the EU's Charter of Fundamental Rights, a means of enforcing politically correct doctrines and other values endorsed by the European nomenklatura.

Phillips' concern that the Charter represents the transformation of the EU from a principally economic organisation to one with a far broader sociocultural remit is echoed by Charles Moore (*Telegraph,* 30 October 2004), who comments that as a result of the agreement:

> Everyone has a right to a "high level" of this and that – healthcare, environmental protection, ciabatta, whatever. It will give the European Court a much wider basis for making decisions. Until recently, most European decisions have been economic. Now they will be cultural. This is about what sort of lives we should lead, and it gives legal authority to European judges and bureaucrats to tell us how to lead them.

For both Moore and Phillips, the idea that the EU should have a role in governing the way we manage 'our lives' is anathema. While they also oppose the deepening of economic integration, there appears to be a qualitative distinction between their opposition to the EU's role in the economy, and their opposition to any form of supra-national competence in broader social issues.

This is perhaps indicative of the more obvious association of the latter with what Zizek (1993: 201) terms the 'national Thing': the unique set of cultural practices which constitute the essence of nationhood. The reference by Moore to 'ciabatta' would also seem to imply a suspicion of curious 'other' forms of 'enjoyment' manifested in the image of the food 'they' eat. The way in which the 'others' choose to organise their enjoyment is as inaccessible to us as ours is to them. For this reason, decisions about morality or lifestyle can only be made within national cultural boundaries, which within the Eurosceptic discourse are synonymous with national boundaries.

Elsewhere, the customs and practices of other Europeans are seen as strange and impenetrable to the British observer. Justin Stares (*Telegraph*, 1 May 2005), for example, dedicates an entire article to the opening of a new 'VIP sauna' installed in the Berlaymont Building: the headquarters of the European Commission. The article purports to be about the excessive benefits of the European political class and the questionable use of budgetary resources. However, alongside the details of how taxpayers' money is allegedly being misspent, there is a deeper sense of cultural 'othering' which runs through the article:

> Ever the masters of punctilious regulation, the European Union's 25 Commissioner have outdone themselves with a code of conduct for their new and beautifully-appointed Brussels sauna. Nudity is de rigueur, according to the Commission's infrastructure office, but bravado is not. "Reckless competition about who stands heat best is out of the question. Leave your clothes in the dressing room- nakedness is natural," the code tells its 18 male and seven female commissioners.

Here, British behavioural norms are implicitly contrasted to a heterogeneous set of 'European' norms. While for the British, bravado and healthy competition are viewed positively, for the European they are to be avoided at all costs. By contrast, there is something seemingly suspicious to the British reader about both safety notices and gratuitous nudity, particularly in a mixed sauna.

Leaving the European Union

By the time of the ToL debates, the idea of the UK leaving the EU had already emerged as a topic of open discussion within Eurosceptic circles. For example, the *Telegraph* ran a series of articles in October 2007, in which the feasibility and desirability of the UK's withdrawal from the EU were debated. Ruth Lea (*Telegraph*, 16 October 2007) and Norman Lamont (*Telegraph*, 17 October 2007) put the economic case for leaving on the grounds that this would free British industry from the burdensome EU, while Martin Howe (*Telegraph*, 19 October 2007) argued that the UK could construct a new relationship with the EU which maintains close ties with the latter, but falls short of full membership. This renegotiated relationship, David Trimble (*Telegraph*, 20 October 2007) suggests, would give the UK government greater control over domestic policy and also greater influence internationally.

These articles are united in their view that the UK's relationship 'with' the EU is valuable, at least in economic terms, but that the political costs and regulatory burden associated with EU membership outweigh the benefits to the UK. In what foreshadows the later Brexit referendum debate and the subsequent negotiations with the EU over a future relationship, there appears also to be a consensus among the commentators cited above that Britain could enjoy the benefits of the single market without necessarily remaining a full member of the EU. Countries such as Norway and Switzerland provide a precedent which the UK could follow in redefining its relationship with the EU. However, as became apparent in the post-referendum debates membership of the European Economic Area would not in fact afford the UK the degree of 'independence' and regulatory divergence sought by these Brexit proponents. These interventions are indicative of the mindset of a large and influential part of the British political class when it comes to Britain's role in the world and its position within the EU. Many mainstream politicians and commentators have never fully reconciled themselves with the fact that Britain is a European country and adhere to an idea of British exceptionalism, whereby the UK is not subject to the structural limitations of other medium-sized powers and can somehow carve out a bespoke position for itself in the world.

In countries such as France and Germany (along with the UK, the most populous member-states, representing the three largest economies), debates would simply not be possible in the way they are in the UK. While it is true that political actors and commentators in France, for example, may advocate reform of the EU or, on the political margins, may oppose its very existence, it is impossible to think that they could advocate the secession of their country from the EU, while expecting the Union to continue to exist in anything resembling its current form. Were France (or Germany) to leave the EU, it would cease to be an EU in anything other than name. There would be no Union left with which to forge bilateral relations in the way in which British commentators argue the UK should. By contrast, it is not only possible to imagine an EU which does not contain the UK, but this functions as the very basis of Anglo-British nationalist discourse.

Britain as Europe's saviour

The idea of the UK as a unique, independent, not truly European nation is closely associated with discourses about its national mission and its relationship to Europe. The Eurosceptic discourse positions the UK playing an almost messianic role in the EU. It is the responsibility of the UK to spread the gospel of sound economic practice and, in so doing, save the Europeans from themselves. Parallels are drawn between the role of economic saviour in which the UK is now cast and its role as a military saviour in previous times. The connection between the role of the UK as military saviour in the past and her present role of economic saviour is nowhere clearer than in the title of Simon Wolfson's article in the *Telegraph* in which he implores his readers to 'Vote No to the Constitution, and Save Europe from Itself (again)' (Wolfson, *Telegraph*, 29 October 2004).

Most obviously, the role of Britain in WW2 is highlighted with great regularity. However, the First World War and even the Napoleonic Wars are also invoked in keeping with the differentiation of the UK from the Franco-German alliance at the heart of the EU. For example, Michael Henderson in the *Telegraph* reminds us how the British 'saved the continent from Napoleon and Hitler' (Henderson, *Telegraph*, 27 October 2007). To underline the point he concludes the article by stating how it was 'our forebears who gave their lives to keep Europe free.' Britain now as then is seen as the final enclave of freedom and liberty in Europe and for this all Europeans ought to be grateful. In a similar vein, a *Sun* editorial from 2005 laments the irony that 'the country which saved Europe during the war' could have its own destiny decided by the French or the Dutch, who, unlike the British, were scheduled to vote on the Constitutional Treaty shortly after the publication of this article (*Sun*, 26 May 2005).

The construction of the UK as Europe's saviour reinforces not only the narrative of British separation from the continent, but also the apparent moral, military and now economic superiority of the UK over continental Europe. Historically, the European continent symbolised a source of conflict and strife. Britain's role was and is to fend off the threat it presents and to intervene to solve the problems it creates. This is fuel to the fire of those who argue that Britain's interests are better served outside the EU. If the threat to the UK in past centuries came in the form of war with neighbouring states, that threat presently comes in the form of stifling regulation and outdated economic policies which find their institutional embodiment in an EU dominated by the same countries who once posed that military threat.

The hegemony of the Eurosceptic discourse

The Eurosceptic discourse outlined above represents the dominant articulation of European integration and the relationship between the UK and the EU within the British media. This is evident in the extent to which Eurosceptic voices are given a platform even in generally pro-EU publications, while overtly pro-European voices are almost completely excluded from Eurosceptic newspapers. Secondly, pro-EU commentators in pro-EU publications devote a great deal of attention to, and often position themselves in opposition to, the Eurosceptic discourse which is evidence of the position of dominance achieved by the latter. The Eurosceptic discourse, therefore, dictates the terrain on which debates about the EU are conducted. It is the default position against which other accounts of the European integration process must position themselves. Those advocating a positive engagement with the EU must first counter the claims of the Eurosceptic discourse, before being able to present their own arguments. However, in reproducing elements of the Eurosceptic discourse, and in positioning themselves in direct opposition to them, commentators in the left-wing press simply serve to reinforce the predominance of the hegemonic discourse.

Finally, as discussed above, the hegemony of the Eurosceptic discourse is evident in the language employed by government officials, whose defensive and confrontational tone mirrors that of Eurosceptic commentators. Their rhetoric presents the government as the defender of the national interest, protecting the British people from the spectre of the EU and fails to make the case for the EU as a mechanism for managing interdependence, resolving conflicts between states and achieving shared political objectives. This may be the result of a conscious decision by ministers to appeal to the editors of Eurosceptic newspapers or to what they perceive as a Eurosceptic public. On the other hand, it may be the result of a more subtle, subconscious process of socialisation, which reflects the extent to which the Eurosceptic discourse informs the most basic assumptions on which the debates surrounding the EU are grounded, and the terms in which they are conducted. In either case, it is further evidence of the hegemony of Eurosceptic discourse within British debates on the EU.

The critical logics of the Eurosceptic discourse

The preceding sections of this chapter have set out the key assumptions of the predominant right-wing Eurosceptic discourses. In terms of social logics, this discourse is grounded on an essentialist nationalism which sees nations as natural and necessary forms of political community and identity. The EU is, viewed through this lens, inauthentic and incapable of engendering the ties between individuals necessary for democratic governance to occur above the levels of the nation-state. In keeping with this, it is constructed either as an international bargaining forum or as an emerging super-state. In both strands of the Eurosceptic discourse, the political logics of the Eurosceptic discourse create a fundamental separation between the UK and the EU – politically, economically and culturally – through the articulation of disparate elements of the EU and its member-states into equivalential chains unified through their shared heterogeneity from the UK, which exists somehow outside of and alongside the EU.

There is a process of cultural homogenisation at work within the Eurosceptic discourse which constructs a common set of European norms against the (incommensurable) British norms, but fails to offer any differentiation between, for example, Spanish and Finnish approaches. In discourse theoretical terms, we again see the predominance of the *logic of equivalence* over the *logic of difference*. Two competing equivalential chains of British and European political, economic and cultural norms emerge in which the shared commonality between the elements of these chains is highlighted, and any internal differences which exist between them downplayed. In highlighting what binds these chains together, what characterises them as British or European, however, we are simultaneously reinforcing their heterogeneity from the 'other,' since it is in their common rejection of that which they exclude that the unifying principle of a discourse is to be found. The effect of this is to create a radical separation between the UK on the one hand and the remainder of the EU on the other through which the former is constructed and reproduced as a political entity for a principally Anglo-British audience.

These logics exercise a powerful and deeply sedimented hold over the structure of British political discourse on the EU and the way in which both elites and citizens think about and discuss these issues. It is through the category of *fantasmatic logics* that we are able to understand the source of their power. It will be recalled from previous chapters that the Lacanian conception of nationalism is inextricably linked to the category of 'enjoyment' (*jouissance*). The process through which the nation and its relationship to the 'other' is constructed centres around the issue of enjoyment, and how this national enjoyment is allegedly under threat from the 'other' whose aims and motivations remain hidden.

The EU, as a supra-national entity, seems to run counter from the most deeply sedimented (nationalist) assumptions about the natural form of socio-political organisation. It is extremely difficult for commentators or citizens to comprehend what it is, or to identify the ultimate destination of the European integration project. In the context of this conceptual confusion, the aims and objectives of the EU become an object of fantasy (Zizek, 1989; Zizek, 1993). In the absence of a clear understanding of what the EU is and does, Eurosceptic discourses attribute to it an alternative set of aims and motivations. This consists of an apparently hidden agenda that runs counter to the interests of the UK, and whose ultimate aim is to control and subjugate the latter.

According to the Eurosceptic discourse, the EU is an international forum skewed to favour other member-states and exploit the UK, and France and Germany use the EU as a means for pursuing their national interest at the UK's expense (while little attention is given to its own bespoke terms of membership). Alternatively, it is an emerging super-state seeking to slowly colonise the UK. From both perspectives, the EU represents the institutionalisation of Britain's subjugation to its rival states. In Lacanian terms, the EU serves as a barrier to the UK achieving its national 'mission' and functions as an impediment to the full realisation of the shared national 'enjoyment.' This represents the 'horrific' dimension of the Eurosceptic fantasy; however there is also a 'beatific' dimension to these narratives (Glynos and Howarth, 2007: 147). Fantasmatic logics are not only structured around loss – and the theft of 'enjoyment' by the other – but around the idea of a mythical 'fullness-to-come,' currently precluded by the presence of a particular obstacle (Glynos and Howarth, 2007: 147; see also (Zizek, 1989: 210; Stavrakakis, 2005: 73). In this context, if the UK were to leave the EU it would be free to pursue its own interests, without the costs and impediments imposed by 'Brussels.'

In both instances, the construction of Britain as separate from Europe is reinforced by the fantasmatic constructions of the excessive enjoyment of the European 'other' and the need to defend the 'British way of life,' be it in the economic or the cultural sphere. The opposition to the ongoing process of European integration may not simply emanate from a utilitarian concern about the effects of a particular economic policy, or the correct level at which decisions on certain issues should be taken, but taps into a deeper psychological attachment to the national way of life, and a concern to protect the national Thing from the strange and threatening practices of the 'other.'

Summary

This chapter examines how long-standing British debates on the EU are founded on an underlying logic of nationalism. The EU is constructed in such a way that renders it amenable to examination within the conceptual vocabulary of the nation-state. The result of this is that the EU is represented either as simply a forum for inter-state bargaining or as an emerging state in its own right. The EU is identified as a hostile 'other' against which 'Britain' is defined. The othering process presents the EU as a politically, economically and culturally heterogeneous entity to the UK. In the Whig narratives which inform the Eurosceptic discourse, the UK is seen as playing a heroic historical role, coming to Europe's rescue in past conflicts and, in the contemporary context, offering an alternative economic model to rescue it from its current mire. Already at this stage, the idea of leaving the EU is a topic of discussion and many of the tropes and contentions that would inform the 2016 referendum campaign are evident in the contributions of those advocating what was not yet known as 'Brexit.' The narratives of separation and threat which constitute the Eurosceptic discourse are underpinned by fantasmatic support structures focused on the 'horrific' realisation of UK's subjugation to the EU, while holding out the 'beatific' possibility of its emancipation from this exploitative relationship. Outside the EU, the UK would be free to pursue its own interests and realise its unique national mission. The next four chapters examine how the Eurosceptic discourse informed, and was reproduced in, the pro-Brexit discourses which informed the 2016 Brexit referendum campaign, while identifying the ways in which new elements were articulated into this discourse to broaden its potential appeal to voters during the short campaign.

6 Social logics of the *Vote Leave* discourse

This chapter and the two following chapters analyse the pro-Brexit discourse evident in the interventions of key figures in the *Vote Leave* campaign in the 2016 referendum. As explained above, the decision to examine the interventions of the principal actors in *Vote Leave* and *Leave.EU* was a result of the different tone and emphasis identified as emerging from each of the campaigns and the different constituencies of potential leave voters to which they principally sought to appeal. Despite these variations, there remain significant commonalities between the campaigns, particularly in terms of the most fundamental assumptions about the political identity of the UK vis-a-vis the EU, which are discussed in subsequent chapters. This chapter focuses on the *social logics*; ie claims about the social world and the political and economic relationship between the UK and the EU. The two subsequent chapters then focus on the political and fantasmatic logics of that discourse. As outlined above, social logics examine underlying assumptions which a discursive-political project makes about the nature of the social world and the social order which it seeks to define.

In keeping with long-standing Eurosceptic tenets, the pro-Brexit discourse is grounded on a radical separation constructed between 'Britain' and 'Europe' in which the latter is seen as the 'other' against which Anglo-British conceptions of the nation and national identity are defined. The pro-Brexit discourse constructs the EU in an overwhelmingly negative light: as being not just undemocratic, but anti-democratic and seeking to exercise ever-greater control over the UK. From this perspective, the EU is not just a foreign power but a quasi-colonial power posing a significant threat to the UK's political freedom. From an economic perspective, the EU supports an outdated and inefficient model opposed by the UK, but which undermines the UK economy.

A key characteristic of pro-Brexit discourses is the ambiguity and elision of different claims about the nature of the EU, its effects on the UK and the consequences of withdrawal. Multiple themes and tropes of the pro-Brexit discourse are often evident simultaneously in highly dense, carefully constructed texts. In addition, social, political and fantasmatic dimensions of the discourse may also co-exist within the same passage. This makes disaggregating and presenting the key tenets of the discourse in a clearly and non-repetitious way highly challenging. The quotes and examples from leave actors' interventions in the Brexit debate provided in this and the following chapters are designed to exemplify specific aspects of the discourse but may also include other dimensions of the discourse discussed elsewhere. However, despite the potential for repetition, the decision has been taken to reproduce longer quotations where needed in order to provide the full context for the arguments being made and to allow analysis of the underlying assumptions on which they draw. The current chapter is structured around the key themes as they emerged in the Brexit discourse, but seeks to highlights parallels with, and continuities from, longer-standing Eurosceptic discourses as evident in previous studies, particularly the analysis of the ToL debates discussed in the previous chapter and elsewhere (Hawkins, 2012; Hawkins, 2015).

The EU as political 'other'

Within the pro-Brexit discourse, there is a clear separation constructed between the UK and the EU, through the language and imagery employed, in ways that closely mirrors longer-standing Eurosceptic discourses. The first- and third-person pronouns, 'we' and 'they,' are used to define the boundaries of the national in-group and have the effect of positioning the EU as a heterogeneous 'other' to the UK, while reproducing the idea of the EU and the UK as internally homogenous entities. In addition, radically different, and mutually exclusive, conceptions of the nature of the EU and its future direction are attributed to these identity positions. This is evident in the following passage from Boris Johnson (*Telegraph*, 22 February 2016, emphasis added):

> There is only one way to get the change *we* need – and that is to vote to go; because all EU history shows that *they* only really listen to a population when it says No. The fundamental problem remains: that *they* have an ideal that *we* do not share. *They* want to create a truly federal union, *e pluribus unum*, when *most British people* do not. It is time to seek a new relationship, in which *we* manage to extricate *ourselves* from most of the supranational elements. [...] *They* have an ideal that *we* do not share. *They* want to create a truly federal union.

In addition, familiar tropes relating not just to the separateness of the UK from the EU, but to the potential threat posed by the latter position the EU as a *hostile* foreign power, despite the now well-worn reference to other EU member-states as 'friends and allies.' As Boris Johnson (*Telegraph*, 22 February 2016) comments elsewhere in the article:

> Whatever happens, Britain needs to be supportive of its friends and allies – but on the lines originally proposed by Winston Churchill:

interested, associated, but not absorbed; with Europe – but not comprised. We have spent 500 years trying to stop continental European powers uniting against us.

The reference to Churchill evokes not just his vision of the UK (via its empire) as separate from Europe in the post-1945 settlement, but draws on the moral authority he has in popular British imaginary as the greatest Prime Minister and perhaps the greatest of all 'Britons.' The canonical position which Churchill occupies in the national consciousness reflects the foundational role and enduring presence of WW2 – and conflict with Europe – in national mythology. As Johnson's intervention here suggests this is a history of conflict and threat which has endured for centuries.

Jacob Rees Mogg (*Mail,* 29 May 2016) also makes reference to past conflicts with European powers. Perhaps unsurprisingly, his reference point is not the 20th-century conflict, but that of the 18th century. With no small amount of irony, given Brexit supporters' depiction of the referendum as a campaign for the UK's independence from the EU (discussed below), his focus is on the wars fought by the UK with rival colonial powers for control of territories and peoples in other continents:

> Providentially, the day of the [Brexit referendum] vote falls on the anniversary of the Battle of Plassey in 1757 when Clive of India's victory over the Nawab of Bengal and his French allies ushered in over a century of unsurpassed greatness for this country. Let us hope history is repeated, and as a people we are as resolute now as we were then.

(Anti-)democracy

A central component of the pro-Brexit discourse is the idea that the EU is not just undemocratic, but anti-democratic. This claim results from an amalgamation of related and overlapping points about the impossibility of democracy above the level of the state (the 'no demos' theory, reflecting the nationalist logic of Eurosceptic discourses); the curtailment of democratic oversight over governance via the transfer of policy competences from the national level where this can occur to the European level where it does not or cannot; and the deleterious effects which EU membership is said to have on the functioning of democratic norms and institutions at the national level.

Michael Gove (*Times,* 16 June 2016), for example, complains about the inability of citizens to influence policies decided collectively within the EU:

> I cannot accept that decisions that intimately affect my fellow citizens [...] should be decided by people over whom we have no control. Without democratic accountability to keep it in check power grows corrupt and complacent. Democratic self-government should be a

principle precious to left and right [...] but there has been a remarkable willingness to surrender control of our nation to others.

Elsewhere in the article, Gove (*Times,* 16 June 2016) argues clearly that, within the EU institutions, the UK is unable to influence common EU policies given the 'unelected' Commission's sole right of legislative initiation and the weak position of the UK in the behind-closed-doors meetings of Council:

> We have no veto over huge swathes of legislation and can be outvoted by a "qualified majority" of other states. And we are. Repeatedly. Britain has been on the losing side of European Council votes more often than any other country. But that is scarcely half the story. Because on many occasions we fold before a vote is taken, knowing we are in a losing minority and resistance is useless.

The preceding passages capture the defensive mindset which sees EU politics as something to be mitigated through the use of the veto and wraps this in the language of conflict and capitulation. It also demonstrates either a lack of understanding of (or deliberately misrepresents) the policymaking process at the EU level by omitting the role of the EP. UK citizens are thus re-presented in the legislative process both via their democratically accountable national officials in the Council, and their directly elected representatives in the EP. Here, Gove reinforces the idea that the EU is a foreign power, in which the UK has no influence. It reflects also one of the main contradictions at the heart of the Eurosceptic movement which has consistently railed against the undemocratic nature of the EU while opposing the extension of powers of the EP, and denigrating the democratic credentials of the latter more generally.

This, in turn, follows from the assumption within Eurosceptic discourses that *real* democracy can exist only at the national level and is synonymous with the Westminster model of executive authority. From this perspective, democratic shortcomings of the EU centre on the apparent inability to vote out, or even identify, the EU 'government.' According to Gove (*Times,* 16 June 2016), the EU has become:

> a living negation of its founding purpose: it was set up as a club for democracies but it is fundamentally undemocratic. [...] Other democratic nations know who is sovereign in their country, whether President or parliament, because they were elected and can be slung out.

Elsewhere, Gove (*Telegraph,* 20 March 2016) repeats that 'we should be free to kick out politicians who have failed, and our membership of the EU means laws and policies are forced on us by people we can't get rid of.'

These quotations reflect a central focus in Eurosceptic discourses, and indeed in wider British political culture, on the ability to 'throw the rascals out.' It is emblematic also of a fundamental, conceptual dissonance that informs British political thought on the EU when viewed through the prism of the highly centralised Westminster model of majoritarian, single-party government and winner-takes-all elections. The more consensus-based model of decision-making – involving multiple parties, institutional actors and power bases – which characterises politics at the EU level appears alien and incomprehensible to those steeped in the British tradition alone. It resembles more closely the political systems of other member-states, whose coalition governments and proportional representation voting systems are seen within Eurosceptic discourses as inferior to the stability of the Westminster model in British political mythology. As Gove (*Telegraph*, 21 February 2016) comments:

> we developed – and exported to nations like the US, India, Canada and Australia – a system of democratic self-government which has brought prosperity and peace to millions. Our democracy stood the test of time. […] By way of contrast, the European Union, despite the undoubted idealism of its founders and the good intentions of so many leaders, has proved a failure on so many fronts.

The dissonance between the UK and EU polities is indicative of deeper, underlying assumptions about the nature of politics and democracy within Eurosceptic and wider political discourses in the UK. Developments since the referendum have underlined the extent to which democracy, from this perspective, is seen as synonymous with empowerment of the executive. Within the Westminster system the government of the day controls parliament by definition. Prime Ministers, and the governments they lead, are appointed, and endure in office, only to the extent that they are able to command a majority in parliament. With a few exceptions seated in the House of Lords, ministers are drawn exclusively from members of the House of Commons. The blurred lines that exist between the executive and the legislative means that democratic government becomes synonymous with executive power within the British political imaginary. Democracy is enacted in the formation of the government. Between elections, however, the will of the government becomes synonymous with the will of the people in ways mirrored by the framing of post-referendum debates on the implementation of the 2016 result. This particular understanding of democracy was clearly revealed by the bombastic speech delivered by former Advocate General Geoffrey Cox on 25 September 2019 in which he branded the parliament in which he stood 'a disgrace' for failing to pass the Government's bill to enact the terms of withdrawal from the EU negotiated by Theresa May's administration. This sees little role for parliament to oversee and hold government to account. Its function is purely instrumental; to enact the government's agenda. From this perspective, the EU system is not just a conceptual challenge but a material challenge to democracy given that it curtails the ability of the executive to act with impunity in areas of pooled sovereignty or shared competence. While these assumptions about the nature of real democracy have been challenged by the devolution in Scotland, Wales and (albeit in unique historical, political and cultural circumstances) in Northern Ireland since the late 1990s, they remain a key structuring element of the Anglo-British political mindset and an important factor in explaining the deeply sedimented and enduring (mis)understanding of the EU in British political discourse.

Given the alleged inability of citizens to shape the direction of EU laws and policies through its institutions, Brexit supporters claim that it is only through referenda that the peoples of Europe are able to push back against the integration process. Even then, though, the results of these are often set aside. As Jacob Rees Mogg (*Mail,* 29 May 2016) comments:

> In recent years, every nation given the opportunity to vote against Brussels has done so, including the Dutch, the Greeks, the French, and especially the Danes and the Irish. [...] Less happy lands without confidence in their abilities have been bullied into voting again. This cannot happen to the United Kingdom.

From this perspective, the British people are seen to have a unique democratic resolve to see their wishes implemented in a way that other, more compliant peoples do not. This reflects the wider construction of the UK as the democratic counterpoint to the autocratic tendencies of the EU:

> We have given so much to the world, in ideas and culture, but the most valuable British export and the one for which we are most famous is the one that is now increasingly in question: parliamentary democracy – the way the people express their power (Johnson, *Telegraph,* 22 February 2016).

Elsewhere, Boris Johnson (*Telegraph*, 20 June 2016) takes the argument a step further, arguing that membership of the EU – and the increasing amount of policy-making which occurs at the EU level, beyond the purview of elected national officials – has undermined people's faith, and willingness to participate, in democratic processes even at the national level:

> People often complain about voting these days. They say it doesn't make any difference. They say that whatever party they choose they get the same old broken promises. In fact, they say there is no point in bothering at all.

Ever closer control

Closely allied to the idea that the EU is anti-democratic is the claim it seeks to exert control over ever-greater areas of UK policy and public life, through the adoption of new powers and the absorption of new areas of policy competence. This includes the UK's loss of global influence which allegedly arises from collective EU representation, in place of separate national delegations, in international fora such as the WTO and other specialist agencies. As with longer-standing Eurosceptic discourses, pro-Brexit discourses are characterised by a reductionist and formalist conception of political sovereignty as an object you possess rather than a process through which effective (and at times collective) policy outcomes are generated. As Michael Gove (*Times,* 16 June 2016) states: 'Sovereignty is not something that can be pooled or shared. Sovereignty is simply another word for control. You either have it or you do not.' This Manichean world view of winners and losers not only misrepresents the EU as a political entity, but also the nature of *de facto*, functional (versus *de jure*, theoretical) sovereignty in a world of complex trans-national interdependencies.

Of central importance to this aspect of the pro-Brexit discourse is the idea that an excessive and ever-increasing volume of UK laws is made by the EU, with different figures given to support the claims about the precise number or percentage of UK laws emanating from the EU. As Boris Johnson (*Telegraph*, 25 April 2016) argues:

> Inch by inch, month by month, the sausage machine of EU law-making will extrude more laws – at a rate of 2,500 a year, or perhaps even faster, once the referendum is out of the way.

Michael Gove (*Telegraph,* 21 February 2016) argues that the very *raison d'etre* of the EU is to accumulate power and identifies the European Commission and the CJEU as the key institutions driving this process forward:

> The EU is built to keep power and control with the elites rather than the people. Even though we are outside the Euro, we are still subject to an unelected EU Commission which is generating new laws every day and an unaccountable European Court in Luxembourg which is extending its reach every week [...]. This growing EU bureaucracy holds us back in every area.

The position articulated by Gove here offers a key insight into Eurosceptics' misunderstanding (or misrepresentation) of the nature of the European integration process. It indicates a key conceptual vacuum within the Eurosceptic world view about the very rationale for the EU's existence which must be otherwise filled. Brexiters do not recognise the EU as a mechanism for managing interdependency and mutual interest between neighbouring states via legal and normative mechanisms for resolving (potential) disputes. But this raises the question of what the EU is then for? If the EU does not exist to manage interdependence and avoid conflict between neighbouring states, then what does it exist to do? It must be about something other than official party line; there must be a different underlying rationale. That 'something' has both benign and malign versions within Eurosceptic discourses. In the former, the EU is seen as the misguided endeavour of well-meaning but naive ideologues, engaged in tragi-comic attempts to build 'Europe.' This is an ultimately futile exercise that can be dismissed and patronised as an eccentric folly rather than having more sinister motives imputed. In the latter, the EU exists simply as a project to assume control over member-states, and the UK in particular. The apparently incessant production of laws is just a way of gaining control over member-states one bill at a time. This fear about the EU's real (hidden) intentions is an example of what Zizek (1993) identifies as the mystery of the other's demand – what do they *really* want from us (*che vuoi*)? – which underlies all xenophobic discourses.

EU as foreign, colonial power

Mirroring the long-standing tropes identified in Eurosceptic discourses, the EU is discussed as if it is a foreign power as opposed to a multi-lateral entity of which the UK is a part. For example, Michael Gove (*Telegraph*, 16 June 2016) comments:

> In America whoever is president, Democrat or Republican, can chart that country's course. They would never accept that judges sitting in a court in Guatemala should be able to strike down US law or that Brazilian and Peruvian Commissioners would draw up the rules on weekly bin collection in Delaware. If Australians and Americans would never accept the loss of democratic control that EU membership requires then why should we?

In this formulation the EU is seen as a neighbouring state and rulings of the Court of Justice being the equivalent of the constitutional courts of these neighbouring states ruling over affairs in the UK. The point of comparison with the UK's current plight in the UK is Australia and the USA underlining the importance of the Anglosphere as an alternative model for the UK to follow outside the EU, which offers greater freedom and autonomy.

In keeping again with long-standing Eurosceptic discourses, the EU is depicted by the Brexit advocates as not just a foreign, but a colonial, power that dictates decisions to the UK and over which the British government is unable to exert any influence. This links closely to the assertions above that the EU is seeking to gain ever greater control over the UK polity. Boris Johnson (*Telegraph,* 22 February 2016, emphasis added) suggests that there is an inevitable movement toward ever more power accumulating to the EU and no mechanism existing to reverse this process:

> It is unstoppable, and it is irreversible – since it can only be repealed by the EU itself. Ask how much EU legislation the Commission has actually taken back under its various programmes for streamlining bureaucracy. The answer is none. That is why EU law is likened to a ratchet, clicking only forwards. We are seeing a slow and invisible process of legal *colonisation*, as the EU infiltrates just about every area of public policy.

The idea of the EU as a colonial power is reflected in the parallels and analogies drawn between the EU and historical examples of totalitarian regimes such as the Soviet Union. As Michael Gove (*Times,* 16 June 2016) comments:

> Lenin famously explained [...] that the essential question to ask about all political arrangements was "who controls whom?" [...] Do we, the people, control the EU's institutions? Or do the people who run the EU's institutions control the policies that affect all of us? Manifestly, it is the latter.

The parallels to the Soviet Union, and the 'kill or be killed' mentality which informs Gove's worldview (or at least his view of EU politics), is indicative of the extent to which the British historical experience of empire shapes the way in which European integration is viewed. Seen through this lens, trans-national governance cannot be conducted on the basis of shared interests and mutual benefit, mediated via consensus-based forms of decision making, but necessarily involves the domination of one party by another. As a counterpoint to the apparently centralising and controlling tendencies of the EU, Gove identifies Australia and America as examples of democratic, self-determining countries which, as Brexit commentators frequently highlighted, owe their unique democratic heritage to the role of the UK in their foundation and the development of their political culture (see also Gove, *Telegraph,* 21 February 2016). This identifies the 'Anglosphere' as an alternative and more natural home for the UK in the world than that provided by its geographically (if not culturally and historically) closer neighbours in Europe.

The EU as economic 'other'

One of the key points of separation between the UK and the EU is the structure and efficiency of the British and European economies, and the underlying economic model on which they are based. Within the pro-Brexit discourse (as in the longer-standing Eurosceptic discourse), the EU, and particularly the Eurozone, represents the institutionalisation of an outdated and inefficient economic model characterised by low growth and high unemployment by misguided policies. As Boris Johnson and Gove (*Telegraph*, 5 June 2016) state:

> [T]he Eurozone suffers from severe economic and institutional problems. It is blighted by low growth and high and rising debts and taxes. Unemployment and youth unemployment are high – at their worst level since the 1930s – in some parts of southern Europe youth unemployment is over 50%. [...] The Eurozone countries are trapped in a low-growth system in which debts are rising remorselessly. This adds to pressures on taxpayers and creates a vicious cycle [...]. The nations of the EU are not creating new technologies and new industries in the way other countries are. [...] That is why there have been no EU equivalents of Apple, Uber, Amazon, Netflix, Google or Facebook. Indeed, the EU's whole regulatory structure works against innovation. The EU now has slower growth than any other continent apart from Antarctica.

This Eurocentric model is seen by Brexiters to be an anachronism in the context of current developments in the global economy. As Michael Gove (*Telegraph*, 21 February 2016) comments:

> The EU is an institution rooted in the past and is proving incapable of reforming to meet the big technological, demographic and economic challenges of our time. It was developed in the 1950s and 1960s and like other institutions which seemed modern then, from tower blocks to telexes, it is now hopelessly out of date. The EU tries to standardise and regulate rather than encourage diversity and innovation. It is an analogue union in a digital age.

In contrast to the 'European' economic model, Brexiters consistently talk up the strength of the British economy and British economic success stories but identify these companies as succeeding in spite of, rather than because of, the UK's membership of the EU. In his various interventions in the referendum debate, Johnson makes repeated references to UK inventor James Dyson – who opposed EU regulations limiting noise outputs from the vacuum cleaners he produces, supported Brexit then relocated his company to Singapore soon after the 2016 vote – and another Brexit supporter Anthony Bamford (of the JCB industrial vehicles company) as evidence that wealth creators and captains of industry share his concerns about the effects of the UK's position within the EU on innovation and jobs.

The single market

While the negative framing of the static European economy in contrast to the superior British model characterised previous iterations of Eurosceptic discourse, they had always (perhaps reluctantly) stated that the single market was of value to the UK, often citing the role of Margaret Thatcher's government in its creation as justification for this. What is new in the referendum campaign was the extent to which Brexit supporters consistently underplayed or dismissed the benefits of the importance of the single market to the UK economy. Leading figures in the leave campaign consistently suggested that its apparent benefits to the UK economy are overstated by remain supporters. Boris Johnson (*Telegraph*, 30 May 2016), for example, argues that countries outside the EU have in fact done better than the UK importing into it:

> We can dismiss most of the claims for the "single market" – too often an excuse for a morass of politically driven legislation that costs UK business about £600 million a week. In the 20 years since the dawn of the 1992 Single Market programme [...] 27 non-EU countries did better [than the UK] at increasing their exports of goods, and 21 did better at ramping up their exports of services. Of course they did: American and other non-EU businesses have excellent "access" to the EU, but aren't wrapped in EU red tape, whereas we have only 6% of companies trading with the rest of the EU – yet 100% of them have to comply with EU law.

At other times, Brexiters argue that the single market, and trade with the EU more generally, is of declining economic importance to the UK in a globalising world in which opportunities for investment and growth increasingly exist outside Europe:

> Britain already conducts more trade outside the EU than any other member-state, and the EU takes an ever-shrinking share of our exports, down from about 55% in 2002 to less than 45% last year. This trend is set to continue, underlining that our greatest opportunity for future prosperity lies in the global economy. [...] The Single Market is touted as one of the greatest benefits of EU membership. But in the 20 years since it came into force our trade with other EU countries has grown more slowly than in the two decades before (Howard et al., *Telegraph*, 15 June 2016).

Consequently, leaving the EU, and thus the single market, should not pose a threat to the British economy, but offer an opportunity to escape the regulatory confines which have held the UK back. As Liam Fox (*Sun*, 14 February 2016) states:

> Not only will Britain not suffer from Brexit, it could provide major economic opportunities. We would lose the heavy burden of regulation imposed upon us by Brussels, but we would also be able to negotiate trade deals with countries where the EU does not currently have them. This includes the USA, China, India, Australia and New Zealand.

The attempts to underplay the importance of the single market and to cite the advantages of being outside its structures represent a departure from longer-standing Eurosceptic discourses which focused on rejection of political union, but conceded the economic advantages of 'the common market.' Even in the Brexit campaign, rejection of the single market was not the universal position of all leave campaigners. As will be examined in subsequent chapters, many were at pains to highlight that they believed the UK could retain unfettered access to the single market even outside the EU, ensuring the benefits of membership while casting off the cumbersome regulatory burden which held the UK back. So-called 'liberal leavers' went even further, advocating continued membership of the EU. Before the referendum campaign, for example, Conservative MEP Daniel Hannan boldly asserted in a now-infamous interview on *Channel 4 News* that 'absolutely nobody is talking about threatening our place in the single market.'

International trade

As the preceding quote from Liam Fox implies, the area in which the UK is seen to be held back most by EU membership, and in which the biggest potential opportunities from Brexit thus lie, is that of international trade. This position is summarised by Boris Johnson (*Independent*, 16 June 2016):

> The EU straitjacket is actually preventing us from engaging with the rest of the world. Locked in the EU, we cannot do free-trade deals with some of the fastest growing economies – in South-East Asia, China, India or the Americas – because our trade policy is entirely controlled by the EU Commission, where only 3.6% of officials come from this country.

The focus on the number of UK officials in the Commission underlines the idea that the EU is a foreign body and that the institutions are a competition for relative advantage between member-states (in this instance through the placement of their officials to pursue their interests) as opposed to the idea of common action for mutual benefit.

This is echoed by Jacob Rees Mogg (*Mail*, 29 May 2016) who argues that the institutions and policies of the EU are fundamentally antithetical to trade liberalisation:

> The UK economy is held back because the EU is not about free trade, but rather a customs union. Buying goods from outside the EU becomes more expensive for Britons, because of the tariffs imposed. Non-EU cars cost about ten per cent more than they need to, which means consumers pay a higher price – handing German car manufacturers better profit margins.

The argument here offers both a highly simplistic critique of external tariffs (which the UK would also put in place as part of an independent trade policy outside the EU) while failing to recognise the significant trade facilitating effects for intra-European trade of being part of a single customs territory (as well as a common regulatory regime in the single market). Moreover, it reproduces again the argument that the EU is a zero-sum game for national advantage, which works to serve the interests of other states (n this case Germany) at the expense of the UK and its citizens.

In contrast to the EU, the UK is seen as naturally inclined to be more internationalist, but held back from realising its potential as a global trading nation by the confines of EU membership. As Boris Johnson (*Express*, 22 June 2016) comments:

> This country has always been at its greatest when we've looked outward, when we've steered a course for freedom and exploration – the great Elizabethan age, the Industrial Revolution, the spirit of Churchill.

The Anglosphere is present again in this dimension of the pro-Brexit discourse as a point of comparison for the position of the UK within the EU. This is evident in a joint article by former Conservative leaders and Chancellors of the Exchequer who lament the decision to hand control of the UK's trade policy to 'Brussels:'

> Since the 1970s, the EU has reached 37 agreements with 54 countries. The largest economies among them are South Korea and Mexico. By contrast, Australia, an economy half our size, has agreements in place with China, the United States, Japan and a host of smaller countries. It is on the brink of signing with India. If we leave, we would regain the freedom to forge deals while continuing to trade freely with the EU (Howard et al., *Telegraph,* 15 June 2016).

It is noteworthy also that Australia is identified as the model which the UK could potentially follow as a free trading nation and India and the USA are identified as potential candidates for future trade agreements. In addition to the Anglosphere, it is emerging economies in Asia, particularly China, which are identified as the key target markets for an independent trade policy. However, little consideration is given to the relative size of the UK economy versus those of China or America and thus the ability of the

UK to achieve its strategic trade objectives (whatever these may be) in any subsequent negotiation.

The Euro as economic catastrophe

The introduction of the Euro as a shared currency now used by 19 EU member-states and the economic and political consequences of EMU play an extremely prominent role in the Brexit debate. The Euro features in multiple overlapping yet distinct ways in pro-Brexit discourses. Firstly, the Eurozone appears in Brexiter discourses as a microcosm of, or a synonym for, the problems of overregulation, slow growth and high unemployment, besetting the wider European economy. The adoption of a 'one-size-fits-all' currency is seen as the (il)logical extension of a misguided ideological project which simply does not (indeed cannot) function when it encounters the necessities of the real world of markets and nations. As Boris Johnson (*Telegraph*, 30 May 2016) captures:

> In the last decade the EU has been suffering from a self-inflicted economic disaster – the Euro. We get inured to some of the figures – the 50% youth unemployment in Greece and Spain – without stopping to think of the individual tragedies; the suicide rates; the inability to get medical treatments; the blighting of young lives. It is a moral outrage [...]. On our doorstep we have a vast and developing tragedy - caused by the folly of trying to impose a single currency on an area with different labour markets and different rates of productivity.

Secondly, previous political debates around the UK joining the Euro are invoked to dismiss economic arguments put forward by remain campaigners about the dangers of Brexit. Brexit advocates make repeated reference to the support for the UK's membership of the Euro previously articulated by many of the same individuals and institutions now advocating that the UK remain in the EU, arguing that they were wrong then and they are wrong now. The predicted economic damage which would result from not joining the Euro when proposals to do so were on the table under Prime Minister Tony Blair, Brexiters argued, did not come to fruition, so similar claims about leaving the EU – articulated in often hyperbolic terms by some remain supporters and economic commentators – could also be disregarded.

The term 'project fear' was coined by Brexit campaigners to capture the sense that 'the remain establishment' was seeking to exaggerate the effects of leaving the EU in an attempt to browbeat the electorate into voting remain. The widespread perception of the relative success of the UK economy, versus continental European economies in the preceding decade, and that the country had been insulated from the 'Euro-crisis' through its maintenance of an independent currency made this a powerful argument for Brexit supporters. The idea of economic contagion from the EU was a common motif in pre-Brexit discourses as in previous Eurosceptic versions. While remaining outside the single currency insulated the UK to an extent against this, concerns were raised that as a member-state the UK would remain exposed to a degree and only by leaving the EU altogether could it completely protect its economy. As Johnson and Gove (*Telegraph*, 5 June 2016) states elsewhere:

> The Eurozone institutions remain broken and have been unable to cope with the Euro's crisis. Despite writing a promise of 'no bail-outs' into the EU Treaties, there have been massive bail-outs. The so-called Stability and Growth Pact was abandoned by Germany and France as well as Greece and Italy and no substitute has been found. The Eurozone banking system remains in crisis and lacks clarity about who is in charge of what. [...] This Eurozone crisis is a disaster for millions of Europeans and it is also a danger to Britain.

Elsewhere, Duncan Smith (*Mail*, 5 June 2016) laments the failure of economic institutions and experts to consider the dangers the Eurozone poses to the UK alongside their forecasts about the potential risks of leaving the EU:

> They have failed to give any weight to the risk to Britain of being tied to the highly unstable Eurozone or to the economic threat posed by Brussels. Research released today details the scale of the risk to our financial services industry, which employs more than two million people throughout the UK and funds 12% of spending on public services.

The third dimension of the Euro in pro-Brexit discourses identifies it as a mechanism of political control employed by the EU. This is in keeping with the identification of the latter as a neo-colonial power discussed above and is examined in the following section.

The Eurozone as disciplinary control

For Brexiters, the Euro represents not just a misguided policy which they blame for the economic problems and high unemployment faced by southern European states such as Greece, but an ideologically driven political project to exert control over specific member-states, with particular negative consequences for the UK. This discourse has two components. Firstly, the Euro is seen as a key mechanism through which to bind Germany to the rest of the continent, which necessitated a deepening of integration that undermined the UK's independence. As Johnson (*Telegraph*, 22 February 2016) comments:

> And then came German reunification, and the panicked efforts of Delors, Kohl and Mitterrand to "lock" Germany into Europe with the

Euro; and since then the pace of integration has never really slackened. As new countries have joined, we have seen a hurried expansion in the areas for Qualified Majority Voting, so that Britain can be overruled more and more often (as has happened in the past five years). We have had not just the Maastricht Treaty, but Amsterdam, Nice, Lisbon, every one of them representing an extension of EU authority and a centralisation in Brussels.

The second component of this discourse sees the Euro as a key mechanism of disciplinary control exerted on Sothern European states in particular by the EU's most powerful, northern European states. As Boris Johnson (*Mirror*, 21 June 2016) comments:

> The Greek people's decisions were ignored by Brussels, which forced its economic medicine down their throats, destroying the hopes of a generation and leaving more than half of young people there jobless.

This is linked, in turn, with the specifically anti-democratic nature of the EU within pro-Brexit discourses. The apparently authoritarian tendencies of the EU are to be seen in the replacement of governments in Italy and Greece during negotiations between member-states, the European Central Bank and the European Commission and the International Monetary fund (the 'troika') over debt restructuring and budgetary discipline in those countries. As Johnson (*Telegraph*, 25 April 2016) comments elsewhere:

> Remember that twice in the past five years, the EU has removed a democratically elected government – in Italy and Greece – and installed Brussels-approved technocrats. It is a narcotic tyranny. They want to go on with the work of building a unitary state, in a way that is anti-democratic and ultimately very dangerous, since it will one day provoke real public anger.

In this context the onus is on the UK to vote to leave the EU not just to protect its own interest but to defend those of the remaining EU member-states, by forcing EU elites to change policy course in the aftermath of a 'leave' vote:

> If we vote Remain, we do nothing to rebuke the elites in Brussels who have imposed the Euro on the Continent, and thrown a generation of young people on the scrapheap, and who are utterly indifferent to the misery they are causing for the sake of their bankrupt ideology.

Yet the principal fear for the Brexiters remains that the Eurozone will seek to exert similar disciplinary control over the UK:

> The Eurozone now has a permanent structural majority in the EU's voting system. We only have 12% percent of the votes (at most 8% in some circumstances). When the Eurozone countries vote together to prop up the broken system, they can impose their will and force us to accept laws that are not in our interests. The recent renegotiation did nothing to change this situation. This has left us dangerously and permanently exposed to being forced to hand over more money and accept damaging new laws.

Underlying the concerns about the effects of the Euro (and the wider effects of the single market) is the idea that the EU wants to lock the UK into the EU system in order to exploit it as a source of revenue for its ideological project. As in the debates surrounding the ToL, the EU is constantly presented as being the EU's paymaster while being marginalised from its decision-making procedures. The sense of economic injustice manifested itself in perhaps the most iconic image, and most effective slogan, of the referendum campaign in which Brexiters claimed on the side of a campaign bus they would get back '£350m a week' from the EU which could be spent instead on 'our' people and 'our' priorities such as the NHS. The narrative of exploitation offers as a plausible response to the Brexiters' underlying question about what it is that the EU wants from the UK. The answer, in this context, appears to be to keep the UK trapped in the EU to foot the bills while systematically undermining its economic and commercial interests.

EU as a source of unlimited migration

The pro-Brexit discourse identifies the EU as a source of unlimited migration which we are simply unable to control while remaining a member-state. As Boris Johnson (*Telegraph*, 12 June 2016) articulates:

> The Remain campaign has failed to answer the fundamental question. How can we control immigration as long as we are in the EU? [...] [Most people] can see that our current immigration policy is unfair and unbalanced and out of control – and they can also see that the Remain campaign has failed for months to answer the fundamental question. How can we control the rate – 333,000 net last year, a city the size of Newcastle – as long as we are in the EU?

In highlighting the rate of immigration, Johnson argues that this arises as a result of fundamental changes in the nature of the EU about which the electorate were never fully consulted or asked to give their consent. The implied conclusion of this is that it is perfectly reasonable for people who have not explicitly acquiesced to this social change to want their views to be heard now:

> In recent years, we have gone through a huge change as the EU has expanded from nine to 15, and now to 28 countries, with 1.25 million people added to Britain's population since 2004 because of the EU's rigid free movement rules. Few people saw it coming and no-one voted for it (Johnson, *Mirror*, 21 June 2016).

Migration and the European economy

The driving force for immigration is identified as the relative weakness of continental European economies and the resulting wage levels and living standards far lower than in the UK, which is thus seen as a land of opportunities for those elsewhere in the EU:

> The UK minimum wage is already the equivalent of €1,529 a month – compared with €215 in Bulgaria and €233 in Romania. Think of that magnetic effect – if we continue, as now, with no way of moderating the tide [of immigration] (Johnson, *Telegraph*, 30 May 2016).

At other times it is the ongoing 'crisis' in the Eurozone which is identified as the specific factor pushing people to move to the UK, which exists as an independent economic sanctuary outside the single currency zone:

> Thanks largely to the decision to keep the pound [...] the UK was a zone of relatively high growth – a comparative *El Dorado* of job creation. This meant that the UK experienced substantial waves of immigration by people in search of work [...]. The British were traditionally welcoming, but they could see the pressures of uncontrolled immigration on the NHS and other services (Johnson, *Telegraph*, 23 May 2016).

This aspect of the immigration discourse thus overlaps with the wider depiction of the (successful) British and (failing) European economic models discussed in the preceding chapter. In addition, it feeds into, and draws on, ideas at the heart of the wider immigration debate that the UK is a uniquely desirable country to live in, and thus the ultimate target destination for migrants, which must be protected and defended from the coming hordes – and preserved for its indigenous people – by robust border defences.

Freedom of movement and asylum seekers

Iain Duncan Smith (*Express*, 1 June 2016) links the issue of freedom of movement to the UK from other EU member-states to the issue of extra-European migration. Concerns about the EU serving as a gateway to 'asylum seekers' and other non-European migrants received significant public attention following the 2015 'migrant crisis' which saw large numbers of people, many escaping conflicts in Syria and elsewhere, moving through central and Eastern Europe via Turkey:

> As our television screens are filled with pictures of thousands of people trying to cross from North Africa into Europe, we are reminded that there is real chaos in the EU – with millions having already crossed into Europe in the last year alone. [...] The EU's disastrous open border policy means that once in, migrants are free to go wherever they want – and many are trying to come to the UK. [...] As the tide of migration surges up through Europe, we in Britain are paying the price of successive governments' woeful neglect of our own coastline – with people-smugglers now landing their human cargo on the beaches of Kent, Sussex and East Anglia.

'Free' movement of people within the EU does not just mean that other EU citizens can come to the UK, but that anyone from outside the EU who has entered its common external border can move on to any other EU country. Duncan Smith carefully name checks coastal areas of the UK likely to contain potential leave voters, linking the issue of immigration to the neglect and underinvestment which these communities feel they have experienced in recent decades.

Liam Fox (*Sun*, 14 February 2016) makes a similar point, arguing that the issue is further complicated by the decision of other member-states such as Germany to grant citizenship to those arriving during the migrant crisis:

> At the moment, we are seeing a huge influx of migrants into continental EU countries from Syria, Pakistan, Afghanistan and Iraq. Countries such as Germany, in which they are arriving, have no idea whether they will turn out to be genuine refugees, economic migrants, Islamist sympathisers or part of terrorist networks. The stark truth is once they get citizenship from any EU country they will have a right to come to the UK if we remain. Up to 3 million migrants are expected to have arrived in the EU by the end of 2016.

According to Fox, this means that immigration into the UK is being determined by policy decisions taken in other European capitals. As such, immigration policy within the EU raises fundamental issues of democratic control. This is echoed elsewhere by Duncan Smith (*Mail*, 5 June 2016), who argues that EU membership means the UK government is unable to deliver its manifesto commitment to cut immigration, thereby undermining support for the Conservative government and the democratic process more generally. In both of these passages, continental Europe, even its largest and most powerful state, Germany, is seen to be poorly, even recklessly, governed. It is a source of chaos and conflict from which the UK must move to insulate itself. As with the introduction of the Euro discussed in the previous chapter, the 'open door' immigration policy is seen to be the product of naïve idealism on the part of European leaders as a result of which the UK will suffer unless it withdraws itself from the political confines of the EU.

Immigration as a security threat

The reference to 'Islamist sympathisers' in the preceding quotation suggests also that this poses a potential security threat to the UK which is beyond the government's control within the EU. Concerns about the security threat posed by immigration from elsewhere in the EU are echoed by Michael Gove (*Mail*, 30 April 2016), who invokes the conflict in the former Yugoslavia as a precedent for the current 'crisis':

> The Yugoslav conflict was a hauntingly sad episode in Europe's recent history and we are still living with its ramifications today – including the consequences of refugee flows, organised criminals exploiting the collapse of state institutions, and Islamist foreign fighters making an ethnic struggle their own personal jihad. [...] The war in Syria has generated a refugee crisis more profound than the problems triggered by the collapse of Yugoslavia. [...] And just as the fate of Bosnian Muslims in the Yugoslav wars inspired jihadists to flock to Europe, so Syria has become the training ground for thousands of Islamist terrorists.

The reference to the break-up of the former Yugoslavia may not have resonated with all readers but was potentially selected by Gove as it is seen as a key example of the EU's failings as a security actor on its own doorstep in which it was necessary for the North Atlantic Treaty Organization (NATO) to eventually intervene. This reflects the long-standing Eurosceptic trope that the EU is unable to guarantee its own security and that it is NATO, and not the EU, which is responsible for the preceding seven decades of peace experienced in Western Europe.

Later in the article, Gove argues explicitly that immigration poses a security threat to the UK and argues that EU inefficiency and corruption means that the UK faces not just uncontrolled legal migration from the EU, but an additional 'influx' of illegal migrants:

> Of all the prisoners in our jails who come from European countries, 10% come from Albania – yet Albania comprises less than half of one per cent of the overall population of Europe. Those prisoners currently cost the British taxpayer almost £18 million a year to keep in custody. And that's before Albanian citizens even have the right to move to the UK! [...]
>
> They are serious criminals who came here on forged Italian and Greek documents. European laws allow anyone with ID cards from EU countries – not even full passports – to enter the UK. Italy's cardboard

documents are a particular favourite with criminals because they can be so easily forged. Last year, there was a 70% increase in the number of people trying to get into Britain with fraudulent European papers. And in the vanguard were Albanian criminals using fake Greek and Italian ID papers. Even if those entering have real documents, we have no effective way of checking whether they have a criminal record.

The EU is thus again identified as corrupt and inefficient; a source of disorder and criminality to which the UK is exposed and against which it must secure itself.

Elsewhere, Gove (*Times*, 16 June 2016) argues, the principle of freedom of movement of people is seen as an article of faith for the state-builders in Brussels. However, this ideological commitment leads to averse and dangerous real-world consequences:

> The EU takes a fundamentalist approach to issues like freedom of movement. So much so that we have given up the ability to deport criminals or keep out terrorists. Abu Hamza's daughter-in-law was found guilty of smuggling contraband into prison and received a criminal conviction that would have enabled her to be deported under English law. But EU law forbade it. [...] The Home Secretary tried to stop him. EU law said she could not. Whatever approach you may take to immigration [...] we are clearly no longer sovereign if we no longer control these ultimate decisions.

This is in keeping with the long-standing Eurosceptic positions, examined in Chapter 5, that the EU is an ideological project, led by idealism (much of it well-intentioned) but which fails to recognise fundamental economic and sociological realities.

As well as a security threat, immigration, and the policy dilemmas which this presents, forces EU member-states, including the UK, to form uncomfortable and compromising political alliances. Addressing the consequences of the 2015 migrant crisis and the subsequent deal struck with Turkey to slow the rate of arrivals into the EU from Anatolia, Boris Johnson (*Telegraph*, 18 April 2016) comments:

> We all know that the original problem was exacerbated by Germany's open-door policy. [...] But it is Turkey's hand on the tap. Erdogan, if he chooses, can allow the trickle to turn back into a flood – with devastating consequences not just for Merkel, but for the whole project of EU integration.

The idea that we are reliant on Turkey to secure our borders in this way appears to Johnson not just to be a compromise but a form of political humiliation. Later in the article, Johnson suggests this reliance on Turkey to help control migration into Europe leads to a kind of moral compromise in which we sacrifice our most fundamental values. He was referring to German Chancellor Angela Merkel's acquiescence in the prosecution of a German comedian for comments made about Turkish President Recep Tayyip Erdoğan. This episode serves to highlight the hypocrisy of the EU's ruling classes which are prepared to sacrifice fundamental rights and principles to protect the ideal of European integration. Moreover, it implies that the UK's own principles and standards are eroded through EU membership and the need to adhere to common policy imperatives. The implication is that, outside the EU, the UK would once again stand up for values like freedom of speech which its neighbours are unable or unwilling to defend.

Summary

The social logics of the pro-Brexit discourse draw on the fundamental dichotomies, and processes of 'othering' between the UK and the EU, evident in longer-standing Eurosceptic discourses examined in Chapter 5 (Hawkins, 2012; Hawkins, 2015). Leave discourses are grounded in an underlying logic of nationalism which provides the lens through which the EU, and politics more generally, are viewed. A fundamental separation is constructed between the UK and the EU as both a political and economic entity. Throughout these interventions, there is a fundamental ambiguity about what the EU actually is. At times it appears to be a bargaining forum, dominated by, and serving the interests of its most powerful member-states, such as Germany. At other times it consists of an unspecified group of actors and officials referred to just as 'them,' but which is certainly not part of 'us.' Elsewhere, it is identified as a hostile, controlling, neo-colonial foreign power. Whereas the UK is democratic; the EU is not just undemocratic but *anti*-democratic, undermining political participation at home and seeking to control the British people through new laws and conventions, which the UK is unable to influence. Similarly, the historical experience of conflict with 'Europe' and of empire, which looms large over British political and popular culture, provides the principal tropes employed to characterise EU politics and to impute motives to the confusing actions of this far-off body.

What underlies the pro-Brexit and wider Eurosceptic discourses is the need to impute alternative motives to the EU which arises from Brexit supporters' rejection of official EU narratives of the European integration project as a peace project designed to manage trans-national interests and interdependencies through formalised institutional structures. This is, in turn, a consequence of the conceptual challenge posed by the complex, multidimensional nature of EU governance compared with the executive control (usually) guaranteed by the Westminster model. The curtailment of government power by EU membership and the identification of democratic accountability with the ability to vote governments out of office means the

EU appears both undemocratic and incomprehensible when viewed through this particular conceptual lens.

From an economic perspective, while the UK is internationalist and forward-thinking, in keeping with the evolving dynamics of the global economy, the European economic model is anachronistic and damaging to its member-states and puts the UK economy at the risk of contagion even outside of the Euro. The UK is held back by being tied to this and being represented by the EU on the global stage. In keeping with the conceptual challenge posed by the EU, and the attempt to discern its hidden motives, the Euro is seen as an ideological project to assert control over the UK.

In other respects, the social logics identified within the pro-Brexit discourse have evolved beyond the tropes identified previously in Eurosceptic discourses. In part, this reflects real-world developments and the attempts to come to terms and make sense of these within the Eurosceptic worldview. The Euro crisis, for example, emerged as one of the predominant issues in European politics in the years preceding the referendum and was an unsurprisingly prominent theme in the campaign. The depiction of the Euro as a form of disciplinary punishment meted out to Southern Europe reflects the wider reportage of this issue in the British media. However, pro-Brexit discourse also departs from the previous Eurosceptic discourse in terms of the extent and the vehemence of the claims made about the EU, particularly the dismissal of the single market – a project driven forward by the doyenne of the Eurosceptics, Margaret Thatcher – as economically unimportant to the UK.

Perhaps the most important element of the pro-Brexit discourse, and the most obvious point of departure from longer-standing Eurosceptic discourses, was the focus on immigration and the EU as a source of unlimited population growth. To some extent, this also reflects underlying social, economic and political development in the UK in the intervening period. EU enlargement occurred in 2004 and in the period analysed in Chapter 5 (up to 2007 when the ToL negotiations concluded) inward migration from the ten new member-states was yet to be activated as a mainstream political issue, as occurred after the success of UKIP at the 2009 European elections. However, the prominence of immigration within pro-Brexit discourses, and the particular articulation of immigration as a policy problem that emerges within these, reflects also the need for the leave elite to construct their narrow interests and objectives – to leave the EU – as a hegemonic political project in which these became synonymous with the concerns and interests of the wider population.

In the period following the 2008 financial crisis and the austerity measures introduced by the UK government in response to this many people in the UK experienced a reduction in living standards and front-line public services which coincided in many contexts with a seemingly rapid demographic change as a result of immigration, mainly from Eastern Europe. This created an intuitive plausibility to the narrative that immigration had placed undue pressure on underfunded schools and hospitals while depressing wages in many working-class occupations. The claims that the UK was unable to limit migration inside the EU thus identified EU membership as a surface of inscriptions for a wider set of social and political grievances and fears, and voting to leave the EU was presented as a way of addressing these.

The overriding message of the pro-Brexit discourse was that the UK had ceded control of its ability to make public policy; to control its economy and public spending; to manage its international relations and trade policy; and, perhaps most pertinently, to limit migration into the country from the EU. Moreover, the EU is seen as a source of chaos, disruption and threat – principally in terms of its economy and as a source of migration – from which the UK must act to protect itself. Voting leave was presented as a way of regaining sovereignty over these areas, with the implicit promise that this would allow governments to take decisions to improve the lives of their citizens. This was summarised in the constant refrain of leave campaigners that they wanted to 'take back control' of the UK's laws, borders and money.

7 Political logics of the *Vote Leave* discourse

The previous chapter identified the *social logics* underpinning pro-Brexit discourses in the lead up to the 2016 referendum. The current chapter focuses on the *political logics* – the *logics of equivalence* and *difference* – at play in constructing the campaign for Brexit as a popular movement able to sew together various disparate interests and sub-populations to create a 'leave' majority – however contradictory, unstable and temporary – on 23 June 2016. As was argued in the Introduction, Brexit was an elite political project centred around a small if expanding faction of the parliamentary Conservative Party, and an associated coterie of interest groups and ideologues, including some of the country's wealthiest investors and political donors who funded both the Brexit campaign and the party. While Conservative Party activists and members were overwhelmingly supportive of Brexit, they represented a tiny if extremely influential proportion of the electorate. Numbering just over 100,000 this constituted an even smaller percentage of the UK population, geographically and demographically skewed to older, white voters in relatively wealthy, non-metropolitan parts of England; i.e. the precise groups most likely to have voted both for Brexit and for Boris Johnson at the 2019 general election (Dorling and Tomlinson, 2020).

The challenge for leave campaigners was, therefore, to construct a sufficiently large coalition of voters to deliver a pro-Brexit majority on polling day. This meant convincing voters beyond the Tory heartlands – people for whom voting for the 'right', or perhaps even voting at all, was anathema – that the Brexit vote transcended party allegiance and traditional left-right dichotomies. This included centrists for whom Brexit may appear extreme as well as those on the opposite end of the political spectrum. While Brexit received some support from the radical left – the so-called 'Lexit' voters – which had assumed greater national prominence under Jeremy Corbyn's leadership of the Labour Party, these actors remained vehemently opposed to political alliances with the Tories. In addition, they needed to convince previous abstainers, and those disillusioned with politics, that unlike normal elections the referendum represented the opportunity to bring about *real* political change. This required the construction of a popular-democratic imaginary which could serve as a surface of inscriptions for myriad hopes,

DOI: 10.4324/9781315098067-7

fears, grievances and aspirations of disparate groups of voters in order that they coalesce around the idea of 'leaving' the European Union (EU).

This chapter will argue that the leave campaign constructed Brexit as a populist insurrection against a political establishment which had neglected the concerns of ordinary people to pursue their own self-interest and ideologically motivated political projects. This requires a subtly differentiated and, at times, contradictory construction of the elite to be developed against which *the people* is defined and called to action. In part, this aspect of the leave discourse draws on established Eurosceptic tropes, such as the aloof, distant 'Brussels bureaucrats,' evident in the ToL discourses examined in Chapter 5. In the Brexit debates, however, the equivalential chain is expanded beyond this to associate the EU and support for remain with a wider and more amorphous category of elite interests. In addition, the key issue in which these discursive techniques come to the fore is immigration.

Constructing the remain elite

Perhaps the most obvious trope in the Brexiters' discourse is the invocation of a vaguely defined EU, or more often 'Brussels,' elite which controls political direction of, and decision-making within, the EU. As in the longer-standing Eurosceptic discourses, it is unclear precisely who belongs to this group and no differentiation is made between the various institutions and actors – located at the supra-national, national and subnational levels – which are involved in EU governance processes. A clear separation is, however, drawn between the governing elites, who benefit from European integration, and those they govern who apparently bear the costs and have no ability to hold them to account. As such, the political logics at play in constructing 'the elite' and 'the people' draw heavily on the social logics examined in the previous chapter, and the assumption about the nature of the EU as an anti-democratic political system bolted onto a failing, anachronistic and punitive economic model set out in the preceding chapter. The following quotations from Boris Johnson are indicative of this theme:

> The choice is clear. You can claim back your democracy and the decisions that affect your lives. Or you can give the green light to the limo-riding classes in Brussels who no one can touch, as they grab more and more power (Johnson, *Mirror,* 21 June 2016).

> If we vote to stay then I am afraid the whole EU caravan carries blithely on; and when I think of the champagne-guzzling orgy of backslapping in Brussels that would follow a Remain vote on Friday, I want to weep. We must not let it happen. [...] People can sense the true motives behind Project Fear. It isn't idealism, or internationalism. It's a cushy elite of politicians and lobbyists and bureaucrats, circling the wagons and protecting their vested interests (Johnson, *Telegraph,* 20 June 2016).

Central to this discourse is the idea that the people are somehow being taken advantage of, laughed at and humiliated by the elites whose lavish lifestyles they fund, and which stand in stark contrast to the daily lives of many voters in austerity Britain.

The national elite

Within pro-Brexit discourses, the equivalential chain of 'the elite' is expanded to include a political and social 'remain elite' or 'remain establishment' at the UK level who share an ideological commitment to the European integration project. This element of the discourse identifies both individuals and institutions whose interests, it is argued, are served by the UK's membership of the EU. Their common interests mean that these national actors are working together with the 'Brussels elite' to maintain the *status quo*, while marginalising the people they govern. This creates the idea of a remain establishment that is part of the European ruling class which shaped and benefits from the EU but that has little in common with, and even less regard for, the ordinary citizens whose lives they govern. From this perspective, the remain elite's motivation for supporting EU membership is not just economic and political self-interest but about their social status within this elite and their ability to deliver the result in the referendum that their peers expect. As Boris Johnson (*Telegraph*, 23 May 2016) claims, it is not just the will to power which explains the British elite's support for remaining in the EU but their vanity and pride:

> As the brow-beating and scare stories intensified, many began to suspect that the government campaign to 'Remain' was driven not so much by an enthusiasm for the Brussels system, but simple fear of the political embarrassment entailed in a Vote to Leave.

Brexit supporters consistently focus on the idea that the 'remain elite' is dishonest and duplicitous, attempting to hide their real aims and motivations for wanting to remain in the EU from the people. A joint article by senior former Conservative ministers identified how different parts of the remain establishment – the institutions as well as the individuals – are working together to promote a false narrative of post-Brexit economic shock:

> There has been startling dishonesty in the economic debate, with a woeful failure on the part of the Bank of England, the Treasury, and other official sources to present a fair and balanced analysis. They have been peddling phoney forecasts and scare stories to back up the attempts of David Cameron and George Osborne to frighten the electorate into voting Remain. To give but one example, yesterday saw the threat of an emergency budget – which was nothing more

than ludicrous scaremongering born of desperation. (Howard et al., *Telegraph,* 15 June 2016).

In addition to their dishonesty, the argument made by leave campaigners that the remain elite were trying to frighten the people into voting remain through the promotion of dishonest and inaccurate economic projections became one of the key tropes of the leave discourse. In an act of almost unprecedented chutzpah given the leave campaign's own claims about the alleged consequences of a remain vote (discussed in the following chapter) they coined the term 'project fear' to simultaneously define and dismiss leave arguments about the costs of Brexit. Along with 'take back control' and '£350 million a week,' this became one of the most widely repeated and effective slogans of the campaign. Jacob Rees Mogg (*Mail,* 29 May 2016), for example, rails against the 'dishonest predictions by the Treasury, and the improper political intervention of the governor of the Bank of England' and its 'Canadian governor' in relation to the potential economic consequences of Brexit. That Rees Mogg here makes explicit reference to the nationality of Mark Carney, the Governor of the Bank of England (without name checking him), is almost certainly not accidental and is a subtle, indirect but pointed reference to a further aspect of the pro-Brexit discourse: the remain elite's interconnection to, and common interests with, a global financial elite.

The global financial elite

A further dimension of the pro-Brexit discourse is the connection to a global financial elite, whose interests are in alignment with those of the 'Brussels' and 'remain' elites. As Boris Johnson (*Telegraph,* 18 April 2016) comments:

> All the usual suspects are out there, trying to confuse the British public, and to persuade them that they must accept the accelerating loss of democratic self-government as the price of economic prosperity. We have heard from the IMF [...], as well as the banks and the CBI, all of whom were wrong about the Euro. Davos man – the kind of people whose club-class air tickets are paid by the taxpayer, all the lobbyists and corporate affairs directors of the big companies.

The class of people who populate these international financial institutions – 'the thousands of Davos men and women who have their jaws firmly clamped around the Euro-teat' (Johnson, *Telegraph,* 25 April 2016) – not only move in the same circles as the Brussels and UK political elites discussed above but benefit from the same system at the expense of ordinary people who, they fear, may finally be able to hold them to account via the referendum. Michael Gove (*Times,* 16 June 2016) highlights the divide between the financial elite and the people, indirectly extending the equivalential chain to include those from the world of private finance and separating the collective interests of those bodies from those of ordinary people:

> We, the people, no more control the EU's operations than we control Goldman Sachs or JP Morgan. Because the people who run the EU are individuals most of us have never heard of, whom we never chose and cannot kick out.

Despite his own elite credentials, and his position within the UK government which is clearly able to exercise influence over the EU, Gove positions himself as part of 'the people' in opposition to the European political and global financial elite he identifies. The reference to Goldman Sachs is particularly evocative as it, more than any other entity, came to symbolise the corrupt and unregulated banking sector which had propagated the post-2008 financial crisis. It became a byword in popular discourse for the unacceptable face of the global capitalist system and took on more sinister connotations in the world of online conspiracy theories. As such, the equivalence claimed between the EU and Goldman was designed to evoke the most visceral forms of indignation among potential leave voters about political institutions which allegedly sustained the business practices that led to such dire financial outcomes for the ordinary people who faced the consequences of the financial crisis.

Big business

Michael Gove's reference to multi-national financial institutions as part of the global remain elite is closely associated with the idea, promoted by leave campaigners, that the EU serves the interests of big business and global corporations, versus those of the people they are meant to represent. As Boris Johnson (*Telegraph*, 15 May 2016) argues:

> Of course, the FTSE100 fat cats will sign up for remaining in the EU: they are getting personally richer and richer [...] while those at the bottom have seen a real terms fall in their wages. It is one of the reasons that the EU has such low innovation, low productivity, and low growth. If you want to back the entrepreneurs, the grafters, the workers, the innovators, the burgeoning and dynamic businesses of Britain then Vote Leave on June 23, and give this cabal the kick in the pants they deserve.

A clear differentiation is made between 'big business' and smaller, local businesses which, like the potential leave voters who may run or work for them, are positioned as the victims of a system which favours only the 'insiders' of the global economic elite. Large corporations have the knowledge and resources to understand the complex EU system and to identify and implement strategies to influence its opaque governance processes. As Johnson (*Telegraph*, 15 May 2016) continues:

> The EU is starting to take on some of the features of an 'extractive' society. It is dominated by a group of powerful international civil servants, lobbyists and business people. These people, on the whole, know who each other are. In the case of big business, they can afford to hire someone to follow the regulation that comes out of Brussels. They can fix a meeting with the Commissioner responsible. They may even meet him or her at some conference or event – Davos being the most famous. In that respect they have an immense advantage over the vast majority of businesses in this country.

The victims of the *status quo* are not just ordinary voters but also much of the business community; especially small local businesses which lack the resources of multi-national corporations to access and influence EU policy making. These firms may well not benefit from cross border trade within the single market but are nevertheless forced to bear the costs this allegedly poses on them. As Johnson continues:

> Most businesses (in fact most Britons) have absolutely no idea who works in the Commission, or how to get in touch with them, and they wouldn't know their Euro-MP from the man in the moon. Only 6% of UK businesses actually export to the EU, and yet 100% of them have to comply with 100% of EU law, whether they are large businesses or small – a regulatory burden that costs about £600 million per week.

As such, small businesses are not identified as being part of the 'remain elite' as is the case with large corporations. Their interests are seen to align instead with those of ordinary people. In the same way that the individuals who may run or work for these local businesses are marginalised and exploited by the remain-supporting political establishment, the interests of these companies themselves are also sacrificed in favour of the industrial establishment. The costs imposed on them and disadvantages they suffer as a result of EU membership compared with their larger competitors are identified as equivalent to those suffered by ordinary citizens with whom they have common cause.

Constructing the (Leave) people

In constructing the 'remain elite,' leave discourses are engaged in a simultaneous process of constructing the idea of 'the people' against which they are juxtaposed. It is in terms of its radical heterogeneity from 'the elite' that the different components of that equivalential chain obtains its meaning as the people. Consequently, some attributes of 'the people' – their marginalisation and exploitation at the hands of a self-interested, plutocratic, trans-national remain elite – have been discussed earlier. However, there are a range of 'positive' characteristics attributed to 'the people' which are examined in this section. These identity positions are an important counterpoint to the sense of anger which narratives of exploitation are designed to generate since they allow the reader to view themselves, not as victims or to experience just the stigma of exploitation but as active agents pushing back against these oppressive elites. This section introduces the concept of 'the (leave) people' to identify the population of potential leave voters *interpellated* ('hailed') into Brexit discourses (Althusser, 1971). The particular idea of 'the people' constructed in leave discourses identifies the popular will as synonymous with the desire for Brexit.

Old-fashioned common sense

A key aspect of the pro-Brexit discourse sought to detoxify the idea of voting leave in the minds of centrist voters who may be reticent about voting leave because of the opposition of the political establishment – and the leadership of the main political parties – to leaving the EU, while the most vociferous support for Brexit was articulated by more extreme or peripheral actors, including Nigel Farage and UKIP. In part, this strategy aimed to create a shared 'social norm' around voting leave by reassuring these voters that other 'people like them' also supported Brexit. As Jacob Rees Mogg (*Mail*, 29 May 2016) comments:

> Outside the political elite, at events across the country, people tell me (quietly, as it is not the fashionable view) that they too want to leave. And in London, I get supportive shouts from people driving lorries and taxis – a somewhat unusual experience for a Conservative politician.

In Johnson's formulation two key target demographics for the leave campaign – quiet, rural, probably older voters out of touch with the latest fads but with a keen sense of their (now unfashionable but deeply held) values, and the urban working classes – are identified. Crucially the fictional voters in Johnson's article, he implies, are not the kind of people who would usually vote Conservative but are supporting his side this time.

Standing up to the remain bullies

A further characteristic attributed to the (leave) people is their steadfastness and resilience in the face of pressure from the establishment to support remain in what the leave campaigners dubbed 'project fear.' It was highlighted earlier that Brexit supporters consistently presented the 'remain elite' as both dishonest and attempting to browbeat voters into choosing the *status quo* through a series of exaggerated claims about the (mainly economic) consequences of a leave vote. This aspect of the leave discourse presents the counterpoint to this through the evocation of a savvy and resilient people able to see through the exaggerations and half-truth to stand up to the remain elite and vote for their own interests, as opposed to those of the political class. As Boris Johnson (*Telegraph*, 12 June 2016) comments:

> We are being bullied and brow-beaten into remaining in this failing system – and I think the public can see through it. As time goes on, I find more and more people can see that.

The use of 'we' in this passage is important as it not only places Johnson, despite being an almost archetypal establishment figure, on the side of the (leave) people. In addition, it positions the leave campaigners as pushing back against the *status quo* on behalf of the people who support them.

These arguments draw on and evoke clichéd aspects of the self-conceptualisation of (at least certain sections and demographics of) the Anglo-British people in which myths of stubbornness and bloody mindedness are the heart of the national character. While these people may be reticent about articulating strong opinions, they are nonetheless clear in their own minds about what they value and what they want. However, to paraphrase the words of leave supporter Iain Duncan Smith in another context, the message to the establishment is that they should not underestimate the determination of a quiet people. As well as insightfulness, the leave people are attributed a steely determination. As Johnson (*Telegraph*, 25 April 2016) argues elsewhere:

> So I gather they think it's game over. The Bremainers think they have bombed us into submission. They think that [...] the British people are so intimidated by these testimonials – American presidents, business leaders, fat cats of every description – that they now believe the British people will file meekly to the polls in two months' time and consent to stay in the EU [...]. If that is indeed the view of the Remain campaign, they [...] are perhaps ignoring the resilience and thoughtfulness of many middle-of-the-roaders.

In keeping with long-standing Eurosceptic tropes, the reference to being bombed into submission evokes images of WW2 and the fetishisation of the 'blitz spirit' at the heart of long-standing Eurosceptic discourses and wider national mythologies.

Jacob Rees Mogg (*Mail*, 29 May 2016) argues that 'project fear' reveals the low regard in which the remain establishment hold the (leave) people; that they do not have the courage of their convictions to vote against the position which their political masters are attempting to force them into:

Now it assumes a nation yellower than a Lib Dem leaflet will be frightened into remaining in the European Union. Virgil's 'Monstrum Horrendum' has been conjured up to cow a people.

The implication of this quotation is that Rees Mogg and his colleagues have much greater faith in the judgement and resilience of the people than their remain supporting counterparts. In keeping with the mannered performativity of the English gentleman that characterises Rees Mogg's carefully crafted public persona, his evocation of Virgil and some superfluous, rudimentary Latin are designed to mark him out as a man of depth, substance and learning whose insights not only can be trusted but would reflect favourably on those wise enough to share them.

Voting 'Leave' as a heroic act

Closely related to the idea of stubborn resiliencies is the idea that voting leave is an act of heroic rebellion. This aspect of the leave discourse draws on the idea that the referendum offers a unique opportunity for the quiet (leave) people to be heard and to intervene to right the alleged wrongs done to the UK by virtue of its membership of the EU and at the hands of the remain elite. Boris Johnson (*Telegraph,* 20 June 2016) identifies the quiet (leave) people as almost a vanguard class with a unique historical mission and one which serves the interests not just of the UK but of those beyond:

Well, whatever you say about this referendum campaign, it is a moment of fundamental decision. You have it in your hands to transform Britain's current democratic arrangements for the better. You can change the whole course of European history – and if you vote Leave, I believe that change will be overwhelmingly positive.

Like the image of the stubborn resilience of the (leave) people, the idea of the British people, as victors and liberators in WW2, striking a blow against an oppressive force on behalf of the peoples of Europe is one of the key foundational myths of the British nation, which is continually reproduced in popular culture. Boris Johnson (*Telegraph,* 6 June 2016) evokes these ideas in an article written from the perspective of an imagined post-referendum future in which the UK had voted to remain in the EU. Describing the period in the lead up to the vote he comments:

You knew that this was the last – the only – chance you would have in your life to vote for change, and to make the powerful listen. This was the moment for Britain to speak for all the people of Europe – everyone enraged with how Brussels works. [...] the dispossessed of southern Europe, their lives blighted by the Euro. This was the chance to fight for the low-paid in the UK, their incomes compressed.

Voting leave here is represented not as an act of narrow insularity but as something with much wider ramifications than for just the UK's 'freedom.' It is in keeping with the UK's mission as Europe's saviour, discussed in Chapter 5, that the British people have the historical responsibility to take such action on behalf of people across Europe and the most marginalised within the UK itself. The idea that this would be the last, or only, chance voters got in their lives to take such action is also noteworthy. It implies though that the (leave) people being *interpellated* into their movement is an older demographic which post-referendum analyses discussed in Chapter 2 suggest had the greatest propensity to vote leave and to vote at all (see Dorling and Tomlinson, 2020).

It is not by accident that the imagery, values and the emotions at the heart of this aspect of the leave discourse relate so directly to those associated with WW2. The target for this messaging was not the generation which experienced the war as adults, since those that did were in their 80s by the time of the referendum and, understanding the realities of European conflict and the reasons for founding what became the EU, were far less likely to vote leave than those a decade younger (Dorling, 2016). Moreover, harsh demographic realities meant this represents a relatively small cohort of voters in absolute terms. The leave voting generation, and the target for these campaign messages, was instead the baby boomers, brought up on their parents' recollections and rationalisations about the war, hagiographic cinematic dramatisations of the Battle of Britain and Whig history served to them in their schoolbooks detailing the great contribution of Britain to the world, but very little about the less noble aspects of its (imperial) history (see Dorling and Tomlinson, 2020).

Immigration as class politics

While the debate on immigration revealed key aspects of the social logics of the pro-Brexit discourse, discussed in Chapter 6, it was perhaps the main issue in terms of which the political logics of the pro-Brexit discourse were revealed, and on which the wider contours of the Brexit debate were defined. In terms of social logics, the UK is seen to have lost control of its migration policy and to be unable to secure its borders as an EU member-state subject to the 'free movement' of EU citizens. Given the invocation of anti-immigrant sentiments as an alternative explanation for the politics of inequality within right-wing populist discourses, the association of EU membership with uncontrolled migration meant voting to leave the EU – and thus to control immigration – became a surface of inscription for a wider set of political grievances. This was particularly the case for those voters who felt their interests were ignored by the political establishment and normal political processes, and who identified the referendum as an exceptional event that may hold the possibility of genuine policy change.

In terms of political logics of the pro-Brexit discourses, immigration served as a key nodal point in the construction of an equivalential chain in which the interests of the (leave) people were identified as synonymous with those of the Brexit elite campaigning to leave the EU. To achieve this, the issue of immigration was discussed through the lens of class politics in which the interests of the 'remain elite' are identified as being in diametric opposition to those of ordinary people. In addition, there is a consistent attempt to present concerns about immigration as legitimate and reasonable in order to detoxify the idea of supporting leaving the EU on these grounds in the minds of centrist or centre-left voters who may be quietly concerned about this issue and/or sympathetic to the leave campaign in other ways.

The key theme in the leave discourse is the idea that immigration serves the interests of the political and economic elites which support remaining in the EU at the expense of the majority of the population. The messaging around this issue is designed to target specific policy issues – principally access to and the quality of front-line public services, employment and wage levels and the availability and affordability of housing – identified as being of key concern to potential leave voters. As Iain Duncan Smith (*Mail*, 5 June 2016) states:

> Those on the lowest incomes suffer the most as a result. [...] It is these people who experience first-hand the pressure on public services – finding their schools full, or while trying to get a doctor's appointment or a toehold on the housing ladder. It is no wonder that a recent poll showed that almost two-thirds of people oppose the current levels of EU migration, while fewer than one-third think it has been good for the economy.

Speaking as someone whose own parents were migrants to the UK, Priti Patel (*Sun*, 1 June 2016) nonetheless seems to concur with this analysis of the alleged economic burden created by migration:

> And hard-working British families see in their daily lives the impact that the loss of control over our borders has placed on the services they rely on. Schools, hospitals, public transport and housing are all struggling to cope with the growing demands placed upon them by immigration. [...] And that may not matter much to the corporate executives in the City, and it certainly doesn't impact on the foreign politicians and big businessmen who seek to lecture us on how to vote, but it matters to the British people.

The invocation of those on the lowest incomes is in part an attempt to focus on this socio-demographic group – who may feel alienated from ordinary political processes – as a key source of potential leave voters. However, the construction of the (leave) people in the context of the immigration debate depends on the positioning of the remain elite as the radical other against which their interests are defined. As Priti Patel (*Telegraph,* 28 May 2016) comments:

> For the millions of Britons who feel the consequences every day, this rate of growth cannot continue. [...] If you have private wealth or if you work for Goldman Sachs you'll be fine. But when public services are under pressure, it is those people who do not have the luxury of being able to afford the alternatives who are most vulnerable. Getting your child a place in your local school becomes more and more difficult; there is more competition for jobs; wages are held down. It's shameful that those leading the pro-EU campaign fail to care for those who do not have their advantages. Their narrow self-interest fails to pay due regard to the interests of the wider public.

Patel's decision to name check Goldman Sachs is noteworthy as it plays a number of symbolic functions. Most obviously, it symbolises the existence not just of a parallel (remain elite) economy detached from the daily lives of the (leave) people but, as discussed in Chapter 6, the idea of an international financial elite whose interests national politicians favour over those of ordinary (leave) people.

Yet there is a deeper symbolic value to this reference. Perhaps more than any other bank, Goldman Sachs became synonymous with the irresponsible business practices that precipitated the 2008 financial crisis. By creating an equivalence between the interests of Goldman (and its executives) and the UK remaining in the EU it creates an association between EU membership and the economic consequences of the financial crisis. It was membership of the EU which allowed the business practices to occur which led the elite to get rich while the ordinary (leave) people paid the price as public services were sacrificed to bail out the banks. From this perspective, leaving the EU can be viewed as a progressive and egalitarian policy designed to rebalance the economy from those who have gained most to those who have suffered the most. Far from being a fringe concern of ideologically driven sovereigntists, self-interested speculators and political careerists, the Brexit movement is motivated by the objective of meaningful social change to improve the lives of the most marginalised groups. At a more visceral level, voting to leave the EU then becomes an act of retribution against the class of people who have exploited ordinary citizens and imposed hardship on them.

Interpellating the Lexit vote

The anti-immigration discourse at the heart of the pro-Brexit political strategy attempts to explicitly target voters who may historically have voted Labour or who feel an often deeply ingrained cultural aversion to allying themselves with a political movement so closely associated with (the right wing of) the Conservative Party. To attract traditional Labour voters, Brexit campaigners sought to identify the Labour leadership as part of the elite who had abandoned ordinary people and the issues they cared about, such as immigration. This created an equivalence between the Labour leadership and that of the Conservative Party which was also campaigning for a remain vote, while positioning the leave campaign as being on the side of these abandoned voters and prepared to address the issues they cared about. As former Home Secretary, David Davis (*Mirror*, 13 June 2016) comments:

> Cameron, Osborne, Brown, Corbyn – it's all the same. It's the haves lecturing the have-nots. It's the elite in their cushy, chauffeur-driven lifestyles, insulated from the reality of mass migration which their people are suffering, telling them they had better back the so called status quo. Shame on Brown and Corbyn, frankly. If they had any self-respect as Labour leaders, they would be standing up for ordinary Brits, not scurrying to Cameron's aid to defend the elitist EU.

The message from Davis is that the political establishment abandoned normal, working-class people, and sacrificed their living standards by failing to control immigration. And the Labour Party, whose very reason for being is to represent the interests of such people, has abandoned them too. The reference to Mr Corbyn symbolises in the minds of some the shift in Labour's political focus away from the everyday lives of 'traditional' labour voters to the issues of concern to those seemingly aloof, metropolitan internationalists such as the MP for Islington North.

Michael Gove (*Mail*, 30 April 2016), meanwhile, allies himself to the Labour MP, Frank Field, seen as a representative of traditional Labour values and policy interests:

> What's interesting is that it has been thinkers on the Left – people whose whole lives have been devoted to supporting the most disadvantaged in our society – who have been ringing the alarm bell this week about the consequences of unfettered free movement. The Labour MP Frank Field […] has devoted his life to the Labour movement. As a welfare minister, and now as Chair of the Commons Work and Pensions Committee, his first concern has been helping the poorest in our society.

In the article, Field is highly critical of UK immigration policy including that of the previous Labour government. In particular, he cites the decision by former Prime Minister Tony Blair not to impose controls on migration during the permitted transition period after the 2004 enlargement and identified this as being a direct cause of pressure on public services. It is again no accident that Mr Field, and his position on the referendum question, is contrasted to

Tony Blair who perhaps, even more than Mr Corbyn, symbolises the political realignment of the Labour Party away from its traditional voter-base.

As well as the appeal to working-class and traditional Labour voters, there is an attempt to underline the concerns about immigration raised also by members of ethnic minority groups. David Davis (*Mirror,* 13 June 2016), for instance, highlights the intervention by 2019 Brexit Party parliamentary candidate, Harry Boparai, during a television debate:

> They had better listen to people like father-of-three Harry Boparai who told the Prime Minister during the EU referendum TV debates that uncontrolled immigration had caused his family's quality of life to plummet.

Iain Duncan Smith (*Mail,* 5 June 2016) meanwhile highlights that the UK's immigration policy within the EU is biased against those from elsewhere in the world:

> Regaining control over borders will mean designing a migration system that serves the economy. Regardless of where people have been born, we will be able to accept them on a points-based system that recognises the skills we need.

While the focus on immigration from outside the EU may simply be an attempt to appeal to non-white voters, it can also be interpreted as an attempt to detoxify the idea of Brexit in the minds of centre-left or left-wing voters who identify as progressives or internationalists. This required the construction of an alternative narrative around the issue of immigration, which became so intrinsically associated with the campaign to leave the EU, by invoking norms of fairness, identifying the ways in which the current situation adversely effects ethnic minority voters, and highlighting that many people from these backgrounds themselves support a reduction in immigration.

Priti Patel is a key figure in this element of the pro-Brexit discourse and is name checked as a source of authority on immigration-related topics in articles authored by other leave supporters, in addition to commenting on this topic frequently herself. As opposed to other leading *Vote Leave* figures, whose attention focuses on a wider range of the issues relating to EU membership, her interventions in the debate deal almost exclusively with this issue of immigration. As the daughter of migrants into the UK, Patel (*Mail,* 27 May 2016) invokes the views of her family as a way of presenting the leave campaign as an inclusive movement deriving support from all sectors of the population:

> The cause of British freedom from the Brussels regime embraces all kinds of people, races, creeds and occupations. My own East-African Asian father is passionately opposed to the EU because he loathes how

it has traduced Britain's democracy and independence. There are businessmen, retired admirals, Labour MPs and top sports stars who are supporting Brexit, not one of them a screeching xenophobe. The insulting idea that racism is the driving force behind the Brexit campaign is increasingly voiced by Remain supporters. [...] But there is nothing remotely prejudiced about wanting Britain to break free from the shackles of Brussels rule and enjoy self-governance, with control over its own taxes, borders, justice, laws and welfare.

This passage is an extremely powerful invocation of the key political messages of the *Vote Leave* campaign. A leading female politician of Asian heritage strongly rejects the idea that white voters motivated to support Brexit due to concerns about immigration can be considered racists. In doing so, she cites the reasons for her own father's support of Brexit, and those of other miscellaneous leave supporters, to identify how the motivations for adopting such a position transcend social and ethnic boundaries and personal biography and are rooted simply in a concern for independence and sovereignty of key levers of policy. In keeping with the analysis earlier, Patel notes that there are Labour MPs, not just those from her own Conservative Party, allied to the leave cause. All this is designed to appeal to mainstream voters who may sympathise with the ideas behind the Brexit campaign but feel uneasy about the associations with more extreme ideologies and movements with which it may be associated in their minds.

Platitudes of reasonableness

Vote Leave commentators repeatedly and explicitly declare that they are in favour of immigration and extol its benefits. For example, Boris Johnson (*Telegraph,* 30 May 2016) reassures readers that he has 'always championed the benefits of immigration, and the ability of talented people from around the world to contribute to the life of this country.' These claims of support for immigration, or the benefits which immigration can bring, however, are almost always qualified in some way, and/or serve as a (sometimes immediate) prelude to discussing the economic and cultural dangers which immigration allegedly poses to the UK. For example, David Davis (*Mirror,* 13 June 2016) expresses empathy with those seeking to move to the UK:

Look, if I was a Romanian or a Greek I would want to come to London. I would want to swap a hard life of earning little more than a few pounds a week for a job earning many times that. Nobody should blame them. But that doesn't make such a system right for us Brits.

The leave discourse functions through a rhetorical distinction between controlled and uncontrolled migration. While the former is beneficial to the

UK, it is the latter which poses danger. This fits with the wider claim of Brexit supporters that the UK must leave the EU in order to be able to re-establish control over arrivals to the UK. Michael Gove (*Mail*, 30 April 2016), for example, declares his support for 'controlled migration' while arguing that 'Britain is strengthened by new people, new ideas and new cultures.' He warns, however, that 'you can have too much of a good thing.' The focus on control over immigration (versus immigration itself) seeks to displace the idea that people oppose immigration *per se*, or do so on the basis of ethnocentric or cultural grounds, and frames the debate about immigration as being instead about a concern for basic democratic norms. For example, Boris Johnson (*Telegraph*, 30 May 2016, emphasis added) argues that:

> People do not necessarily object to immigration, and *certainly not to the immigrants themselves*. They object to the absence of democratic consent. There is no balance or discretion in the policy, because we do not control it – and the only way to take back control is to vote Leave on June 23.

Here, there is an obvious attempt to depersonalise anti-immigrant sentiments and thereby to play down the extent to which those concerned about immigration may be motivated by individual racism. Elsewhere, Johnson (*I*, 16 June 2016) distinguishes between the legitimate concern for democratic control with more extreme, genuinely anti-immigration forces and the potential emergence of radical, right-wing parties if these 'legitimate concerns' about immigration from the political centre are not listened to:

> I am pro-immigration; but I also believe that it should be controlled, and done with democratic consent. It is that lack of control that has caused such public disquiet [...]. Indeed, it is only by taking back control that we can spike the guns of those political forces that are truly hostile to immigrants.

This reframing of the immigration debate is designed to appeal to centrist or moderate voters who may feel concerned about immigration but uncomfortable with, or unwilling to confront, what this may say about them and their beliefs. By shifting the focus of the debate onto issues of democratic control, it allows potential leave voters who may be sympathetic to the campaign, and its stance on immigration, but concerned about the association of the campaign with more extreme political positions, to reconcile their decision to vote leave with their own political and moral self-conception. It is noteworthy that the intervention above is taken from *The I* whose left-of-centre readership is the target demographic for such reassurances. An almost identical form of words was used in another article by Johnson in the *Mirror* (21 June 2016), another left-of-centre, formally EU supporting paper whose readers may be facing similar internal dilemmas. However, similar arguments are evident also in the right-wing press. Writing in the *Telegraph* (20 June 2016), Boris Johnson is similarly indignant about the aspersions allegedly cast on leave voters by the remain campaign:

> Remainers are now desperately trying to suggest that anyone who wants to Leave is somehow against the spirit of modern Britain; against openness, tolerance, decency. What nonsense – and what an insult to the people of all races and parties and ages and beliefs who simply want to take back control of this country's democracy.

This aspect of the leave discourse has a collective as well as an individual component. Leave campaigners also argue repeatedly that the UK is a tolerant and welcoming place for immigrants. Priti Patel (*Sun*, 1 June 2016), for example, argues that this meant that people like her own parents were able to come to the UK and makes lives for themselves:

> Britain is a brilliant, open-minded country – and migration has undoubtedly brought significant benefits throughout our history. We have a long and proud record of welcoming migrants – as my parents can attest.

Given her own biography as the daughter of immigrants to the UK, this argument has a particular normative weight when articulated by her. However, Patel (*Telegraph*, 28 May 2016) is keen to assert also that migration in not an unbounded good and needs to be controlled and managed:

> Britain has a long and proud record of welcoming migrants. They have made many positive contributions to our economy. But the impact of uncontrolled immigration from the EU has placed new pressures on our country.

It is noteworthy also that she emphasises that it is immigration specifically from the EU which is the source of concern. This framing, and Patel's role in the leave campaign more generally is indicative of attempts by the *Vote Leave* campaign to appeal to non-white voters and to frame the debate about immigration in terms of fairness to migrants from all backgrounds, particularly those from the Commonwealth whom, it is argued, are unfairly discriminated against by the current immigration system which creates preferential access for EU citizens. Overall, these interventions are designed to counter accusations that opposing immigration is insular and xenophobic by appealing both to readers' national pride and positive self-conception and detoxifying the idea of voting to leave the EU among undecided voters and those outside the main demographic to which *Vote Leave* sought to appeal.

Summary

It is in terms of the political logics that the differences between the Brexit discourse and longer term Eurosceptic discourses are perhaps most evident. This perhaps reflects the evolution of a broader political disposition, evident principally in the print media, into a concrete political campaign needing to deliver a majority vote. The success of the leave campaign depended on its ability to present Brexit as a surface of inscription of multiple, disparate and at times contradictory political constituencies and interests. Leave campaigners understood also that the equivalential chains they were building did not necessarily have to endure beyond 23 June. They simply needed to assemble a temporary coalition of voters able to deliver a majority on polling day. This required them to present 'Brexit' as a surface of inscription for a range of plausibly associated grievances and political objectives, which would expand the appeal of the project far enough and for long enough that more people would turn out (or cast their postal ballot in advance) for leave than for 'remain.' Ultimately, as the referendum result indicates, these efforts were successful and the analysis above demonstrates how they sought to assemble their majority.

While many of the key assumptions about the heterogeneity of 'Britain' and 'Europe' evident in longer-standing Eurosceptic discourses were evident also in the leave campaign, the focus shifts toward constructing an equivalence between the 'Brussels elite' and the political elites in the UK and a global business and financial elite. A radical heterogeneity is constructed between these national and trans-national, remain-supporting elites, on the one hand, and the (leave) people on the other. The *Vote Leave* campaign sought to appeal to a wider constituency of voters beyond ideological Eurosceptics concerned about the dry, opaque or abstract debates about 'sovereignty,' including those uninterested in the EU and those perhaps unengaged with politics in general. Aware of the increasing concerns about the accessibility and quality of essential public services (such as health care and education) as a result of austerity and the increasing salience of immigration as a policy issue in the preceding decade, Brexit campaigners sought to link the issue of leaving the EU to potential leave voters' concerns, fears and resentments which emerged from the lived experience of their daily lives. The referendum was presented as a unique opportunity for genuine political change which the political system and normal democratic processes had consistently failed to deliver. It was an opportunity to finally make the uninterested political elite – who seem to care more about their counterparts in Brussels or big business than the citizens they are supposed to represent – address the issues of ordinary voters whose problems and opinions had been marginalised and ignored. The political logics underlying the pro-Brexit discourses thus took on the structure of a classic populist narrative of an honourable people abandoned and exploited by a distant and self-interested elite whose interests are served by the EU. From this perspective, voting leave offered not just the chance for a better life but, at a more visceral level, the chance to punish the distant elites who ignore and disdain them.

The success of the leave campaign in constructing 'remain' as an elite project was no small achievement given the personnel leading the *Vote Leave* campaign, drawn from the highest echelons of the political establishment and the Conservative Party hierarchy. The move was so successful that definition of the elite become almost tautological, with support for remain become the defining characteristic of membership of the elite which was recast in cultural (as opposed to an economic or political) terms. Conversely, rejection of the 'establishment' position of remaining in the EU identified campaigners as being on the side of the people. This led to the almost surreal situation in which teachers, trade unionists and residents of some London boroughs which are among the most deprived in the UK were dismissed as the elite by expensively educated ministers and advisers, while they and the millionaire hedge fund managers funding their campaign were able to position themselves as men (and in some rare cases women) of the people. The definition of the elite in these terms though resonated with the sense of cultural alienation identified in the studies discussed in Chapter 2, which as much, if not more, than economic marginalisation was found to be a key motivating factor for many leave voters to reject the *status quo*.

From a discourse theoretical perspective, the success of the leave campaign lay in their ability to rearticulate the interests of key sections of the population through the identification of 'the people' with support for Brexit. In this way voting leave became not just a rejection of the political settlement, the policies of austerity or the societal changes caused by immigration, but an act of rebellion against the elites who had brought these things about. However, the leave campaign had to ensure those drawn into this transient leave coalition were not just convinced by their arguments but sufficiently motivated to convert their support into action and to actually vote 'leave' on polling day. The following chapter examines the ideological and motivational aspects of the pro-Brexit discourse in greater detail through the concept of *fantasmatic logics*, which are key to understanding the effectiveness of this political movement in mobilising turnout.

8 Fantasmatic logics of the *Vote Leave* discourse

The Lacanian idea of fantasy is central to the critical logics approach to social and political explanation. The development of the concept of *fantasmatic logics* represents arguably the most significant intellectual development in post-Laclau and Mouffian DT and one of the most useful tools for policy analysts working in this tradition to deconstruct and explain contemporary social and political phenomena. While *social logics* examine the contours of social order and *political logics* help us to define the political fault lines and forms of contestation through which hegemonic political projects emerge and are reproduced, *fantasmatic logics* explain the emotive power that discourses are able to exercise over their adherents. As such, it is key to explaining both the stickiness, or longevity, of highly sedimented social orders and the strength of attachment to the ideals which they are able to engender in those *interpellated* into the subject positions they offer.

Understanding the emotional/fantasmatic investment in a given meaning structure or order of discourse is, therefore, a key step in understanding the ways in which new social movements, such as the pro-Brexit coalition, can be built and mobilised. Fantasmatic logics are constructed along two, often symbiotic, axes. The *horrific dimension* of fantasmatic logics tells of a future catastrophe which will come to pass if a specific course of action – integral to the present social order and the political formations that sustain it – is not taken. The *beatific dimension*, meanwhile, paints a picture of a utopian future that will come to pass if certain conditions prevail and certain choices are taken. This chapter applies the concept of fantasy, and the horrific and beatific dimensions of fantasmatic logics, to understand the power of leave discourses and their ability in the 2016 referendum to motivate people to choose a course of action with such uncertain consequences and potentially damaging repercussions for their country and their individual lives. Having analysed the horrific and beatific narratives of the pro-Brexit discourse, the final section of the chapter argues that EU membership is experienced as a form of national (and vicariously personal) humiliation by Brexit supporters and that this forms a key motivational dimension for potential leave voters.

DOI: 10.4324/9781315098067-8

Horrific dimension: 'hard' remain

The first aspect of the horrific dimension of the pro-Brexit discourse relates closely to the analysis of the EU presented in Chapter 6 on social logics, which identify the EU as a dysfunctional, punitive and anachronistic polity overseeing a failing economic model. Despite this, it is claimed the EU is able to exercise increasing control over ever-greater areas of British life, while forcing the UK to fund its harmful, ideological project. These fantasies of exploitation and subjugation are facilitated within the 'intentional vacuum' that exists at the heart of Eurosceptic and pro-Brexit discourses. In other words, there is a failure within the Eurosceptic worldview to comprehend the reason for the EU's existence and the purpose it serves. Its sharply nationalist assumptions provide a limited conceptual toolkit through which to make sense of the EU, often defining it as a foreign power more akin to a (hostile) neighbouring state than a multi-lateral organisation of which the UK was a member. Moreover, the EU's complex, multi-level and poly-institutional governance structure in which power is distributed between multiple actors and decision-making fora provides a conceptual challenge for those whose conception of politics is grounded in the Westminster, majoritarian system. This is particularly the case for those socialised into the mythology of the UK political tradition and isolated from contact with other political traditions and systems by the verbal and cultural mono-lingualism, which characterises much of the political class and UK society more generally. This leads Eurosceptics to question and reject the rationale for the EU's existence and search instead for the *real* motivation behind it. Instead of a legalistic order to manage interdependence, resolve conflict and project collective interests between neighbouring medium-sized powers, it is seen as a plot by individual states to control their neighbours or by a faceless ruling class to reduce independent nations to regions of a federation. The EU as a conceptual challenge emerges as a fantasy object for Eurosceptics as they seek to work out what 'they' really want from the UK.

In keeping with this fundamental discursive structure, a recurrent theme in the pro-Brexit discourse was the future direction of the EU and the apparently secret plans for further integration after the referendum. Leave campaigners argued that a vote to remain in the EU would lead to a rapid acceleration of the European integration process by a newly emboldened Brussels bureaucracy and their allies in the UK remain establishment. This position is referred to here as the *hard remain* discourse. As Boris Johnson (*Telegraph*, 20 June 2016) summarises:

> [I]t is an illusion to think that if we vote to Remain, we are somehow opting for the *status quo*. The *status quo* is not on offer. If we stay in, we will be engaged willy-nilly in the desperate attempt to keep the Euro together, by building an economic government of Europe.

This is mirrored by a group of other senior Conservative Brexiters:

> The key thing to remember is there is no status quo option. There are two possible paths. We can remain anchored to a declining economic power with a tottering currency, bound by all the EU's laws, with little influence. This master-servant relationship makes no sense for Britain (Howard et al., *Telegraph*, 15 June 2016).

This argument goes hand in hand with the assertion that the British people are being somehow duped by their political masters about the future which awaits them if they elect to stay in the EU. As Boris Johnson (*Telegraph*, 25 April 2016) informs his readers:

> For more than a year now, Brussels has been in a self-imposed lockdown. Nothing must be done to frighten the children. The British referendum – that embarrassing and tedious genuflection to democracy – must be safely won; and then they will get their plans out of the drawer and get on with the business of building a federal super-state.

The clear sense which emerges from this is of a deceitful and duplicitous political establishment unwilling to be honest with people about their true plans and the consequences for people's lives.

As well as the generalised speculation about deeper integrations, there are repeated references to specific policies that are apparently planned for the post-referendum period. One key example of this is the claim that there are plans afoot to create a European army. As Jacob Rees Mogg (*Mail*, 29 May 2016) comments:

> The revelation that plans for a European army have been deliberately kept under wraps until after the referendum simply shows the ambition of those who seek a single European state, and the cunning manner in which they aim to achieve their objectives. It is not the democratic will that must prevail, but rather the master plan.

Liam Fox (*Mail*, 12 June 2016) meanwhile focuses on financial regulations:

> Plans by the European Commission to harmonise our insolvency laws, our company laws and our property rights through single market legislation where we have no veto have brought shivers through the business community, who are becoming less and less sure about the case to remain. But there is worse to come.

Boris Johnson (*Telegraph*, 6 June 2016) links the emergence of and EU-level defence capability to the weakening of NATO. The latter is a key point of reference in Eurosceptic discourses, which identify NATO, as opposed to the

124 *Fantasmatic logics of the VL discourse*

EU, as responsible for the unprecedented and unbroken 70-year period of peace in Europe following the end of WW2:

> It now seems – hey presto – that Britain's budgetary contributions will go up, to more even than £350 million per week. There are plans for a European army, it emerges, that will undermine NATO.

As in the preceding quotation, it is a point of universal agreement among leave advocates that remaining in the EU will lead the UK's contributions to the EU budget to increase – beyond even the much vaunted figure of £350m – in order to pay for the 'hard remain' policy agenda. Johnson and Gove (*Telegraph*, 5 June 2016) claim that 'the Commission has delayed publishing its budget until after the referendum,' for fear that the implied increase in UK contributions, and threat to the totemic British rebate, may deter people from voting remain.

In addition to these alleged new policy initiatives, leave supporters argue that a vote to remain in the EU will further undermine the ability of the UK to protect its interests within the EU which, for Brexiters, is equated with their ability to prevent further integration or the adoption of common policy measures through veto powers. According to four former Conservative leaders and Chancellors, this is due to a reduction in decision-making via unanimity (and thus with a UK veto):

> Within the EU, our influence will decline remorselessly. The growth in the number of decisions taken by Qualified Majority Voting will inevitably mean the UK is outvoted by Eurozone countries ganging up to rescue the single currency (Howard et al., *Telegraph*, 15 June 2016).

Liam Fox (*Mail*, 12 June 2016), meanwhile, argues that the ToL grants the Commission unprecedented powers to monitor and intervene in the economic policies of member-states:

> A provision in the Lisbon Treaty called 'the rule of law mechanism' allows the Commission to determine if elected governments are 'deviating from the common constitutional traditions of all member states'. This allows the members of the European Commission, each of them unelected, to determine whether an elected government is legitimate.

In keeping with long-standing Eurosceptic tropes about 'the EU juggernaut' (Hawkins, 2012), the sense created in the pro-Brexit discourses is of a political system with its own internal dynamic moving inexorably forward but over which the UK is able to exercise little or no control. Instead, it is governed by people fundamentally alien to the British with whom they have little in common. As Boris Johnson (*Telegraph*, 20 June 2016) comments:

If we vote Remain, we stay locked in the back of the car, driven by someone with an imperfect command of English, and going in a direction we don't want to go.

Johnson's image is powerfully evocative of the sense of fear and disempowerment we would experience (or may have actually experienced) in such a scenario. It builds also on established tropes of cultural othering evident in the Eurosceptic discourse which may manifest themselves most obviously, or frequently, in the daily lives of his readers in the spoken language of the people with whom they come into contact. Perhaps most importantly in terms of the content of this chapter, it relates to the idea of the unknown desire of the other, discussed in Chapter 3, which permeates and empowers the pro-Brexit and longer-standing anti-EU discourses.

The Eurozone

As was examined in Chapter 6, the apparent economic and political dangers posed to the UK by the Eurozone are a key component of the leave discourses. This includes a series of claims about the future direction of the European economy, the political responses to this and how they will impact on the UK. As well as speculation about the negative economic consequences of the Euro, the leave campaigners claims that there will be an inevitable need for extensive political integration to manage the ongoing crisis surrounding the European currency. As Boris Johnson argues, this will inevitably lead to greater costs for the UK and a loss of political control:

> the next step – post the UK referendum – is to try full-bore to create an "economic government of Europe", using the single-market institutions, in a way that will inevitably drag us in – and for which the UK taxpayer will end up paying. This "political union" will be both horrifically anti-democratic and expensive for us, too (Johnson, *Telegraph,* 30 May 2016).

As in the examples cited above, these moves are seen to be being deliberately delayed until after the referendum in an attempt to hide the UK's fate from the electorate and thereby influence the result. Johnson reiterates this point in an article written from an imagined post-referendum future in which the UK had voted to remain, a literary device which provides his speculation about future developments with a greater air of inevitability:

> In their desperation to save the Euro, the Brussels authorities had set an ambitious agenda to go further and faster with a United States of Europe. Reading the fine print, the British discovered that there was nothing they could do to veto such moves – towards a fiscal and

political union [...]. Nor could they stop further centralisation from applying to Britain (Johnson, *Telegraph*, 23 May 2016).

These concerns are echoed, in even more hyperbolic terms, by Iain Duncan Smith (*Mail*, 5 June 2016) who claims that the existence of the Euro will be used as a pretext by 'Brussels [...] for eradicating the independence of nations and creating a single federation in the Eurozone.'

Elsewhere, it is claimed further integration is needed to reassure Germany and to guarantee its political and economic commitment to EMU. As Boris Johnson (*Telegraph*, 25 April 2016) comments:

> the Commission wants to have a new European approach to company law, to property rights, to every aspect of employment law. Why? Because if the Germans are to be persuaded to engage in a perpetual bankrolling of the less prosperous regions of the EU, then they want proper Germanic rules to enforce good behaviour. He who pays the piper calls the tune. And Brussels can see only one way to save the Euro – and that is to get Germany to pay, and therefore to allow Germany to call the tune.

This implies that the UK's independence in these policy areas will have to be sacrificed to save the EU's ideological commitment to the Euro. Similarly, it identifies the EU as serving interests of the largest and most powerful member-states. The implication is that special arrangements are made to reassure Germany and protect German interests while the UK is told just to get on with it and pay the bill. It is with no small measure of irony that the UK had clearly the most bespoke arrangement of any member-state with its membership of the EU characterised by an almost constant series of renegotiations and opt-outs from Margaret Thatcher's demand that she 'wants our money back' at the Fontainebleau European Council meeting of 1984, through John Major's agreement that the UK would not be obliged to participate in EMU or the social chapter of the Maastricht treaty, up to David Cameron's short-lived, unimplemented renegotiation of the UK's terms of membership before the 2016 referendum.

Opening the floodgates

The issue of future enlargement of the EU to the East – and particularly the prospect of Turkey, as a populous country of principally muslim citizens joining – is identified as a key threat facing the UK if it votes to remain in the EU. More specifically, enlargement is identified as an inevitable source of additional immigration to the UK as the populations of these countries will enjoy free movement rights as EU citizens. As Boris Johnson (*Telegraph*, 30 May 2016) argues:

> It is likely to get worse, with nearly 90 million people from Turkey and four Balkan countries being lined up for EU membership and free movement. That will bring competition for jobs and pressures on hospitals, schools and housing that we can only guess at.

This, Johnson argues, will simply exacerbate the pressure on public services, further depressing the living standards of ordinary people. Priti Patel (*Sun*, 1 June 2016), meanwhile, argues the UK is already funding these countries, moving toward accession:

> If we remain in the EU the situation is only likely to get worse. British taxpayers are already paying nearly £2billion for Albania, Macedonia, Montenegro, Serbia and Turkey to join the EU.

As in Johnson's intervention, Patel then exaggerates the likelihood and consequences of these countries acceding to the EU and follows this with inaccurate claims about the UK's ability to influence these decisions inside the EU:

> The European Commission is accelerating these plans and is in the process of extending visa-free travel to the border with Syria and Iraq. I'm afraid that I completely fail to see how or why this is a sensible policy. The truth is that we can do nothing about this for as long as we remain in the European Union – the only way to take back control of our borders and immigration is to vote Leave on June 23.

The Eastern expansion of the EU is presented as a realistic, short-term prospect despite accession negotiations with Turkey having stalled in the decade preceding the referendum with little possibility of further progress. In addition, it is simply untrue that leaving the EU strengthens the UK position in this regard since, as a member-state, the UK has a veto over any future enlargements. Patel also links the idea of enlargement to the ongoing wars in Syria and Iraq which were identified as key factors behind the 2015 migrant crisis. Enlargement, she implies, is akin to moving the UK's external border to the edge of these conflicts zones and thus will lead to a potential surge in asylum seekers from there coming to the UK.

Michael Gove (*Mail*, 30 April 2016) also presents enlargement as posing a security threat to the UK in very similar terms:

> The states now negotiating to join the EU include Albania, Serbia and Turkey – countries with poor populations and serious problems with organised crime, corruption, and sometimes even terrorism. We have to ask ourselves, is it really right that the EU should just continue to expand, conferring upon all new member states all the rights of

membership? Do we really think now is the time to contemplate a land border between the EU and countries like Iran, Iraq and Syria?

In addition, Gove suggests that the countries now being considered to join the EU do not share the democratic and wider social norms of current EU member-states and thus enlargement risks importing corruption and organised crime. Later in the article he links the potential for Montenegro to accede to the EU to the Balkan conflict of the early 1990s:

> Montenegro, [...] unfortunately, has mafia gangs, a reputation as a centre for money-laundering and a record for narcotics trafficking. The Prime Minister, Milo Djukanovic, has been a leader of the country almost continuously for the past 30 years. He started as a Communist apparatchik and friend of the murderous Serbian dictator Slobodan Milosevic. But today he is a fan of the European Union and chummy with EU power brokers.

Despite the obvious hyperbole and inaccuracies in these projections of the EU enlargement and the consequences for immigration, the *Vote Leave* discourse sought to insulate this from criticism from remain voters by invoking the experience of the 2004 enlargement which, from, not by argued, had led to much higher levels of migration to the UK than had been predicted. As Priti Patel (*Telegraph*, 28 May 2016) comments:

> the public have lost trust in politicians being able to control immigration. Before the EU expanded to include countries in Eastern Europe, Brussels and the then Labour government claimed immigration from these new member-states would not be significant. But instead we have seen hundreds of thousands of people entering this country.

The horrific dimension of the pro-Brexit discourse recast the referendum debate to position remaining in the EU as the risky option – the leap into the unknown – as opposed to leaving. The idea of remain being the *status quo* option was dismissed and a secret agenda for further integration and enlargement was presented as being the inevitable fate for the UK inside the EU. The generally low levels of understanding about the EU within the UK, and the apparently extensive transformations to the organisation which have occurred in recent decades, meant that this speculation about the future direction of the EU by leading Brexit supporters had a certain plausibility. This discourse resonated also with long-standing Eurosceptic tropes about Europe as a source of threat, disorder and conflict discussed in previous chapters. Faced with an uncertain future within the EU, the 'safe' option, it was argued, was for the British people to get out while they can.

Beatific dimension: taking back control

The horrific dimension of the leave discourse focuses on the idea that the UK is somehow out of control of its own destiny; that EU membership represents a fundamental undermining of its sovereignty at the hands of a foreign, quasi-imperial power which seeks to exert ever greater control over, and extract ever more resources from, the UK. Consequently, a key focus of the beatific component of this discourse is the ability of the UK, and its people, to 'take back control' of their destiny. As Boris Johnson (*Express*, 22 June 2016) summarises there are explicit foci on the ability to decide certain laws, control immigration and decide how to allocate financial resources:

> On June 23 we have the chance to take back control of our destiny and our place in the world. With control of our trade, our borders and our democracy we can prosper as never before. [...] we will get back all that money to spend on our priorities such as the NHS and cutting VAT on energy bills for pensioners – which the EU, you won't be surprised to know, forbids us from doing.

This is echoed by Michael Gove (*Telegraph*, 21 February 2016):

> We can take back the billions we give to the EU, the money which is squandered on grand parliamentary buildings and bureaucratic follies, and invest it in science and technology, schools and apprenticeships. We can get rid of the regulations which big business uses to crush competition and instead support new start-up businesses and creative talent. We can forge trade deals and partnerships with nations across the globe, helping developing countries to grow and benefiting from faster and better access to new markets.

For Liam Fox (*Sun*, 14 February 2016) this is not just a pragmatic concern, or about democratic control, but is of existential importance to the UK's claims to be an independent country:

> I believe that a country that cannot make its own laws and control its borders is not a free and independent nation. I want Britain to be free to take advantage of new economic opportunities and independent of outside controls. We must not give in to the fear mongers. It is time to take control. Time to leave and be free.

Perhaps the key area in which advocates of leaving the EU sought to reassert control was immigration and they repeatedly proposed the alternative of implementing what they claimed would be a fairer system based on the example of Australia. As Boris Johnson (*Telegraph*, 20 June 2016) comments:

We can take back control of our borders, and install an Australian-style points-based system that is fair both to people coming from the EU and from non-EU countries.

This sentiment was echoed by Michael Gove (*Mail*, 30 April 2016):

And we can develop a more humane and rational policy on who is allowed to live and work here – extending a helping hand to genuine refugees in peril, while attracting the top international talent that will really strengthen our economy. [...] It would empower us to rescue the most vulnerable across the globe, liberate us to forge new alliances and trade deals, strengthen us to stand up more vigorously for the rule of law and human rights worldwide, and re-invigorate our democratic institutions.

While Gove presents a partly moral argument for a reformed, independent immigration policy, as part of a reoriented foreign policy, migrants are seen in transactional, functional terms; as a resource which can benefit the UK economy and, by extension, the indigenous population. This is echoed by Priti Patel (*Sun*, 1 June 2016):

We would prioritise people coming here based on their skills, not on where they happen to have been born. We would be getting the brightest and most productive people contributing to our economy rather than unlimited numbers of often unskilled migrants from Europe. It will be fairer, it will be better for the economy, and we will be in control.

This meritocratic, reformed migration system, it is claimed, will protect the interests and improve the living standards of the key demographics targeted by the leave campaign who perceived themselves to be negatively affected by immigration, particularly those relying on front line public services. Similarly, it opens the possibility that those from non-European backgrounds may actually find it easier to come to the UK.

Elsewhere Patel (*Telegraph*, 28 May 2016) reassures EU citizens in the UK as well as British migrants to the EU that their rights would be protected under a future migration regime (although it is obviously not within the gift of the UK government to guarantee the status of its citizens abroad):

there would be no change in the status of people who have already exercised free movement rights. That would provide stability and reassurances to the 1.3 million British expats living elsewhere in the EU, as well as to employers in Britain who have already hired European workers. But swift changes would be required to control future numbers coming in and to accelerate the removal of EU migrants who are not exercising free movement rights or who have been convicted of serious criminal offences. [...] Such a system would support economic growth while protecting schools, the NHS, housing and infrastructure.

The contradiction here is obvious that Patel seeks the ability of the UK government to remove EU citizens from the UK after Brexit while guaranteeing it would be impossible for the remaining 27 member-states to do the same to UK citizens living elsewhere in the EU. Moreover, she appears unaware that a wide degree of discretion is available to national governments to police the residency (and remove EU citizens) even within the EU.

The pro-Brexit discourse identifies immigration as a key social, economic and cultural challenge faced by the UK which has led to inadequate public services, housing and job opportunities, as well as declining real-terms wages and living standards. In reality the causes of these issues are multiple and complex. One key factor though is the policy of austerity pursued by the UK government since 2010 which has led to significant reductions in funding of public services and welfare programmes which were supported by the leading Conservative figures in the *Vote Leave* campaign. The remedy they present for the hardship many people are experiencing in their daily lives is not a repudiation of the policy regime they contributed to implementing and maintaining, but a reduction in immigration which, they claim, would alleviate demand for the public services they have failed to fund. It is only by leaving the EU, they argue, that the UK would be able to cut net migration, thereby freeing up resources for hospitals and schools, while increasing demand for labour and raising wages for those already here.

In reality, a reduction in immigration would increase not relieve pressure on public services as immigrants are both net contributors to the UK public finances and a significant proportion of the workforce in front line service delivery. Moreover, the loss of so many young, dynamic, talented people would have a wider negative, macro-economic effect which, allied to the wider effects of Brexit on inward investment, would lead to an overall decrease in the size of the economy and thus public spending capacity. Yet the anti-immigration discourse has a seductive plausibility to it based on simplistic but intuitive notions of supply and demand which clearly resonated with the lived reality of at least key sections of the electorate.

Brexit as national renewal

A key component of the *Vote Leave* discourse was the apparent ability of Brexit to raise the spirits of the country and lead to a renewed sense of national purpose and belief. Boris Johnson (*Telegraph,* 23 May 2016), writing from the perspective of an imagined post-Brexit future, captures this sentiment:

> The British felt suddenly and unexpectedly galvanised – with a renewed confidence in their democracy, and excitement about the new opportunities for global trade and partnership. The Brexit vote was followed by a powerful campaign for reform in Europe, and a widespread euphoria that at least one population had plucked up the courage to say that the emperor had no clothes. After only a few years it became increasingly hard to find anyone who would confess to having voted Remain.

The imagery employed by leave supporters suggests that the UK has been infantilised or emasculated through its membership of the EU. They present Brexit as an antidote to this malaise which will force the country to stand on its own two feet and control its own destiny. As Jacob Rees Mogg (*Mail*, 29 May 2016) comments:

> Those who want to vote Leave have a passion for freedom, while the remainers merely say 'always keep a hold of nurse for fear of finding something worse'. Inevitably there will be a level of uncertainty if we leave, although the collapse of the Euro would also have a profound effect on us if we vote Remain to pick up the pieces.

An almost identical image is used by Boris Johnson (*Telegraph*, 22 February 2016):

> This is a moment to be brave, to reach out – not to hug the skirts of nurse in Brussels, and refer all decisions to someone else.

The imagery of 'nurses' used here invokes wider right-wing discourses about the apparently corrosive social and moral effects of the 'nanny state' and the culture of reliance this creates in those reliant on public services. It is with no small degree of irony that it is Jacob Rees Mogg – who famously took his own childhood nanny with him on the campaign trail during a previous general election campaign – and others from the same social milieu, in which such forms of paid childcare are common, who should be the ones to employ this metaphor. However, it is a common trope of British political discourse that those with the means to afford actual nannies are the most severe critics of the metaphorical state nanny.

Brexiters are highly critical of remain campaigners, whom they accuse of talking the country down or lacking faith in the UK's ability to govern its own affairs outside the EU. As Boris Johnson (*Express*, 22 June 2016) states:

> My view is that Britain is poised for a new age of confidence. [...] The fundamental choice in this referendum is between people who believe our country is capable of running itself and people who want to outsource our future to unelected Brussels bureaucrats. [...] The Remain

camp will not get away with running Britain down by saying we can't manage our own country. I believe Britain will have the confidence to take back control and Vote Leave tomorrow.

The implication of this statement is that the 'lack of belief' in the UK demonstrated by the remain elite is somehow responsible for the UK's current failure to function at its full potential. Talking down the country, they imply, becomes a self-fulfilling prophecy. The focus on positivity and belief in the UK and its people though has a resonance beyond simply the claims that the UK could function more effectively economically and politically outside the EU. This has a powerful emotive force which speaks to people's self-identity mediated through their perception (and the perception of others) of their country. In other words by encouraging people to think positively about the country, leave supporters encourage the public to think positively about themselves also. In contrast, remain supporters, whose caution about leaving the EU is presented by Brexiters as negativity and doubt, are accused of lacking faith in the people of the country. From this perspective, it is easy to see how voting leave became a more positive and inviting proposition for those unsure how to evaluate the more substantial claims about the merits of leave or remain. The positive tone became a heuristic device that encouraged people to vote for how they would like the future to be (and how they would like to view their country and themselves) as opposed to what the future may more realistically hold for them and their co-nationals.

In keeping with this, the pro-Brexit discourse continually invokes the idea that the UK is a great and unique country. Leave campaigners frequently rehearse what they argue is the unique economic, political and cultural contribution of the UK to the world. For example, Michael Gove (*Telegraph*, 21 February 2016) sees this as evidence why it must flourish outside the EU:

> We are the world's fifth largest economy, with the best armed forces of any nation, more Nobel Prizes than any European country and more world-leading universities than any European country. Our economy is more dynamic than the Eurozone, we have the most attractive capital city on the globe, the greatest 'soft power' and global influence of any state and a leadership role in NATO and the UN. Are we really too small, too weak and too powerless to make a success of self-rule? On the contrary, the reason the EU's bureaucrats oppose us leaving is that they fear our success outside will only underline the scale of their failure. [...] We set up the first free parliament, we ensured no-one could be arbitrarily detained, we forced our rulers to recognise they ruled by consent not by right, we led the world in abolishing slavery, we established free education for all, national insurance, the NHS and a national broadcaster respected across the world.

The idea of the UK as a unique and special country goes hand in hand with the idea that its natural position and role in the world is that of a global leader, serving as an example for other nations to follow. As Gove comments elsewhere in the article:

> But by leaving the EU we can take control. Indeed, we can show the rest of Europe the way to flourish. Instead of grumbling and complaining about the things we can't change and growing resentful and bitter, we can shape an optimistic, forward-looking and genuinely internationalist alternative to the path the EU is going down. We can show leadership. Like the Americans who declared their independence and never looked back, we can become an exemplar of what an inclusive, open and innovative democracy can achieve.

Boris Johnson (*Telegraph*, 20 June 2016) even seems to suggest that the UK can somehow lead the reform of the EU from outside:

> Now is the time to believe in ourselves, and in what Britain can do. Of course we can continue to provide leadership and support for Europe – but inter-governmentally, outside the supranational EU system.

The idea that the UK could lead the reform of the Eurozone, having fought to detach itself from any obligations in relation to it, even as a member-state, seems highly unlikely. Yet it exemplifies both the hubris of British exceptionalism and the fundamental contradictions which characterise the pro-Brexit discourse. At the heart of this is the claim that the UK's interests are undermined by its membership of the EU; that the UK is constrained politically and economically by the Brussels machine; that it has no power to influence decision-making or to control the political direction of the EU. At the same, though, they claim that the UK is uniquely blessed, that its achievements surpass those of other countries meaning that it alone can shake Europe from its current malaise. The UK thus appears to be both powerless to defend its interests within the EU, but able to assert its dominance over the EU. While the UK is controlled by the EU as a member-state it would emerge as a leader of other nations and a feared competitor outside its institutional structures. This fits in with the underlying assumption of the pro-Brexit and longer-standing Eurosceptic discourses discussed in Chapter 6 that the fundamental purpose of the EU (what they *really* want) is to restrain and control the UK to protect its institutions and member-states from the cold wind of competition that it would otherwise supply. The fact that the UK is unable to exert its unique capabilities via the channels provided by the EU, as other lesser countries such as France and Germany seem able to do, is because the whole project is working against it, by design.

The beatific dimension of the pro-Brexit discourse is thus centred around an idea of democratic, economic and political renewal for the UK. This is, however, framed in vague and abstract terms. Little attention is paid to the specific changes to be made to the UK's democratic culture, or the trade objectives that will be pursued, and similarly little explanation is given for why membership of the EU prevents these projects from being pursued under the *status quo*. It implies also a return to the UK's historical position as a global leader; not a supplicant to the governance of Brussels. This in turn draws on the idea of empire – and the subject positions of the oppressor and the oppressed – as the enduring metaphor through which trans-national government is understood in Eurosceptic discourses.

The lyin' and the unicorns: all the benefits and none of the costs

The faith of leave advocates in the UK's prospects outside the EU is matched only by the faith they exhibit in the ability of the UK to negotiate a favourable future relationship with the EU. In keeping with their generally bullish positivity and the criticism of remain naysayers outlined above, the *Vote Leave* discourse is highly dismissive of the idea that the UK may lose out through Brexit. They consistently argued that the UK can maintain any benefits of EU membership, which they grudgingly conceded, while jettisoning the costly or unfavoured aspects that they detailed at length. This phenomenon is captured by Boris Johnson's claim that the UK 'can have its cake and eat it' in the pro-Brexit world. His opponents were more sceptical, dismissing the different versions of Brexit he and his colleagues were promising voters as 'unicorns' in that, as attractive and enticing as they may seem, they simply didn't exist and couldn't be delivered.

Brexit supporters consistently argued that the UK would be able to negotiate an even more favourable relationship with the EU as a newly independent country. As Boris Johnson (*Telegraph*, 5 June 2016) comments:

> Countries across the world enjoy trade with the EU without being part of the EU. Trade does not require this country to give away permanent control of issues as diverse as immigration and the regulation of cancer drugs. [...] It is in everyone's interests to do a free trade deal. There is a free trade zone from Iceland to Turkey. This will not end just because Britain decides to take back control and be a normal self-governing democracy.

This is echoed by Iain Duncan Smith (*Mail*, 5 June 2016):

> We also need to bury the Remain camp's assertions that the EU will lock Britain out of trade if we leave the single market. The day after Brexit, we will still have access to the same market of nearly 500 million people that we did the day before. Europe will not start a suicidal trade war with Britain when we buy nearly £70 billion more from the EU than we sell to them.

136 *Fantasmatic logics of the VL discourse*

The faith in the inevitability of a favourable future relationship with the EU being negotiated is rooted in the idea that the UK runs a trade deficit with the EU, thus making a deal more important to the EU than the UK. As Liam Fox (*Sun*, 14 February 2016) argues:

> At the moment, we import far more from the rest of the EU than we export. For every £3 worth of exports we sell them, we buy £5 worth from them. Are we really to believe that Chancellor Merkel would tell BMW or Mercedes to stop selling cars to us if we were to leave? Would President Hollande tell Beaujolais producers not to sell wine to the Brits. Of course not, the arguments are nonsense.

Similarly, Fox argues that hard economic reality will dictate that investment continues to come to the UK because of its superior economic model:

> Project Fear will tell us that investment in the UK will dry up if we leave. Yet major international companies are already making clear that they invest in the UK because of our better economic conditions and the quality of our workforce. For example, [...] the announcement that it [Toyota] will keep making cars in Britain even if voters opt to leave the EU is of tremendous importance.

Beyond the realms of trade, Liam Fox (*Sun*, 14 February 2016) argues that the UK's position as one of the leading military and strategic powers in Europe will provide an additional rationale for the EU to conclude a comprehensive future agreement with the UK, in order to guarantee its own security interests:

> The other great, and possibly most ridiculous scare story from Project Fear is that we would be less safe and secure outside the EU. They say we would not have the same intelligence cooperation with other EU countries if we were to leave. Really? Britain has the best intelligence services in Europe and a unique relationship with American intelligence. Are we really to believe that the French and German governments would reduce cooperation in the fight against terrorism and put their own citizens at greater risk just to punish Britain for leaving the EU? It is just not credible. In fact, the opposite is true.

EU membership as humiliation

Humiliation is one of the most powerful human emotions. A sense that someone's dignity has been removed, their humanity has been diminished, or that they are not being treated with due respect is an incredibly powerful driver for individuals to react and to defend their self-worth. Often this will have dramatic and damaging long-term consequences for all parties involved. The decision of the UK to leave the EU is an act of long-term economic and political significance for the UK itself and for the Union from which it is departing. Despite the assurances of leave campaigners, any decision of the magnitude of Brexit represents a degree of uncertainty and risk about the settlement which will follow it. The motivation for undertaking such a project, for accepting the uncertainty that follows – even if you have the faith articulated by Brexiters in the unique qualities of your country and the resourcefulness of its people – must be hugely powerful.

In the preceding sections we examined the horrific and beatific dimensions of the fantasmatic support structures which underpin the pro-Brexit discourse in the lead up to the 2016 referendum. While the former predicted the further diminution of the UK's political freedom and democratic accountability and the undermining of its economic interest as a result of the inevitable deepening of integration that would follow a remain vote, the latter juxtaposed this with a utopian vision of a newly empowered and self-confident Britain continuing to enjoy the benefits of EU membership, and access to its single market, while trading globally and providing political leadership to the world. However, we can only fully understand the emotive force of the *fantasmatic logics* underpinning the leave discourse by understanding the way in which membership of the EU was experienced by many of its greatest opponents and their supporters who turned out to vote for their cause in June 2016 as a fundamental humiliation. Moreover, given the elided boundaries between the national and personal self-images discussed above, which characterise the leave discourse, this was experienced as a visceral and personal humiliation by leave supporters. Consequently, the act of voting to leave the EU became an act of both national and individual reassertion in which this humiliation is finally vanquished.

The humiliation trope is evident repeatedly in pro-Brexit and longer-standing Eurosceptic discourses. According to Boris Johnson (*Express*, 22 June 2016), the very act of joining the EU was borne of humiliating desperation and the disregard for the UK shown by the European elites was evident from the very start of the UK's membership:

> This country has always been at its greatest when we've looked outward […]. That was not the Britain which joined the Common Market in 1973. Europe was streaking ahead. The bulldog had lost its bounce. It was the year of power cuts and butter coupons for pensioners. Winston Churchill inspired the British to never accept defeat. On the day we joined they even managed to hoist the Union Jack upside down over Brussels, a signal for a ship in distress.

Since then, the fear of humiliation has come to define the way in which the UK's position within the EU is viewed by opponents. From this perspective, the UK's interests and concerns are ignored or disregarded by 'Brussels' and the British government is cowed and unable to defend its interests. As Johnson (*Telegraph*, 25 April 2016) states elsewhere:

> Eventually – when we are unable to take [the volume of immigration from the EU] any more – the UK will utter a faint sheepish cough of protest. Please sir, we will say, raising our hand in the EU Council, we need reform. [...] REFORM? they will say [...]. REFORM? But you just had reform.

This sense of emasculation and disempowerment mirrors the infantilisation of the UK discussed above. The apparent failure of David Cameron's attempt to renegotiate the UK's terms of membership of the EU that concluded in February 2016 is seen as a further humiliation for the UK and the contempt with which it is treated by other member-states:

> Like many others, I was optimistic the Prime Minister would win a good deal in his renegotiation with Brussels. Sadly, it wasn't to be. If we stay, the EU will be after extra cash from us, not least to bail out the Euro. We beg to give them less, they demand we hand over more (Johnson, *Express*, 22 June 2016).

The idea that Cameron's renegotiation was a humiliating defeat is echoed by Liam Fox (*Mail*, 12 June 2016):

> the sight of a British Prime Minister taking the political equivalent of a begging bowl around European capitals, asking Luxembourg and Slovenia if we could please change some of our own minor welfare laws, resulted in the process itself becoming the story.

For Fox it is clear that having to engage with other member-states as equals represents a form of humiliation. From the examples cited, this seems to be particularly true with regard to smaller or newer member-states which lack the grandeur and status of the UK in the exceptionalist narratives of the Eurosceptic movement.

Michael Gove (*Mail*, 30 April 2016) picks up on the theme that the EU sees the UK simply as a cash cow which the EU and its dominant member-states use to bail out their currency and to fund their pet projects such as enlargement:

> Every week we send £350 million to the EU. And now millions of your hard-earned taxes are being directed to these five prospective members. [...] This bounty will be our greatest gift to Albania since the comic talent of the late Sir Norman Wisdom. That country's improbable national hero, lit up the dark days of Stalinist dictatorship. Indeed, I wonder if the Albanian people are now convinced that Britain's

Foreign Office is full of Norman Wisdom characters, lovable chumps whose generosity and good-heartedness make them easily gulled into accepting all sorts of bad advice. How else could they explain their good fortune in being on the receiving end of a £2 billion Balkan bonanza?

Not only is the EU taking advantage of the UK, but those member-states benefitting from its largesse are laughing at the UK's credulousness at agreeing to such manifestly unfair arrangements.

The idea of the UK as a patsy, which other countries treat with contempt, extends beyond simply the UK's experience in the EU, to its treatment by other powerful states, including what many leave supporters would regard as its principal ally: the US. Perhaps the clearest example of how the sense of humiliation underpinned leave discourses and was used to motivate its supporters came with the visit of President Barack Obama to the UK in April 2016. His statement on that visit that, unlike the EU, the UK would be at the 'back of the queue' for a post-Brexit trade deal with the US, was to become one of the most iconic events of the referendum campaign. While remain campaigners hoped this would encourage voters more inclined to value the UK's 'special relationship' with the US over those of its closest European neighbours to see the connection between the UK's position in the EU and its trans-Atlantic relations, it had precisely the opposite effect. As Boris Johnson (*Telegraph,* 25 April 2016), commented:

> One senior public servant [...] texted me after the US intervention and said he had been so outraged at President Obama's "back of the queue" remark that he had instantly decided to vote Leave.

The sense of indignation that the President would attempt to pressure British voters or presume to know what is in the UK's interest is key to understanding the visceral response to Obama's intervention, which received a similar response across the leave-sympathetic media. This is perhaps best captured by Jacob Rees Mogg's (*Mirror,* 27 March 2016) intervention on the event, who sees Obama's comments as the latest in a long line of perceived slights and humiliations for the UK at the hands of a US political class indifferent to British interests:

> It is wonderfully arrogant and presumptuous of a foreign leader to think that he can lay down the law for the United Kingdom, as if we were a colony of the United States. [...] Perhaps Obama just doesn't like Britain. [...] In a symbolic move, one of his first acts was to remove a bust of Churchill from his office. [...] Some of the people around him have long been hostile to this country [... and] IRA sympathisers in the 1980s.

140 *Fantasmatic logics of the VL discourse*

Later in the article, Rees Mogg is equally dismissive of the value of the UK's alliance with the USA:

> The special relationship has long been overrated. It works if the UK is a US poodle, as it was when Tony Blair backed George Bush over Iraq. It rarely does the other way round. Even so, US Presidents usually take the trouble to give something to their loyal ally. The occasional dog biscuit has been thrown our way. Obama has not done that [...]. No self-respecting Briton will be told what to do by such a man. His condescension will inspire our wish for liberty.

The key theme running through the leave discourse is of the UK as a country which is no longer treated with the regard it deserves, even by its closest allies. The idea that Obama's slight will drive the British public to vote for Brexit implies that the reason why the UK is no longer taken seriously on the global stage is that it has sacrificed its independence, and with this its international standing, as a member-state of the EU. As in the beatific component of the discourse discussed above there appears to be a contradiction between the idea that the UK is a uniquely special country worthy of status and respect but at the same time denigrated and dismissed by more powerful actors. In all instances it is EU membership which is seen as holding the UK back from reaching its potential and fulfilling its national mission. From this perspective, therefore, Brexit symbolises the casting off of this humiliation and decline and the reassertion of the UK as a great power.

Summary

The fantasmatic component of the pro-Brexit discourse juxtaposed the horrific prospect of remaining in the EU with the beatific narratives of the potential future which awaited a newly emancipated and rejuvenated UK outside the EU. Brexit supporters, perhaps concerned by the incumbency bias in referenda as risk-averse voters opt for the *status quo*, sought to recast remaining in the EU as the step into the unknown, while assuring their audience that the UK would continue to enjoy all the advantages of EU membership, but none of the costs, from outside. This focused on the apparently secret plans for the EU to assume control over new areas of policy, most notably the formation of a European army, the economic dangers of cross-contamination with the economic travails of the Eurozone and the threat of increased volumes of inward migration as a result of the apparently inevitable eastward enlargement of the EU.

In contrast to this Brexit offered not just the opportunity to regain control of the UK's capacity to make its own laws, direct its own economy and control immigration, it was argued that this would come at no cost and the UK could enjoy even more advantageous terms of engagement with the EU from outside its structures. This new-found freedom would act as a form of national moral (as well as economic and political) renewal in which the British people would feel a new sense of pride and belief in their country. This functioned as the antidote to the perceived humiliation and subjugation which the UK, and by association its people, had suffered as a result of EU membership. These discourses offered an attractive and engaging proposition to voters which stood in contrast to the defensive rationalism of much of the remain campaign, which was reflected in the consistently higher levels of turnout among leave voters and in leave areas. The following chapter examines the interventions in the referendum campaign by Nigel Farage.

9 Nigel Farage and *Leave.EU*

The preceding chapters analysed the pro-Brexit discourse of senior political figures in the Electoral Commission's officially designated leave campaign group, *Vote Leave*. Absent from the analysis so far is thus any consideration of the interventions of perhaps the key figure in bringing about the UK's exit from the EU, Nigel Farage. As explained above, the decision to examine these strands of the leave discourse separately was due partly to the presence of multiple, UK-wide leave campaign groups, most notably *Vote Leave* and *Leave.EU*. However, it reflects also the difference in tone and emphasis between these groups and the core socio-demographic groups to which they sought to appeal. The findings from the analysis suggest a high degree of similarity between the *Vote Leave* and *Leave.EU* discourses to the extent they can be meaningfully thought of as constituting a single 'pro-Brexit' discourse, or at least representing closely related variants of a core underlying discourse. In part, this reflects a move by *Vote Leave* in the final weeks of the campaign to shift further onto the terrain of *Leave.EU* and to focus increasingly on the issue of immigration. Yet some noteworthy differences between the two most prominent leave campaigns were evident, and are examined below. It is important to emphasise the centrality of Nigel Farage to *Leave.EU*. Unlike *Vote Leave* which counted multiple prominent political figures within its ranks, *Leave.EU* functioned essentially as a vehicle for Farage. Thus the following sections analyse Farage's contributions to the referendum campaign. While the analysis in this chapter focuses principally on the unique aspects of Farage's discourse, it seeks also to identify the similarities which existed between this and the *Vote Leave* discourse examined in the preceding chapters in terms of the social, political and fantasmatic logics.

Social logics

Farage's interventions reproduce and reinforce the social logics evident in the *Vote Leave* discourse and in longer-term Eurosceptic discourses. Writing on the eve of the referendum, the following passage reads like a checklist of the key tropes examined in the preceding chapters. The various strands of

DOI: 10.4324/9781315098067-9

this discourse are densely interwoven and ambiguously elided and are thus hard to disaggregate. It is, therefore, quoted at length as almost an exemplar of both the form and content of Eurosceptic ideology:

> We are just hours away from the opportunity of a lifetime: the opportunity to get our country out of the European Union and in doing so get our borders back, our democracy back and for us to embark upon an exciting future as an independent nation. [...] We will exit a failed political union, one which is now a disaster zone. We see a migrant crisis utterly out of control. We see a Eurozone crisis causing human misery on a shocking scale. And we see an outdated organisation that has no answers when it comes to many of the problems in the modern world.

In addition, Farage articulates the economic arguments against migration and the populist separation between the elites and the people:

> I've heard a lot through the course of this campaign from the wealthy establishment about GDP. About maintaining the status quo. Well that might be all right for them with cheaper nannies and chauffeurs but it isn't what's in the best interests of ordinary British workers. Open-door migration has suppressed wages in the unskilled labour market, meant that living standards have fallen and that life has become a lot tougher for so many in our country. We must leave the European Union so that not only can wages increase for British workers but so that living standards rather than declining can start going up. The wellbeing of those living and working in our country matters to me more than GDP figures. The EU's open borders make us less safe.

And he adheres also to the hard remain thesis put forward by *Vote Leave* campaigners that there are secret plans afoot for a further, unavoidable deepening of European integration:

> We know that the European Union is hell bent on further, deeper centralisation. Indeed, the plans for a full EU army have been put on ice only until the very day after the referendum. It is clear that the EU nationalists are biding their time, waiting for a remain vote before they hike up the EU's budget that we will have to contribute more towards and they will also reveal their full military ambitions (Farage, *Express*, 21 June 2016).

Farage here summarises the idea that the EU is a harmful, foreign body whose immigration policy and failed economic model weakens Britain economically and politically and undermines its security. The EU serves the interests of the remain establishment while undermining those of the (leave) people. From this perspective leaving the EU represents a moment of national salvation and renewal as the country takes back ownership of its borders, its laws and its destiny. The alternative is a future of deepening integration, enlargement to the east and accelerated immigration.

Political logics

The parallels between Farage's interventions and those of the leading *Vote Leave* campaigners, in terms of constructing Brexit as an anti-elitist project and as a surface of inscription for wider political grievances and demands, are clear to see. Yet there are important specificities to Farage's discourse that are worthy of closer attention. As regards political logics, these come to the fore in Farage's particular invocation of the (leave) people.

Ordinary decent people

It is in terms of the political logics of the leave discourse that Farage's contribution is most important. While Farage shares with the *Vote Leave* discourse the fundamental populist assumptions of the (leave) people fighting back against a corrupt and self-interested (remain) elite that seeks to exploit them, the specific contours of 'the people' in Farage's discourse differ in subtle but important ways from the analysis presented in previous chapters. This reflects the particular focus of each of the main leave campaigns, on slightly different sub-populations and target audiences.

The equivalential chain which Farage seeks to construct is based around the idea of 'ordinary decent people' in opposition to the elite. The precise definition of these people, and the terms used to identify them, vary at times across his interventions but they share certain characteristics associated with social class, ethnicity and age that frame their lived experience of modern Britain. For example, in the following excerpts, detailing his campaigning tour across the UK, Farage comments:

> We began the week in Barking and Dagenham which is now the fastest-changing borough in the whole of the country. There are plans to increase the housing stock by 50% in the next 15 years. Dagenham is the frontline of the immigration debate in this country (Farage, *Express*, 25 May 2016).

Elsewhere, Farage comments:

> It is interesting to note that many people on the side of remain are those that are comfortable in their lives and whilst very few believe in the EU flag, the anthem, or want a European Army, they seem scared to rock the boat. The leave side is very different. None more so than in Dagenham, in the East End of London. The response I received on the

streets and in the pubs of Dagenham was passionate, strong and unforgettable. A lot of people from lifelong Labour families are committed to leaving the European Union. They have seen their wages driven down, struggled to get their children into their school of choice and are seeing parts of East London change beyond recognition. I suspect for many of them, even if they were asked to walk through hot coals to get to the ballot box, they probably would (Farage, *Express*, 4 May 2016).

The invocation of Barking and Dagenham, a quintessentially working-class borough in outer London, alongside the reference to 'lifelong Labour families,' evokes the idea of a marginalised, and specifically white, working-class population ignored and neglected by the political class. Their implicit concerns about the area 'changing beyond recognition' and the issues around accessing public services which have accompanied this change is a thinly coded message to white working-class voters that Farage understands their concerns about immigration and will seek to address these. Interestingly, the idea that Dagenham is at the 'frontline of the immigration debate' again employs the language of war which permeates Eurosceptic discourses.

This language creates an association between controlling immigration and leaving the EU as two fronts in a broader culture war in which ordinary decent (implicitly white, working class) people reassert their interests against a ruling class that has favoured the interests of both European elites and migrants over them. And the steadfastness and bravery of the people there recalls deeply sedimented national myths about the resilience of working-class Londoners during 'the blitz.' To push back against the *status quo* is presented not just as a way of improving their economic conditions but of recapturing this fighting spirit, and with this their dignity following the humiliation and degradation suffered by their communities.

Of all parties and none

In the above quotation about Farage's encounters with the people of Dagenham, his suggestion that voters would 'walk through hot coals' to vote in the referendum is interesting as it suggests that people who may ordinarily not be inclined to vote are highly motivated to do so on this occasion. Farage's campaign explicitly sought to gain support from previously politically unengaged people. He argues that the leave campaigns:

have reached out directly to those who have not typically engaged in British politics, holding packed public meetings across the United Kingdom with speakers from all parties and none, creating a mass movement of supporters who want out of the European Union (Farage, *Telegraph*, 6 April 2016).

Similarly, the recognition in the passage cited above that many of his sympathisers in Dagenham were previously Labour voters is indicative of his desire to sanitise the idea of voting leave for those who may associate this with the Conservative Party or other elitist institutions from which they feel alienated or unwilling to align themselves:

> Though Conservative figures and voters are of course vital in order to win this referendum, the vast majority of those who will be eligible to vote did not vote Conservative. The leave side must reach out across the spectrum to Labour voters, to those in the trade union movement and to non-voters. […] The public at large are not interested in Tory bickering. They want to know how and why we would thrive outside of the European Union if they are to vote for Brexit (Farage, *Express,* 11 May 2016).

In an attempt to address this issue, Farage along with Conservative MP Tom Pursglove and Brexit-supporting Labour MP, Kate Hoey, announced a series of rallies, to garner cross-party, grassroots support for the leave campaign:

> This is why we are announcing a historic cross-party public meeting to discuss the referendum […]. Throughout the land, MPs and MEPs from all parties will come together, along with thousands of local people, to fight for Britain's national interest […], and side by side with those with no party affiliation […]. We will stand shoulder to shoulder putting country before party. For it is only by leaving Westminster and taking the debate across the country that we will win. No matter which political party you are in, this […] is the moment in which we can break the mould, free our country from the grip of the EU and transform the nation's prospects for the better (Farage et al., *Telegraph,* 7 January 2016).

In this quotation, the idea of 'ordinary, decent' people is replaced by that of 'local people.' The former, like the latter, evokes a specific demographic which perceives themselves as being somehow marginalised and ignored by the political classes. It suggests a non-metropolitan 'silent majority,' in the heart of Middle England (outside of Westminster), whose values and concerns are not taken seriously by the political class, but who now have an opportunity to assert themselves by acting together in the referendum campaign.

War and legacy for the Brexit veterans

As well as their appeal to the white, working class, traditional Labour voters a key target demographic for *Leave.EU* was older voters. Farage's interventions consistently sought to evoke a connection between the referendum and the past sacrifices of generations in ways which were designed to appeal to older voters who overwhelmingly voted leave in the referendum:

> So many fought and died to preserve our democracy. It is precious. Yet our birthright has been handed away by the political establishment. Central to my vision of Britain after June 23 is that our Parliament is sovereign, empowered and able to make all of the big decisions (Farage, *Telegraph,* 10 June 2016).

> A few days after the referendum it's the 100th anniversary of the Battle of the Somme. We should never forget just how much generations have sacrificed. Our democracy is precious and our right to self-determination is one which has been given away by the political class to the EU and bureaucrats such as Jean-Claude Juncker. We must seize this chance, this opportunity to take it back. After all, what sort of future do we wish to leave our children and grandchildren? (Farage, *Express,* 21 June 2016).

In keeping with long-standing, Eurosceptic tropes, the key reference points from the UK's past are the two world wars and the metaphor of the UK's engagement with the EU is of conflict with Europe. Farage argues the memory and sacrifices of previous generations who fought these wars – the parents and grandparents of the main demographic groups who voted for leave (Dorling and Tomlinson, 2020) – have been somehow sold out by the political class via the UK's membership of the EU. This is a generation that feels it inherited the legacy of WW2 only to see the freedoms won in that conflict be given away. What is more, it calls on them to consider whether they will hand down as much to the next generation as their predecessors did to them. This imbues the referendum campaign with a visceral sentimentality and invokes the idea of the nation as a transcendental entity through which the departed live on in the world. Voting leave to save the nation thus becomes tied in not only with ideas of debt and obligation to their parents and children but with ensuing their mark in posterity.

Voting 'leave' in the referendum becomes also an opportunity for voters, in rebelling against their leaders, to replicate the heroism of these previous generations at the same time and vanquishing their betrayal. At a time in life when they may be reflecting on the legacy they will leave in the world potential leave voters are told they can seize back control of their country in order to pass this on to their children and grandchildren. The act of leaving the EU is thus elevated to an act of ultimate defiance through which each of these Brexit heroes will live on as part of a newly 'independent' UK.

Man of the people

The construction of ordinary, decent people depends also on the construction of Farage himself as one such person. He does this through a series of coded messages, seemingly unrelated to the issue of Brexit itself. Farage, like *Vote Leave* campaigners Boris Johnson and Jacob Rees Mogg, has developed a carefully crafted public persona over a number of years intended to appeal to potential UKIP and, latterly, leave voters. The construction of Farage as a man of the ordinary, decent (leave) people depends of course on a process of othering against the 'remain elite' as the heterogeneous counterpoint. While in *Vote Leave* discourses, and frequently also in Farage's interventions, the othering between the (leave) people and the (remain) elite is structured in economic (that the elite reap the benefits of EU membership while the people pay the price) or political terms (that national elites serve the interests of the Brussels machine or big business as opposed to their people), for Farage this 'othering' has a prominent cultural component. Given Farage's own biography as an upper-middle-class privately educated scion of the home counties who, before entering politics, worked in 'the city' – ie at the very heart of the establishment he now derides – his public persona focuses instead on his everyman credentials. More specifically these are associated with his drinking and smoking habits which identify him as a 'normal' person and perhaps serve as a potential point of commonality with working-class voters to whom he seeks to appeal. In contrast to Farage, the jovial *bon-vivant*, the elite are seen as po-faced and dull As Farage (*Express,* 18 May 2016) himself comments:

> I do think this referendum campaign, which is going to be very long, needs livening up. That's why I'll be soon be touring the country in a double-decker bus, taking to the streets, visiting the big towns and cities and speaking to as many people as possible. While this is a serious debate and is the most important political decision of our lifetime, there is nothing wrong in having a bit of fun during the campaign.

Whereas Johnson and Rees Mogg present themselves as differently mannered pastiches on the archetypal English gentleman, Farage presents himself as a lovable rogue, never happier than with a drink and a cigarette in his hand, rejecting the hectoring calls of the 'nanny-state' for him to improve his lifestyle. Describing his experience of the campaign trail, Farage (*Express,* 25 May 2016) tells readers:

> I'm feeling real energy and passion around this tour already, though I'm not sure that my GP would approve of the diet of pork scratchings and Mars bars but (sic) I feel years younger.

Farage's ostentatious rejection of perceived medical wisdom – as with his previous questioning of the evidence of smoking-related harms – functions not just to buttress his everyman credentials, but as a coded message to his supporters about his willingness to transgress broader social norms associated with 'political correctness' and 'health and safety.' The latter represents the world of behavioural control imposed on a generation of men who (among certain social classes at least) have never previously experienced a challenge to their authority or been held to account for their behaviours, opinions and utterances in the micro-level context of their daily lives. In flouting norms about smoking, diet and lifestyle, Farage is sending a message to his supporters that he is prepared also to transgress other (from the perspective of his adherents equally oppressive and pointless) norms around equality, respect and inclusivity for non-white, non-British, non-male people, who have historically lacked the privileges of those who look and sound like Farage.

You are not allowed to talk about (anything except) immigration now

Nowhere are Farage's credentials as a 'man of the people' more clearly flagged than on the subject of immigration. While, as examined in preceding chapters, immigration was presented as an issue of class politics by the *Vote Leave* campaigners, the willingness of leading figures in that movement to engage with this topic was, in the build-up to the referendum and the initial stages of the campaign, a point of contention with *Leave.EU*, with *Vote Leave* adopting this as a key talking point only later in the campaign. As Farage (*Express,* 11 May 2016) comments:

> I've been absolutely clear that the issue of EU open door immigration will be the defining issue of this referendum campaign. Indeed, it is the number one issue in British politics and the one that can win this referendum [...]. I am therefore pleased that the senior Conservatives on the Leave side [...] are all now talking about this issue. Indeed, much of the language I have used over the years on the over-supply in the unskilled labour market and the damaging impact of mass EU migration is now being used by others on the leave side.

Farage thus identifies himself as the person who was brave enough to talk about these issues when no one else would and who forced the hand of others, more centrally embedded in the political establishment than he, to take on this issue of such importance to the (leave) people. In this example, it is evident that the construction of the elite within Farage's discourse differs subtly from that of *Vote Leave* commentators. Whereas the likes of Boris Johnson position themselves against the remain establishment and on the side of the people, Farage is initially sceptical about their credentials as true Brexiteers. It is only in accepting his specific conception of Brexit, and the opposition to immigration at the heart of this, that the equivalential chain starts to expand to accommodate these Conservative grandees within the (leave) people. From Farage's perspective, anti-immigration becomes the existential issue at the heart of the leave movement. To support leave is to oppose immigration by definition. And it is only in your opposition to immigration that you can be admitted to the (leave) people.

In contrast to the ordinary, decent (leave) people – who live the consequences of EU membership and particularly of uncontrollable migration in their daily affairs – Farage claims that the (remain) elite are either unaware of the effects of their political decisions on ordinary people or unwilling to admit to them since they themselves benefit from the current policies. One example of this is the sense of cultural alienation and economic disadvantage which many potential leave voters experience in their own country due to the presence of non-English speakers and the availability of alternative sources of labour from elsewhere in the EU. Farage (*Express*, 11 February 2016) speaks directly to the concerns of these people:

> Worse though are today's revelations that for some vacancies advertised on the Government's Universal Jobmatch website, such as painting and decorating, some employers are demanding applicants speak a foreign language. This is yet another example of how our own citizens are once again suffering due to the foolish stupidity of the pro-EU political class.

In another example, Farage (*Express*, 27 April 2016) identifies what he argues are the wider social and cultural effects of immigration:

> I've often spoken about opening the door to Romania and Bulgaria and been vilified by large sections of the political and media London luvvie classes. I recommend they all go and visit Page Hall, a suburb of Sheffield. Over 800 Roma people have been moved into the area. The overall state of decline, the rising crime and the closure of local businesses has to be seen to be believed. To be fair David Blunkett has spoken out about this.

The invocation of David Blunkett, seen in some quarters as authoritarian former 'New' Labour Home Secretary, is again designed to detoxify the idea of voting leave to control immigration for Labour voters. The implication is that, while the leave campaign is so deeply associated with the political right, its ideas may not be that far removed from the Labour governments these people may have voted into office. Farage continues using the example of a local pub, a potent symbol for a particular kind of cultural Englishness to which Farage has consistently sought to appeal, to exemplify the erosion of traditional social institutions and the interests of those who run or use them, as the result of (uncontrolled) immigration:

> I visited a pub where I had to press a bell to be seen through the window to judge whether I could be let in. The landlord says that on winter days if the door is open, 20 or 30 people will come in with their prams, with

others youngsters running around and sitting in the warm for the day with no one buying a drink. The family that run this pub feel totally abandoned by the local authorities and the police. And I must say I felt very sorry for them. So the next time Mr Corbyn or others in our political set that like open door immigration because it provides them with cheaper nannies and cheaper chauffeurs tell us how good this new development is, I will think of Page Hall and its beleaguered residents.

Interestingly, the then Leader of the Labour Party, Jeremy Corbyn – whose left-wing views on foreign policy and other key-value issues proved to be anathema to the precise electoral demographics sought by Farage, UKIP and *Leave.EU* – is positioned firmly on the side of the political elite; benefiting from immigration and oblivious to the concerns of the (leave) people. Farage's contention that leave campaigners just have to tell the truth is important also. It recognises people's concerns about migration as being both sincerely held and valid, and places Farage again on the side of the people against the elite. He is willing not only to listen to their concerns on immigration but to take them seriously and to believe them; not ignore or dismiss them as the 'remain elite' have done. The reference to nannies and chauffeurs, the economic perks of immigration enjoyed by the (remain) elite as an explanation for their support for EU membership mirrors arguments put forward by *Vote Leave*. Farage's intervention here, as with his visit to Dagenham discussed above, is, however, more crassly evocative of the alleged consequences of immigration for (white) working-class people.

Whereas *Vote Leave's* arguments are couched in more neutral, transactional, often economic terms – that people just want access to high-quality public services – and are accompanied by platitudinous reassurances about campaigners' sense of fairness or internationalist credentials, Farage offers few such caveats. His interventions, like *Leave.EU's* now infamous, immigration-related poster ('Breaking Point') revealed during the referendum campaign, functioned as powerfully impactful vignettes which resonated with the lived experience of his target audience and the emotional responses – of fear, anger and indignation – which these triggered.

Graphic images and narratives are able to engender often visceral emotive responses in people, which are far more impactful than depersonalised statements of fact or statistics in shaping opinions and perceptions. This is particularly the case where they reinforce and confirm previously held biases and opinions and tap into a perceived sense of injustice. It is easy to see, therefore, how Farage's anecdote from Sheffield which confirms what 'everyone knows' about how migrants exploit their 'hosts' and lack respect for 'our' ways (symbolised by the great British pub), even more than *Vote Leave's* acknowledgement of people's 'legitimate concerns' about immigration – let alone the remain camp's sober macro-economic forecasts – was able to motivate those who had never voted, or abandoned politics, to 'walk across hot coals' to get their country back.

As well as highlighting the disadvantage faced by the (leave) people at the hands of the (remain) elite and the uncontrolled migration they have facilitated, Farage underlines that Brexit offers a definitive solution to this. It creates the opportunity to redress the balance in favour of ordinary, decent people and that he and his *Leave.EU* colleagues will make this happen:

> I believe in a future for our country where we make our own laws, negotiate our own global trade deals and control our own borders, a Britain where we start putting our own national interest and the British people first (Farage, *Express,* 2 February 2016).

Farage's offering is not just that leaving the EU will improve the lives of ordinary, decent (leave) people directly, but that it will punish those undeserving of the privileges they are currently seen to enjoy. It will force UK politicians to address the perceived unfairness of the *status quo.* This implies not just 'levelling up' the living standards for those outside the (remain) elite, but a punitive disciplinarity for those identified as the source of the current economic inequalities, be they the powerful elites or the marginalised groups, particularly immigrant populations, who these elites are seen to favour over their 'own' people, who get more than they deserve and more than the (leave) people feel they themselves are given. The power behind Farage's discourse, its key emotive force, lies not in the beatific promise of a better life for the (leave) people, but in the prospect of suffering for those excluded from the equivalential chain of the people. For it is not simply as economic disadvantage that EU membership is experienced but as humiliation or exploitation.

The disciplining of the outsiders is to be enacted through punitive reforms to the immigration system, including the end of freedom of movement for EU citizens and tighter controls on other arrivals. As Farage (*Telegraph,* 10 June 2016) states:

> My vision for our post-Brexit migration system is really quite simple: an Australian-style system that allows those we need to come with work permits, but which brings down numbers significantly to sensible levels. [...] By taking back control of our borders, our country can gain all the benefits of migration while ensuring that never again do our own people have their living standards pushed down.

While the preceding quotations appear superficially quite benign, drawing on the example of a close cultural cousin, Australia, and Farage paints his proposals as being moderate and 'sensible,' the substantive changes advocated are extensive and represent a fundamental change in status for EU migrants at least. They would no longer be able to enter the UK as citizens – with the rights which that entails under EU law – but are repositioned instead as economic commodities, regulated through 'work permits' which, implicitly, (and unlike citizens' rights) can be withdrawn at any time. The reference to the living standards of 'our own people' never again being pushed down asserts the idea of a clear, nationally-oriented social hierarchy. In light of the racialised overtones of the concept of 'ordinary, decent people' discussed above, this implies also an ethnically oriented social hierarchy which would favour the interests of white British voters over those considered to be less British than them, or not British at all. This offers to return to the (leave) people not just economic well-being but a sense of dignity and empowerment derived from a newly re-assertive ethno-national superiority.

Fantasmatic logics: the national is personal

One of the key themes which runs through Farage's interventions in the referendum campaign is the idea that the elite do not believe in the UK and its ability to prosper as a truly independent country outside the EU. This mirrors elements of the *Vote Leave* discourse which identified Brexit as a form of national moral renewal and the chance to unleash the potential of a newly self-confident UK as a global trading power, while assuring readers that the UK will enjoy all the same benefits of EU membership – or get an even better deal – outside. Remainers' concerns about potential downsides of leaving or the ability to deliver the relationship with the EU promised by leavers is dismissed as 'project fear.'

Setting aside the relentless, fear-laden messages about future EU enlargement and associated immigration to the UK, Farage differentiates what he claims is the positive, hopeful message of the leave side with the apparent pessimism and negativity of leading remainers. Referring to an exchange with then Liberal Democrat leader and remain supporter, Nick Clegg, who had warned about the potential economic consequences of a leave vote, Farage (*Express,* 7 February 2016) comments:

> But then something struck me. I realised from the tone of Mr Clegg's voice that what he actually meant was that he didn't think we were good enough. Our pro-EU political class don't think we are good enough to make our own laws, run our own country and to act in our own national interest. [...] It's a very good thing that in 1940 we had politicians with genuine patriotic courage. This time it is not the politicians that can save this country but the people, if they have the self-confidence and believe in Britain.

In positively asserting the strengths of the country, Farage is in line with other pro-Brexit voices who complained, before and after the referendum, that 'remainers' do not believe in Britain. However, Farage's discourse goes a step further, equating the apparent lack of faith shown by the remain elite in the country as an economic and political actor, with their lack of faith in *the people* of the country. In so doing, Farage creates a powerful emotive link between the abstract and the personal. Thus, in warning about the uncertainty of leaving the EU, or presenting evidence about the consequences for UK diplomacy and trade that may come from this, remainers were guilty not just of talking down the country but of denigrating and undermining its people. Farage by contrast not only believes in the British people but positions himself to be one of them through his use of the third person plural:

> [the UK's renegotiation of its EU membership in February 2016] is mere window-dressing from an establishment who just don't think *we* have what it takes to run our own affairs. [...]

> David Cameron [...] has shown that he just doesn't believe *we* are good enough to blaze our own trail in the world (Farage, *Express,* 2 February 2016, emphasis added).

> [Mr Cameron and George Osborne] don't think Britain is good enough to thrive outside the EU [...] The hopelessly pessimistic Remain side say *we* can't do any better than we are at the moment. I am far, far more optimistic about this country and its future outside of the EU. Let's make June 23 our Independence Day (Farage, *Telegraph,* 10 June 2016, emphasis added).

The use of the term 'we' is powerfully ambiguous in these formulations. On one level it could simply refer to the UK and its collective population; that the UK 'has what it takes' to form its own diplomatic alliances and trade relationships outside the EU framework. Another interpretation, in keeping with the analysis presented above, is that this formulation creates a divide between the remain elite and 'we' the (ordinary, leave) people in which Farage positions himself. In contrast to remainers, Farage asserts forcefully that he – as one of them – *does* believe in Britain and the British people:

> I believe we are good enough. I believe in the British people. I believe in Britain. So on Thursday vote to leave the European Union and let's make it our Independence Day (Farage, *Mirror,* 20 June 2016).

> we can do better than this, provided we have the guts to ignore our rulers and stand up for ourselves and ordinary people next Thursday (Farage, *Express,* 15 June 2016).

> This is a once-in-a-lifetime moment. I believe in this country and its people. We are good enough to thrive on the world stage representing ourselves, our interests and our beliefs as a self-governing nation (Farage, *Express,* 21 June 2016).

Farage's invocation of the people here mirrors the *Vote Leave* discourses in identifying leaving the EU as an act of (heroic) rebellion leading to the potential glory of independence. It shares their belief in the determined resilience of the British people to 'stand up' for itself. The idea that the UK is 'big enough' reflects also the idea of EU membership as infantilising and holding the UK back from growing and reaching its potential. As such they replicate both the beatific and horrific dimensions of the fantasmatic logics of the *Vote Leave* discourse.

However, there is a third, more radical interpretation of Farage's interventions: that the specific terminology he employs is crafted to trigger a particular emotional reaction in the key demographics to whom he, and his various political vehicles, are designed to appeal. The key phrase in the excerpts cited above is that the elites think 'we' are 'not good enough.' This is a highly evocative and emotive turn of phrase which speaks to people who are – or perhaps more importantly feel they are – disempowered or marginalised; people who believe their ideas, values and priorities are ignored or denigrated by mainstream politicians. Perhaps because of their age, their opinions are seen as old-fashioned or having no place in the modern world. In one intervention, Farage (*Express,* 7 February 2016; emphasis added) addresses these people directly:

> The Britain Stronger in Europe campaign […] are using a series of threats to make you think that *you're not good enough* and we're not good enough to survive on our own. They clearly do not believe in our country's ability to be an independent, self-governing nation. Well I jolly well do.

For people who feel that they are, or are seen as, 'not good enough' – who may have been told this repeatedly by authority figures such as teachers and employers and other 'elite' figures – it is easy to see how the sight of a politician speaking directly to them, recognising their most intimate fears and desires and offering to redress the perceived injustices wrought on them by the modern world is powerfully appealing.

This may be particularly the case for older (white, male) voters who may once – perhaps for the majority of their lives – have felt empowered and seen their views reflected in mainstream society and politics. With age, however, they have felt themselves and the values they represent being slowly eased from centre stage. For these sub-populations, following Farage and voting 'leave' functions both pragmatically and emotively. Leaving the EU thus offers not just the prospect of the UK recapturing its lost status in the world, but of restoring ordinary, decent (leave) people to the position of social pre-eminence which they feel is rightfully theirs. It offers them a potential resolution to the fundamental and visceral sense of dislocation which they feel with the world.

Summary

A key aspect of the *Vote Leave* discourse was the ability to connect the perceived fate and injustices of the UK within the EU with the lived experiences of potential voters and through appealing to ideas of national identity. People derive a vicarious sense of pride and emotional well-being through the positive affirmation of the identity groups with which they associate themselves, with the nation being recognised as one of the most ubiquitous and powerful forms of identity. There was constant repetition of past glories and the enduring status of the UK in the world by leave supporters, allied to the idea that the UK was being held back by EU membership and could achieve even more beyond its confines. On one level, the self-congratulatory and revisionist narratives of Britain's greatness sought to engender a positive emotive response in voters. However, the fantasmatic dimension of these discourses functioned also on a deeper psychological level. Pro-Brexit discourses sought to *interpellate* the (leave) people into an equivalential chain in which their own everyday, lived experiences of feeling marginalised, disempowered and out of control were projected on to the fantasmatic representation of the UK's own humiliation and exploitation within the EU. Brexit – and the delusionally optimistic evocations of the future that awaited the UK outside the EU – offered people not only the opportunity to experience pride in the idea of a strong and powerful Britain but also an outlet for reconciling their own personal, internal, and viscerally experienced, traumas. When viewed in this way it is unsurprising that the cautiousness and reticence of the remain campaign about the unknown risks was unable to match the lure of the leave campaign who offered their subjects such internal reconciliation.

10 Conclusions

This book sought to understand and explain the decision by the UK electorate on 23 June 2016 to vote to leave the EU through the application of the critical logics approach to social and political explanation (Glynos and Howarth, 2007). The latter provides a conceptual framework, comprising *social, political* and *fantasmatic* logics which is able to explain the normative assumptions, political alliances and affective investments which underpin and sustain political projects such as Brexit. While the argument presented here is framed in terms of 'the UK' and the interventions by campaigners in the lead up to referendum were couched in terms of 'Britain' this study is really about England; the most populous part of the UK which, outside the major conurbations, voted overwhelmingly for Brexit. More specifically, it is about the increasing assertiveness of a politicised form of Englishness. However, in keeping with the terminology employed in this book, this is not articulated in terms of an explicitly *English* national identity, but instead as an Anglo-centric conception of Britishness. This English-nationalist conception of Britain – Anglo-Britain – in which the multi-national character of this hybrid state is elided out, is constructed as an internally homogenous entity defined in opposition to a radical, European 'other' which finds its political manifestation in the institutions of the EU. Thus, while the Brexit vote has implications for the entire UK, it was a project whose origins lie in Anglo-Britain. It was delivered principally by an English electorate, albeit with some support from voters elsewhere in the UK, particularly in Wales and amongst the unionist population in Northern Ireland.

Brexit as a hegemonic project

The argument presented in this book starts from the position that Brexit is an elite-led project whose origins are to be found in the Eurosceptic movement which emerged on the right-wing of the Conservative Party in the early 1990s in response to the negotiation and ratification of the TEU. Historically, anti-EU sentiment is not confined to the political right with left-wing critiques of the EU as a 'bosses club' predating the UK's accession to the EU, through the 1975 referendum campaign – in which senior Labour figures such as Tony Benn campaigned to leave the EU against the committed 'pro-marketeer' Margaret Thatcher – and remaining prevalent to this day in certain sections of the Labour Party and the trade union movement. Right-wing opposition to European integration in the UK also pre-dates the events of the early 1990s, finding perhaps its clearest or most salient manifestation in the speeches and writing of Enoch Powell (see Wellings, 2019). However, what we have come to term 'Euroscepticism' and its key assumptions and ideologies (as opposed to wider anti-European concerns and movements) is a historically specific phenomenon rooted in the British Conservative Party which has since become more widely applied as a label to describe anti-European parties and movements in the UK and beyond (see Spiering, 2004; Taggart, 1998). It was the experience of the Maastricht era, and the organised rebellions in parliament against the government of John Major, which fuelled the emergence of political Euroscepticism as a self-conscious political movement and the interpellation of key actors into this who would work subsequently for the objective of holding and winning a referendum on the UK's membership of the EU.

While the emergence of the Eurosceptic project occurred against the backdrop of an overwhelmingly hostile and media environment (Anderson and Weymouth, 1999; Gavin, 2000; Ichijo, 2002; Daddow, 2012; Hawkins, 2012), 'Europe' remained a low salience issue for the overwhelming majority of voters. The challenge for the Eurosceptic ideologues, having manoeuvred effectively to gain their referendum, was to construct a majority for their project on polling day (see Clements et al., 2013; Carl et al., 2018). The embedded nature of Euroscepticism (Usherwood and Startin, 2013), however, meant there was an available pool of what is termed in this volume 'latent' or 'intuitive' Eurosceptics, who could potentially be mobilised to the cause of leaving the EU in the context of a focusing event such as the referendum campaign which would dominate news and media cycles. To achieve this, however, required the construction of an expansive political imaginary able to tie the issue of EU membership to a wider range of political issues, of higher salience to the electorate – principally immigration, post-austerity economic insecurity and public services – and convince sufficient numbers of voters to support exiting the EU as a proxy for their fears, anxieties and frustrations.

Ford and Goodwin (2014) have argued analogously that the emergence of UKIP as an electoral force, at least in European elections, in the decade preceding the publication of their work can be explained at least in part in terms of voter 'supply.' That is to say the increasing emergence of a pool of voters – mainly older, less educated white men – dissatisfied with the political and economic *status quo* who felt disenfranchised from, or neglected by, mainstream political parties economically and culturally (and indeed the political system *tout court*) and thus sought alternative forms of political representation. UKIP emerged as a radical alternative party which spoke to the concerns and values of this voter pool not just about the EU but a wider set of issues associated with the unwanted social and cultural changes they saw occurring around them, and which functioned as an outlet for their rejection of the entire political establishment. Unsurprisingly, support for UKIP was also one of the strongest predictors of voting leave in 2016, suggesting that the same grievances with the *status quo* lay behind the referendum result. And a significant body of scholarship, reviewed in Chapter 2, has emerged suggesting that the same socio-economic and demographic factors identified in UKIP supporters apply also to an important section of the Brexit coalition. Yet UKIP support has never approached anything like a majority of voters in national elections so, by definition, a winning coalition in the referendum had to expand beyond the core UKIP vote.

As Dorling and Tomlinson (2020) have demonstrated it is not possible to explain the referendum result purely in terms of the 'left behind' thesis. Focusing on the demographic characteristics and geographical distribution of the Brexit vote – the *absolute* numbers of voters in each category and location – there were simply not enough voters within the left behind categories to deliver a majority for leave (as UKIP's vote share would indicate). The leave coalition included also wealthy, socially conservative voters outside the most deprived socio-economic brackets, including in the wealthy and populous south of England, who had remained loyal to the Conservative Party in elections before and after the referendum result. Put bluntly, it was Tory Middle England that delivered Brexit (Dorling and Tomlinson, 2020). While some issues which emerged in the referendum campaign would have been of concern to potential leave voters across the board – less affluent Conservative voters, for example, may have had concerns about public services and social conservatives about immigration – a subtle differentiation was required in communicating to these different constituencies. While some were attracted to the plain speaking of Nigel Farage, others may have been concerned about associating themselves with a political movement outside the mainstream. This mirrored earlier tensions within UKIP between those seeking to attract former Conservative voters and those who sought instead to engage working-class former Labour voters (Ford and Goodwin, 2014).

In order to assemble their transient electoral coalition, the leave campaign had to engage these different constituencies and sought to appeal to different voters in different ways. Most obviously, the existence of two principal campaign groups (and myriad smaller entities with differing degrees of separation from these) reflected the desire to be all things to all people. Notwithstanding the considerable similarities which existed between *Vote Leave* and *Leave.EU*, in terms of their representation of the EU and its radical heterogeneity from the UK, important differences existed between the campaigns in terms of the content and outlets of their messaging.

The key figures in *Vote Leave*, such as Boris Johnson and Michael Gove, were cabinet ministers who attempted to present Brexit as a reasonable and pragmatic choice within the policy mainstream, often in the pages of the newspapers of record for the Conservative establishment such as the *Telegraph*. *Leave.EU*, in contrast, operated as a vehicle for the more controversial and *soi-disant* anti-establishment campaigner, Nigel Farage. His messaging was designed to appeal explicitly to the concerns of the 'left behind' on immigration, public services and culture change, often in the pages of the mid-range *Express*. Perhaps most effectively Farage succeeded in making the personal political by creating a powerful emotive connection between the feelings of personal disempowerment and marginalisation experienced by those who felt they had been 'left behind' and the alleged position of the UK in the EU. Thus by voting for the UK to 'take back control' they were acting vicariously to reassert control over their own lives.

Brexit as populist insurgency

Despite the differences in tone and presentation between the two leave campaigns and the symbolic importance of their respective figureheads, Johnson and Farage, to their electorates, it is important not to overstate the differences which existed between the two campaigns. They shared a fundamentally nationalist political ontology in which the nation – Anglo-Britain – is the only legitimate political community and the only level of abstraction at which democratic governance can exist. They assumed also a radical separation between the UK and the EU in which the UK is not a European country, but exists instead in its own neo-Churchillian, postcolonial circle of influence, alone in the North Atlantic but connected to the Anglosphere by its bonds of language and history (see Wellings, 2019). In terms of their political logics, both campaigns embraced a more overt and assertive form of anti-elitist populism (see Mudde, 2004; Wodak, 2020) than was evident in previous studies of Eurosceptic discourses in which national, global and financial elites are articulated into an equivalential chain with the established tropes of the Brussels bureaucrats and European elites. In opposition to the corrupt, self-interested ruling classes emerges the ordinary, decent (leave) people as the embodiment of the true national interest, represented by the anti-elitist elites at the head of the two campaign groups. Nowhere were these populist dichotomies more obvious than on the topic of immigration, which became perhaps the predominant issue of the campaign (Evans and Menon, 2017). While this had been a consistent theme for *Leave.EU* throughout the campaign, it became a key focus also for *Vote Leave* in the final weeks before polling day as their messaging converged.

Previous studies indicate that voting intentions may not have shifted significantly during the referendum campaign or in the immediately preceding years (Clarke et al., 2017; Evans and Menon, 2017; Evans and Prosser, 2016), suggesting that the debate around the EU, despite being a low salience issue, had become deeply sedimented. In addition, the outcome of the referendum suggests – as opinion polls had consistently identified in preceding decades – that public opinion on the EU had become structured by, or at least in ways which reflected, embedded Eurosceptic discourses on the nature of politics, the EU and the position of the UK within it, or perhaps more accurately in contrast to it. Consequently, the leave campaigns were able to draw on the key assumptions of this discourse which structured 'common knowledge' about, and perceptions, of the EU.

Where the short campaign did perhaps prove decisive was in terms of turnout, with the more effective mobilisation of voters in leave areas versus remain-voting areas of the country proving a decisive factor in the result (Goodwin and Heath, 2016; Dorling and Tomlinson, 2020). The leave campaigns succeeded in generating an affective investment in the act of voting 'leave' not matched on the remain side which drove their supporters to the polls and which proved sufficient to overcome the 'bias' enjoyed by the remain campaign as advocates of the *status quo*. Thus, explaining the outcome of the referendum campaign requires an explanation of the affective 'grip' of leave arguments over their supporters. The leave campaign succeeded in redefining 'remain' as the radical or dangerous option due to the apparent risk posed to the UK by the 'hard remain' agenda being held back by 'Brussels' till after the referendum. The referendum result reflects also the lukewarm, concessive nature of pro-Europeanism in the UK over decades (Hawkins, 2012; Daddow and Gaskarth, 2011) that failed to make a robust, positive case for the UK's membership of the EU (or even to explain adequately what it is). It was a consequence also of the ability of anti-EU campaigners to assert discursive hegemony over the public sphere, meaning that the discursive space in which debates on European integration were conducted were structured by Eurosceptic norms and assumptions in which the only legitimate defence of the UK's position as a member-state became that it was a 'necessary evil' (Hawkins, 2012). It is unsurprising, therefore, that the proposition of voting for an imperfect, opaque inevitability failed to enthuse voters to turn out in the summer rain and cast their vote. In contrast, the leave campaigns were able to imbue their movement with the sense of being a radical and emancipatory insurgency against a corrupt elite and failing institutions in ways that are revealed through the discourse theoretical concept of *fantasmatic logics*.

The EU as conceptual challenge

The EU poses a key conceptual challenge to the nationalist logic of Eurosceptic discourses. Less than a state but more than an international organisation, the EU has been identified as a unique (*sui generis*) political entity designed to respond to the unique historical circumstances from which it emerged. Its aim was to create interdependencies and manage conflict between powerful and wealthy states whose disputes had given rise to centuries of armed conflict which reached their apogee with WW2. The idea of the EU as a peace project which emerged in the aftermath of Europe's greatest catastrophe simply does not translate into British political discourse as was evident from the widespread outrage which greeted the EU award of the Nobel Peace Prize in 2012.

The narrative of the EU as a peace project runs counter to key foundational myths of modern Britain: that WW2 represents the highpoint of the British national mission, not a moment of defeat; that the UK as the victor in that conflict does not carry the moral baggage or weight of history of those countries it fought against; that Europe is a source of conflict and disorder from which the UK must insulate itself; that Britain's place in the world is not alongside its closest geographical neighbours but those it is tied to through the post-colonial bonds of language, culture and tradition and which stood with the UK in WW2.

Consequently, the fundamental motivation for European integration in countries which experienced the defeat or devastation of WW2 or which have emerged from subsequent periods of totalitarianism (i.e. in Southern and Eastern Europe) is absent in the UK (Diez-Medrano, 2003). Instead, EU membership is experienced not as recovery or regeneration but as loss and humiliation. Joining the European Community in 1973 represented an admission of defeat; a desperate attempt to find a new context in the world after the loss of empire and the degradation of what was once the most powerful economy on the globe. Membership of the EU continued to symbolise this humiliation and loss of control in the minds particularly of older citizens but also, albeit less overtly, in the unconscious assumptions structuring political and wider societal discourses.

The EU as a polity poses other conceptual challenges to those, in politics and the media, schooled (only) in the norms and practices of the Westminster model of government and politics. British political discourse is structured by an Anglo-centric form of political 'mono-lingualism,' which reflects the actual mono-lingualism of most political actors and commentators, as well as the wider population of the UK. This manifests itself in an inability to engage with the institutions of the EU or to understand its activities outside the conceptual framework supplied by Westminster politics and the wider norms and assumptions of the British political system. The widespread incredulity and incomprehension which met the formation of the coalition government in 2010 demonstrated how this can affect even analysis of their home turf. The seemingly opaque structures, institutions and processes, involving a shifting array of policy actors, which make up the EU's complex system of multi-level governance, simply cannot be deconstructed and domesticated within the analytical framework of the Westminster model. From this perspective the EU appears not just undemocratic but anti-democratic, not only because of the 'no demos theory' emanating from the Eurosceptics' foundational nationalism but because it does not resemble or appear to behave like a 'real' democracy (such as the UK).

In particular, there is a recurring rhetorical focus on the absence of a single, identifiable EU government which can be voted out of office, reflecting the British understanding of democracy as executive power held in check only by periodic and decisive elections. The European Parliament, meanwhile, is denigrated and derided by Eurosceptics as a pale imitation of the House of Commons and (partly because of this) is ignored by many voters. Yet the assumed compliance of the legislative to the will of the executive at Westminster means this is arguably less representative of its electorate than the EP within the normal legislative procedure and in its oversight of the budget and external agreements including free trade agreements. It is not by accident that the only other political system and electoral process covered with any seriousness in the UK (that of the USA, and mainly then the Presidential elections) is that which has the closest resemblance to the Westminster majoritarian system and is accessible to those who (only) speak English. The absence of equivalent analysis of either EU level affairs, or those of other EU member-states goes some way to explaining the incredibly low levels of understanding of the EU in the 'don't know, don't care' capital of the EU (Geddes, 2003), and the failure to see democratic process at the supra-national level, or across the channel, as equally valid and worthy of respect. From this perspective not only is democracy only possible within the nation-state, but real democracy exists only in one state, and perhaps one other to which the mother of parliaments gave birth.

The other lens through which the EU is viewed is that of empire. It is evident in pro-Brexit discourses that the racialised concept of the 'Anglosphere' – the majority-white, post-colonial states such as Australia, Canada, New Zealand and the USA emerging from the British empire – is identified as an alternative context for the UK to exist in the world outside the EU, or as a model for the UK to follow. Indeed, the Anglosphere emerged as a key conceptual component of Eurosceptic discourses which allowed them to function as a repository for the Anglo-British identity positions in which an emergent, post-devolution political Englishness finds its expression. As Wellings (2019) has argued, the conceptual slippage between ideas of Englishness and Britishness reflects inherent tensions between the creation of an explicitly English nationalism and the desire to maintain the UK, and the associated ideas of Britishness, as a apolitical community. Similarly, while Scottish (as well as Welsh and Irish) nationalism is articulated as a rejection of the political subjugation of an Anglo-dominated UK, the demographic, cultural and political dominance of England means the UK simply cannot function as the hostile 'other' to English nationalism. Consequently, English nationalism has found its identity in the form of Anglo-Britain, and the rejection of the repressive EU as the 'other' against which it is defined (Hawkins, 2012; Welling 2019).

Yet empire features in another more fundamental way in the referendum campaign, as in longer-standing Eurosceptic discourses, by providing the basic metaphor – of the dominator and the dominated – through which the EU and all international politics is understood. The British historical experience of trans-national governance is that of empire and, more specifically, imperial domination. This provides the conceptual prism through which the EU is viewed. Since the UK does not enjoy a position of dominance within the EU, having to compromise and negotiate as it does, it is assumed by Eurosceptics that it must therefore be subjugated (Hawkins, 2015). If it is not the master, it must be the servant. To draw analogies with contemporary social movements, the UK suffers from a form of 'post-imperial privilege' in which equality feels like repression. Interestingly, it is in part at least the same demographics (older, white, men) who have felt alienated by the recent call for greater racial and gender equality, who have been the most prone to oppose processes of European integration and the UK's membership of the EU. Indeed, a key component of the 'left behind' thesis, discussed in Chapter 2, is that it is feelings of cultural, as much if not more than economic, marginalisation which have led these groups to abandon the political mainstream for parties like UKIP and, latterly, to vote to leave the EU (see Goodwin and Health 2016; Sobolewska and Ford, 2020).

The final conceptual challenge posed by the EU relates to its motivation and purpose. Rejecting the foundational narrative of the EU as a peace project, as a means of managing interdependency and mitigating conflict or of constructing a democratic supra-national polity creates an intentional void at the heart of the EU project which Eurosceptics must seek to fill in other terms. As Zizek (1993) argues all nations are founded on the oppositional rejection of an allegedly hostile 'other' seen to threaten the nation or to present an object to achieving the national mission. This leads to the construction of fantasmatic and often racist myths about the real, but hidden intentions of those identified as the nation's 'others.' Within Eurosceptic discourses of British national identity, and within pro-Brexit interventions before the referendum, the EU functions as the other against which the UK is defined, but its intentions remain unclear. Just what is it *really* for? What do *they* really want? The idea of collaboration between neighbours, as political equals and for mutual gain, simply does not translate into the Eurosceptic world view, informed by the adversarial nature of Westminster politics, its winner-takes-all elections and its scepticism of coalition and compromise. The long shadow cast over this is the spectre of Empire. Seen through this prism the lofty ideals of the European project are either well-meaning but futile idealism, or subterfuge to hide more sinister motives. This scepticism about what the EU is *really* about creates a space which must be filled by alternative accounts of the EU's *raison d'être*. It is this space which is populated by the conspiratorial narratives promoted by the fantasmatic logics underpinning the pro-Brexit discourse. And it is this fear about the EU as an alien political entity which means that Brexit is not seen as the endgame by some Eurosceptics. Their goal was not simply to extricate the UK from the EU but to fundamentally undermine and existentially weaken the latter. The extent to which this version of Brexit comes to the fore will be crucial in determining the degree to which future UK governments pursue policies of constructive engagement or active divergence from the EU.

The EU as fantasy object

Not only is the EU politically, economic and culturally heterogeneous to the UK – the other against which Anglo-Britain is defined – it is identified as a source of conflict, disorder and threat from which the UK must insulate itself, drawing on a deeply sedimented topography of war and imperial conquest. From a political perspective, the EU looms across the channel as a quasi-imperial or neo-colonial power seeking to assert ever greater control over the UK. Yet it is perhaps in the area of economics that the division between the UK and the EU, and the threat posed to the former by the latter come into the starkest relief. As Zizek (1993: 203) argues, nationalist discourses attribute to the 'other' an excessive 'enjoyment,' often centred round their relationship to work. The European economic model involves a very different approach to free-market principles and the role of the state in regulating economic activity. Workers in the UK enjoy – and expect – lower levels of social protection and labour-market regulation than those in continental Europe. The two economic models, therefore, represent entirely different attitudes to work or, in Lacanian terms, different forms of enjoyment and processes for regulating this enjoyment. By attributing to the 'European' economies a strange and threatening form of work as 'enjoyment,' the coverage in the right-wing press operates not simply at the level of discursive separation but draws on an underlying fantasmatic support structure.

In this context, the EU, and the European economic model, function as an impediment to the realisation of the British national 'mission.' If it were not for the EU, it is argued, the UK would be even stronger and even more successful; it would achieve its rightful position in the world. The narrative constructed here suggests the possibility of the UK as a fully reconciled society once this impediment to its progress is overcome (see Glynos and Howarth, 2007: 147-8). This in turn holds out the possibility of a stable social order able to confer on the subject the fully-constituted identity it seeks. In this sense, the construction of the EU as economic impediment taps into the fundamental 'lack' at the heart of the subject, something which may help us better understand the strength of emotion which anti-EU discourses are able to generate.

The fantasmatic dimension of the pro-Brexit discourse identifies both a horrific account of the future which awaits the UK inside an unreformed, post-referendum EU and a beatific account of the apparently glorious future which would await the UK outside the confines of EU membership.

The horrific dimension of the narrative focuses principally on the idea of a 'hard remain' agenda according to which there would be a significant acceleration and deepening of integration following a remain vote which exists already in secret plans being held back from the public until the vote has been navigated. This focuses on plans to harmonise various aspects of economic policy, to expand QMV at the expense of the UK veto in the Council and, perhaps most controversially, the formation of a European army. It is in terms of immigration, associated with the allegedly inevitable eastward enlargement of the EU, however, that the fantasmatic logics resonated most effectively with its target public. Brexit campaigners focused consistently on the pressures that would be placed on frontline public services by population increases, the suppressive effect of new sources of labour on wages and the security threat posed by the arrival of criminal gangs and Islamic insurgents via the EU. These narratives resonated with wider feelings of cultural alienation and xenophobia identified among certain key demographics opposed to the EU and targeted by the leave campaigns (see Ford and Goodwin, 2014; Evans and Mellon, 2016).

In contrast to a future of decreasing political and economic autonomy and increasing immigration, the leave campaigns painted a utopian picture of the UK as an independent country. The UK would be able to make its own policies, govern its own economy, set its own trade policy and, crucially, control immigration while ceasing payments into the EU budget which could instead be spent on domestic priorities. At the same time, the UK and its citizens would be able to maintain all the current benefits it enjoyed as an EU member-state, reflecting the extent to which this discourse was characterised by a logic of British exceptionalism and an overestimate of its relative political and economic power vis-à-vis the EU. The implication throughout these contributions was that a political system which had prioritised 'others' could be realigned to serve the interests of what is termed here the (leave) people. Perhaps most crucially there was a punitive aspect to these discourses. Those who had been unfairly privileged – the national, European and global political and financial elites, as well as the outsiders they favoured over their 'own' people – would be taught a lesson. The tables would be reversed so the system would be made to work for the deserving majority not the undeserving minority.

Throughout the contributions analysed EU membership was experienced as a form of national humiliation from which the UK could finally free itself through the referendum. This invests the act of voting leave with huge emotive force: as an act of national salvation undertaken by a heroic vanguard people. Furthermore, leave campaigners succeeded in linking the act of national humiliation to the personal experiences of potential leave voters, many of whom were drawn from economically marginalised subpopulations (see Goodwin and Heath, 2016) or from sectors of society who *felt* they had been economically or culturally marginalised (see Dorling and Tomlinson, 2020). This included the older, socially conservative usually male voters whose ideas and values they felt were denigrated and ignored by the political establishment or were out of sync with a rapidly changing and often confusing world (see Goodwin and Milazzo, 2016). Nigel Farage, in particular, sought to create an association between the national and the personal, arguing that the lack of faith shown by the 'remain elite' in the UK's prospects outside the EU was actually a reflection of their lack of faith in the British people. Thus leaving the EU took on the significance of an act of national as well as individual renewal, which like nationalism more generally operated at a visceral, emotive level (Stavrakakis, 2005).

Compared with the often dry, technocratic and defensive discourses of the remain campaign, which focused largely on the economic case for remaining in the EU – something which failed to resonate with voters who felt they had not shared in the economic spoils that had supposedly arisen from EU membership – it is easy to see how the leave discourses were able to *interpellate* voters into their quasi-revolutionary movement. They offered exciting change where remain could speak only of an unsatisfying, imperfect but necessary *status quo*. In this respect, the referendum campaign reflected the inadequacy of the pro-European movement in the preceding decades, their failure to engage voters and the abdication by mainstream political actors of their responsibility to explain what the EU is, why it exists and its importance to the UK. There had been a systematic failure to redefine the UK as a European country and create a self-conscious European movement before 2016. Ironically, it was with the leave vote itself, and the sudden wave of concern this sent through sections of the population, that woke these latent Europeans from their lethargy and led to the emergence of what were perhaps the largest demonstrations of pro-European sentiment seen in any member-states in the people's vote marches in October 2018 and March 2019. Furthermore, the 'remainer' versus 'leaver' divide (and the wider set of values with which these are associated) has become a defining cleavage in British politics and supplied the conceptual vocabulary in which much subsequent political debate has been couched (see Sobolewska and Ford, 2020).

Contradictions and choices in the referendum and beyond

Glynos and Howarth (2007) argue that contradiction is one of the markers of ideological and fantasmatic discourses. The pro-Brexit discourse, as with longer-standing Eurosceptic discourses, is based on a number of seemingly contradictory positions about the UK and the EU. Most notably it is argued that the UK is at one and the same time the helpless victim of its controlling European overlords and a uniquely gifted and resourceful country which has an incomparable record of achievement and the ability to act as a global economic and political leader. While Brexiters may argue that it is EU membership which guarantees the former and precludes the latter, this leaves open the question as to how the UK ended up in (what was to become) the EU and why it is unable to pursue its interests within it. At the same time, the EU is depicted as politically corrupt and economically feckless, reliant on the UK to fund its ideological projects, most notable the Euro. Despite its outdated economic model and sclerotic institutions, the EU is apparently able to dominate and control the UK corralling it into ever closer political union on the inevitable path to a European super-state.

At the same time, there was a complete failure within the referendum debate to clarify the choices which leaving the EU would imply. The leave campaigns presented Brexit as being both an essential rupture with an unsatisfactory *status quo* while reassuring voters that nothing would change, at least in terms of the apparent benefits of EU membership. The period after the 2016 referendum was characterised by many of the themes and tropes which had characterised the short campaign and the longer-standing Eurosceptic discourses. In an article published four days after the referenda, Boris Johnson (*Telegraph*, 27 June 2016) restated his confused or misleading belief that the UK would maintain the same benefits it enjoyed as an EU member-state:

> I cannot stress too much that Britain is part of Europe, and always will be. There will still be intense and intensifying European cooperation and partnership in a huge number of fields [...]. EU citizens living in this country will have their rights fully protected, and the same goes for British citizens living in the EU. British people will still be able to go and work in the EU; to live; to travel; to study; to buy homes and to settle down [...] there will continue to be free trade, and access to the single market.

At the same time, the UK would be able to negotiate a fundamentally new political and economic relationship with the EU and the rest of the world:

> The only change - and it will not come in any great rush - is that the UK will extricate itself from the EU's extraordinary and opaque system of legislation: the vast and growing corpus of law enacted by a European Court of Justice from which there can be no appeal [...] to pass laws and set taxes according to the needs of the UK. Yes, the Government will be able to take back democratic control of immigration policy [...]. Yes, there will be a substantial sum of money which we will no longer send to Brussels, but which could be used on priorities such as the NHS. Yes, we will be able to do free trade deals with the growth economies of the world in a way that is currently forbidden.

This intervention is indicative of the wishful thinking or misunderstanding which not only characterised the referendum debate but would come to frame the post-referendum negotiations on the UK's withdrawal from the

EU and the subsequent discussions on the future trading, and broader strategic, relationship between the UK and the EU.

Beyond Brexit

The period after June 2016 was characterised as much by internal negotiations within the UK, within Parliament and even within the Conservative Party as it was by negotiations between the UK and the EU as policy actors who had promised mutually exclusive outcomes from the referendum debate were slowly forced to acknowledge and confront the implications of the decision the UK had made and the choices which this implied. In her Lancaster House speech in January 2017 Prime Minister Theresa May committed the UK to leaving both the EU customs union and the single market while setting out her desire for a unique and special partnership with the EU based around enduringly close trade and security relationships. The contradictions between divergence from and proximity to the EU, and their confrontation with the realities of what this divergence implied for the UK economy and for the position of Northern Ireland within the UK, resulted in the compromise agreement negotiated between members of her cabinet at Chequers in July 2018. The latter proved to be unsustainable within May's cabinet even before its first contact with the EU negotiating team leading to the resignations of both Brexit Secretary, David Davis, and Foreign Secretary, Boris Johnson, within days of the plan's announcement. May's critics on the right of the Conservative Party, and the hard-line members of the European Research Group, rejected May's plan for a 'backstop' agreement which would see the UK remain in a customs union and follow a common regulatory rule book with the EU until such time as a workable alternative solution could be found to avoid the implementation of a customs and regulatory border between the UK and the EU on the island of Ireland.

Throughout the negotiations May was criticised for not negotiating hard enough with the EU, for not insisting that the UK's demands would be met. This mirrored the criticisms of David Cameron during the re-negotiation of the UK's membership terms in February 2016; that he had asked for too little and conceded too much. The implication in both instances was that the UK was in a position of relative strength versus the EU and would be able to dictate the terms of its future relationship. This belief was reflected in the various claims that the UK held all the cards in the negotiations and that the EU would be forced to acquiesce to the UK's demands by German car makers and Italian vintners dependent on access to the British market. It reflected also the repeated claims in the referendum campaign about the UK superior economic model and the inherent weakness of the EU as a political actor, which would be unable to maintain a coherent front in negotiations with the UK.

The replacement of Theresa May as Prime Minister and her lead negotiator, Olly Robbins, by Johnson and David Frost in July 2019 was driven in part at least by the belief among Conservative Eurosceptics that if the UK negotiators were to stand firm, the EU would ultimately concede. In the end, Johnson traded May's 'backstop' – seen as a large concession by the EU side – for a 'front stop' in which Northern Ireland would effectively remain in the EU customs union and large parts of the single market, with a *de facto* regulatory and customs border with Great Britain being erected within the Irish sea. This maintained the open border on the island of Ireland and thus the UK's obligations under the 1998 Good Friday Agreement; but it had potentially huge ramifications on the territorial integrity of the UK and the operation of its own internal market. The cleavages between EU member-states – who demonstrated unwavering solidarity with a small member-state such as Ireland – and the resultant capitulation in the face of British demands again failed to materialise. Yet many of the issues within the withdrawal agreement remain live politically at the time of writing and negotiations between the UK and the EU to define the obligations of each party under the agreement, and manage its implementation, continue via the Joint Council established to manage this process.

The negotiations on the future relationship between the UK which began following the UK's exit from the EU on 31 January 2020 were characterised again by the belief that the UK would be able to set the terms of debate and that interests within EU would prove too disparate and weak to hold its common position. The negotiation continued to the very final days of the transition period which ended on 31 December that year, with the agreement only agreed politically between the UK government and the European Commission (on behalf of 27 EU member-states) on 24 December. This necessitated an emergency sitting of the permanent representatives to the EU (COREPER) on Christmas day to sign off the agreement on behalf of the Council and to authorise its provisional application just seven days before it came into effect on 1 January 2021. At the time of writing, only days after the last-minute deal was brokered, the Trade and Cooperation Agreement (TCA), an Association Agreement on the basis of Article 217 TFEU, still awaits formal ratification by the EP.

The implications of the agreement for trade and other interactions between the UK and the EU and its long-term sustainability thus remain unclear. The content of the agreement though reflected UK demands and the negotiating parameters mandated to the EU's lead negotiator, Michel Barnier, by the member-states. In return for tariff- and quota-free access to the EU single market (for goods meeting rule of origin requirements), the EU insisted on the inclusion of so-called 'level playing field' requirements on social and environmental standards and on state aid along with dispute resolution and enforcement procedures in case of infringements by either party. While the TCA creates an important framework for future engagement between the UK and the EU, many questions remain about its practical consequences for exporters and others and for the long-term viability of the new *status quo* it brings into effect.

Already in early January 2021 the border frictions created by the additional administrative requirements for exporting into the EU single market and customs union (as opposed to within them) appear to be having a significant trade diversionary effect for both UK exporters and those outside the UK unable or unwilling to comply with the red tape now involved in accessing the UK market. This includes significant difficulties receiving goods sent from Great Britain in Northern Ireland which for most intents and purposes remains in the EU regulatory orbit and subject to its customs code. Given the specific history of this province, the situation should supermarket shelves remain empty and existing supply chains break down could be the catalyst for significant political fallout from the TCA, which speaks to the wider instability of the agreement. The fishing industry, which featured so prominently in Brexit debates and was so totemic Eurosceptic mythology, has been so devastatingly affected in certain sectors by the new export barriers to its main European market that discussions about increased catch quotas may be moot by the time these are renegotiated in five years' time.

The intention or ability of the UK government to diverge from EU regulatory standards over time, potentially triggering retaliatory action from the EU, is unclear at this time but the decision to diverge, should it arise, could lead to further conflict between London and Brussels. Early signs suggest that the current UK government intends to pursue a policy of at least symbolic divergence from the EU, although it is impossible to know what the political consequences of this will be and if this approach will endure over time. It is, however, possible that such an approach, even at a rhetorical level, may undermine attempts to maintain vital economic and diplomatic relations with the EU on which the UK's prosperity and geopolitical influence depend. The multiple mechanism through which the agreement can be unilaterally cancelled by each of the parties, as well as the 5-year revision clause add to the sense that this agreement represents not an end point but a marker post in, and a structure to facilitate, a continually evolving UK-EU relationship. This model is reminiscent of the consistent state of flux, or punctuated equilibrium, which characterises Switzerland's relationship with the EU. As such the UK may find itself in a state of perpetual renegotiation with the EU, the dynamics of which may emerge only later in light of future political developments.

What is certain is the EU will remain a central reference point for UK policy-making and political debate. The UK formally regained control over certain aspects of public policy and its trade regime on terms largely dictated by the EU and its capacity for action domestically and internationally will continue to be structured by its relationship with the EU – albeit without the ability any longer to influence the policies of the latter. Many Brexit supporters will comes to understand the distinction between *de jure* and *de facto* sovereignty in the context of regional and global interdependency.

The widely predicted collapse by the EU and its last minute acquiescence to the UK's demands in the TCA negotiations, which Brexit supporters had continually predicted over the preceding 4 years, again failed to emerge. A key question is how and why Eurosceptics arrived at their apparently unshakable, yet misguided, faith in the ability of the UK to secure favourable terms of departure from, and future engagement with, the EU despite the obvious asymmetry between the parties in terms of size and power. The answer to this lies in the analysis presented above and in the preceding chapters. The EU exists as a conceptual anomaly within the nationalist logic of the Eurosceptic and pro-Brexit discourses. It is a collective entity made up of sovereign states, which remains less than a state itself (although the horrific-fantasmatic dimension of those discourses identify this as the ultimate *telos* of the European integration process). From the Euroscpetic perspective, which sees national interest in narrow, atomised and zero-sum terms, they believe that national imperative of these states must ultimately trump the solidarity of the collective. The ability to gain an advantage over a neighbour (i.e. through cutting side deals with the UK) will win out over their pursuit of common interests (i.e. protecting the integrity of the single market). This is the same logic through which they argued that the UK must escape the confines of the EU to gain its advantage and achieve its own national mission. Their mistake was to assume that this understanding of international politics and European integrations was shared beyond its border or represented a necessary and universal logic.

This mindset explains also why Brexit supporters, in the immediate aftermath of the referendum result, declared with joyful anticipation that the EU would not exist in ten years' time. Having seen the example of the UK, they believed, other states would be moved to follow suit. From their perspective this reflects the necessary logic of the nationalist world view. For those who see the EU as the latest in a long line of (unsuccessful) imperialist attempts to suppress the nation, as the natural and necessary form of political community, the EU *must* eventually fail. Nationalist sentiments and self-interest *must* eventually come to the fore and the structures around them collapse. In reality, the experience of Brexit has proved to be a sobering lesson for nationalist politicians across the EU, even populist movements highly critical of the EU have rowed back from the previous flirtations with cessation. The enduring solidarity with Ireland and between member-states has arguably left the EU stronger and more coherent, with a clearer sense of common identity and purpose than before Brexit. This should not lead to complacency as the subsequent difficulties faced by the EU in responding collectively to the Covid-19 pandemic demonstrate. Yet Brexit serves as a stark warning to other European peoples that the political reality outside the EU differs greatly to the rhetoric of utopian nationalists. As with the effective creation of a self-conscious European movement, and the foregrounding of previously latent European identities, seen in the UK, it is the great irony of Brexit that it has also reinforced and reinvigorated the

European integration project whose demise its supporters both predicted and sought to precipitate.

Contribution and limitations

The argument presented above adds to the previous literature on the referendum, particularly those studies which seek to place the result in its wider historical, cultural and discursive contexts (see Gifford, 2014; Wellings, 2019). It attempts to explain the appeal of the Brexit project – its underlying assumptions and the societal divisions it constructed – to the population of lower-middle-class Tory and more marginalised voters in provincial England identified by Dorling and Tomlinson (2020) as the key constituents of the Brexit vote. In addition, it adds to studies on the ideological underpinning of right-wing populist and anti-European movements by providing an in depth case study of the UK referendum debate experience (Vasilopoulou, 2018). In particular, it adds to the literature from critical discourse analysis on the language of right-wing populism (see Wodak, 2020), albeit from a slightly different theoretical starting point (and using the associated conceptual vocabulary). It builds also on previous studies of Eurosceptic discourses (Hawkins, 2012, 2015) and on the language of Brexit undertaken in the field of linguistics (Koller et al., 2019) by placing the Brexit debates in their wider discursive context.

While the study offers a detailed analysis of pro-Brexit discourse by key actors in the main two campaigns it excluded wider contributions such as those from the right-wing supporting commentariat and the newspaper opinion pages which were examined in previous studies. In addition, it excluded online content including the key campaign grounds of social media advertising. Nevertheless, the argument presented here focuses on the structure and content of leave arguments and their affective hold in terms of the critical logics as opposed to analysing the reception of particular forms of advertising and engagement on the recipient populations for which an analysis of Facebook content, for example, would have been more relevant. The analysis is also circumscribed by space available in a single volume and the resources available for a study such as that from which this book emerges. As such, it was not possible to present a close linguistic analysis of the contributions which fully exhausted their relevance to the referendum debate as discursive artefacts. Finally, the analytical categories employed here – the critical logics – sometimes require a false distinction to be drawn between different aspects of the pro-Brexit discourse. In reality the social, political and fantasmatic logics elide, overlap and are mutually reinforcing in a way in which it can be difficult to capture in the linear form of a monograph. As far as possible, the text assembled seeks to avoid repetition and overlap or the inclusion of superfluous or irrelevant material at different stages of the argument but the densely structured nature of the articles examined means it is difficult to strike a balance between precision and context. For this reason longer passages are at times quoted to show the interplay of different aspects of the discourse.

Summary

This book aimed to contribute to our understanding of the factors leading to the UK's vote to leave the EU on 23 June 2016 through a critical discourse analysis of the contributions of the main leave campaigners in the lead up to the vote. Through the concepts of *social* and *political* logics it examined the key assumptions and claims of the leave movement about the nature of the social and political worlds; the relationship between the UK and the EU; the expansive hegemonic project to deliver a majority coalition of voters by presenting the EU as a surface of inscription for a wider set of political grievances structured around a fundamental populist narrative of the exploitation of the people by a remote and self-interested elite. Finally, it offered an account of the affective hold of pro-Brexit discourses in terms of their *fantasmatic* logics, which contrasted a horrific future of domination and immigration inside the EU with the sense of political, economic and moral rejuvenation precipitated by Brexit. While EU membership can signify the rejection of a non-democratic past (eg Germany, Spain, Portugal, Greece) or the return to the European political mainstream (eg the post-communist states of central and Eastern Europe) or the insulation from trans-European conflict (eg France, Netherlands, Belgium), the defining metaphor of EU membership in the pro-Brexit discourses was the humiliation which the EU's institutional structures came to symbolise. Brexit, therefore, represented the final casting off of the UK's subjugation and exploitation by a European continent of which it was not truly part. The ability of Brexit supporters to connect the national with the personal means this was experienced by these voters at the most visceral level and the heroic act of voting leave became an act of personal as well as national salvation.

References

Alaimo, L. S. & Solivetti, L. M. 2019. Territorial Determinants of the Brexit Vote. *Social Indicators Research*, 144(2), 647–667.
Althusser, L. 1971. *Lenin and Philosophy, and Other Essays*. London, UK: New Left Books.
Anderson, B. 1991. *Imagined Communities*. London, UK: Verso.
Anderson, P. & Weymouth, A. 1999. *Insulting the Public?: The British Press and the European Union*. Harlow, UK: Longman.
Arnorsson, A. & Zoega, G. 2016. *On the Causes of Brexit*. Munich, Germany: Ludwig-Maximilian University.
Aspinwall, M. 2000. Structuring Europe: Powersharing Institutions and British Preferences on European Integration. *Political Studies*, 48(3), 415–442.
Aspinwall, M. 2004. *Rethinking Britain and Europe: Plurality Elections, Party Management and British Policy on European Integration: Plurality Elections, Party Management and British Policy in European Integration*. Manchester, UK: Manchester University Press.
Azrout, R., Van Spanje, J. & De Vreese, C. 2011. Talking Turkey: Anti-immigrant Attitudes and Their Effect on Support for Turkish Membership of the EU. *European Union Politics*, 12(1), 3–19.
Bache, I. & Jordan, A. 2006. *The Europeanization of British Politics*. London, UK: Palgrave Macmillan.
Baker, D., Gamble, A. & Ludlam, S. 1993. 1846... 1906... 1996? Conservative Splits and European Integration. *The Political Quarterly*, 64(4), 420–434.
Baker, D., Gamble, A. & Ludlam, S. 1994. The Parliamentary Siege of Maastricht 1993: Conservative Divisions and British Ratification. *Parliamentary Affairs*, 47(1), 37–60.
Baker, D., Gamble, A. & Seawright, D. 2002. Sovereign Nations and Global Markets: Modern British Conservatism and Hyperglobalism. *The British Journal of Politics and International Relations*, 4(4), 399–428.
Bar-On, T. 2008. Fascism to the Nouvelle Droite: The Dream of Pan-European Empire. *Journal of Contemporary European Studies*, 16(3), 327–345.
Becker, S. & Fetzer, T. 2016. Does Migration Cause Extreme Voting? *CAGE Online Working Paper Series*: CAGE.
Becker, S., Fetzer, T. & Novy, D. 2017. Is the Brexit vote disconnected from the European Union? In: Beck, T. & Underhill, G. (eds.) *Quo Vadis? Identity, Policy and the Future of the European Union*. London, UK: CEPR Press.

Beecham, R., Slingsby, A. & Brunsdon, C. 2018. Locally-varying Explanations Behind the United Kingdom's Vote to the Leave the European Union. *Journal of Spatial Information Science*, 16, 117–136.

Bennett, S. 2019. Values as tools of legitimation in EU and UK Brexit discourses. In: Koller, V., Kopf, S. & Miglbauer, M. (eds.) *Discourses of Brexit*. London, UK: Routledge.

Betz, H. 1994. *Radical Right-Wing Populism in Western Europe*. US: Palgrave Macmillan.

Billig, M. 1995. *Banal Nationalism*. London, UK: Sage.

Boomgaarden, H. G., Schuck, A. R. T., Elenbaas, M. & De Vreese, C. H. 2011. Mapping EU Attitudes: Conceptual and Empirical Dimensions of Euroscepticism and EU Support. *European Union Politics*, 12(2), 241–266.

Bootle, R. 2007. EU Treaty Threatens Economic Freedom. *Telegraph*, 22 October 2007.

Bouko, C. & Garcia, D. 2019. Citizens' reactions to Brexit on Twitter: A content and discourse analysis. In: Koller, V., Kopf, S. & Miglbauer, M. (eds.) *Discourses of Brexit*. London, UK: Routledge.

Bracher, M. 1996. Editor's Introduction. *Journal for the Psychoanalysis of Culture & Society*, 1.

Braun, V. & Clarke, V. 2006. Using Thematic Analysis in Psychology. *Qualitative Research in Psychology*, 3(2), 77–101.

Buckledee, S. 2018. *The Language of Brexit: How Britain Talked Its Way Out of the European Union*. London, UK: Bloomsbury.

Bustikova, L. 2009. The Extreme Right in Eastern Europe: EU Accession and the Quality of Governance. *Journal of Contemporary European Studies*, 17(2), 223–239.

Butler, J., Laclau, E. & Žižek, S. 2000. *Contingency, Hegemony, Universality: Contemporary Dialogues On The Left*. London, UK: Verso.

Cap, P. 2019. 'Britain is full to bursting point!'. Immigration themes in the Brexit discourse of the UK Independence Party. In: Koller, V., Kopf, S. & Miglbauer, M. (eds.) *Discourses of Brexit*. London, UK: Routledge.

Carey, S. 2002. Undivided Loyalties: Is National Identity an Obstacle to European Integration? *European Union Politics*, 3(4), 387–413.

Carey, S. & Burton, J. 2004. Research Note: The Influence of the Press in Shaping Public Opinion towards the European Union in Britain. *Political Studies*, 52(3), 623–640.

Carl, N., Dennison, J. & Evans, G. 2018. European but Not European Enough: An Explanation for Brexit. *European Union Politics*, 20(2), 282–304.

Carreras, M. 2019. 'What Do We Have to Lose?': Local Economic Decline, Prospect Theory, and Support for Brexit. *Electoral Studies*, 62, 102094.

Cecil, N. 2004. The EU is Out to Destroy Britain. *Sun*, 1 December 2004.

Chapman, J. 2007. Brown to Fly Out for the Great EU Cave-In. *Mail*, 18 October 2007.

Charteris-Black, J. 2019. *Metaphors of Brexit: No Cherries on the Cake?* London, UK: Palgrave Macmillan.

Christin, T. & Trechsel, A. H. 2002. Joining the EU?: Explaining Public Opinion in Switzerland. *European Union Politics*, 3(4), 415–443.

Clarke, H., Goodwin, M. & Whiteley, P. 2017. *Brexit: Why Britain Voted to Leave the European Union*. Cambridge, UK: Cambridge University Press.

Clarke, H. D., Goodwin, M. & Whiteley, P. 2017. Why Britain Voted for Brexit: An Individual-Level Analysis of the 2016 Referendum Vote. *Parliamentary Affairs*, 70(3), 439–464.

Clements, B., Lynch, P. & Whitaker, P. 2013. The low salience of European integration for British voters means that UKIP will have to expand their platform to gain more support. Available from: https://blogs.lse.ac.uk/europpblog/2013/03/08/low-salience-european-integration-british-voters-ukip-expand-platform-support/.

Conti, N. 2003. *Party Attitudes to European Integration: A Longitudinal Analysis of the Italian Case*. Brighton, Sussex: Sussex European Institute.

Copeland, P. & Copsey, N. 2017. Rethinking Britain and the European Union: Politicians, the Media and Public Opinion Reconsidered. *JCMS: Journal of Common Market Studies*, 55, 709–726.

Curtice, J. 2016. Brexit: Behind the Referendum. *Political Insight*, 7(2), 4–7.

Daddow, O. 2012. The UK Media and 'Europe': From Permissive Consensus to Destructive Dissent. *International Affairs*, 88(6), 1219–1236.

Daddow, O. 2015. Performing Euroscepticism: The UK Press and Cameron's Bloomberg Speech. In: Tournier-Sol, K. & Gifford, C. (eds.) *The UK Challenge to Europeanization*. London, UK: Palgrave Macmillan.

Daddow, O. & Gaskarth, J. 2011. Introduction: Blair, Brown and New Labour's Foreign Policy, 1997–2010. In: Daddow, O. & Gaskarth, J. (eds.) *British Foreign Policy*. London, UK: Palgrave Macmillan.

Davis, D. 2016. The people want Brexit and elitist politicians need to start listening to them. *Mirror*, 13 June 2016.

De Saussure, F. 1974. *Course in General Linguistics*. London, UK: Fontana.

De Vreese, C. H. & Boomgaarden, H. G. 2005. Projecting EU Referendums: Fear of Immigration and Support for European Integration. *European Union Politics*, 6(1), 59–82.

De Vreese, C. H., Boomgaarden, H. G. & Semetko, H. A. 2008. Hard and Soft: Public Support for Turkish Membership in the EU. *European Union Politics*, 9(4), 511–530.

Demata, M. 2019. 'The referendum result delivered a clear message': Jeremy Corbyn's populist discourse. In: Koller, V., Kopf, S. & Miglbauer, M. (eds.) *Discourses of Brexit*. London, UK: Routledge.

Derrida, J. 1978. *Writing and Difference*. London, UK: Routledge.

Diez-Medrano, J. 2003. *Framing Europe: Attitudes to European Integration in Germany, Spain, and the United Kingdom*. NJ, USA: Princeton University Press.

Diez, T. 1999. *Die EU lesen: Diskursive Knotenpunkte in der britischen Europadebatte*. Opladen, Germany: Leske und Budrich.

Dorling, D. 2016. Brexit: The Decision of a Divided Country. *BMJ*, 354, i3697.

Dorling, D. & Tomlinson, S. 2020. *Rule Britannia: Brexit and the End of Empire*. London, UK: Biteback Publishing.

Duncan Smith, I. 2016. The only way to bring order to our borders is to quit the EU. *Express*, 1 June 2016.

Duncan Smith, I. 2016. We need Aussie rules to close British door on mass immigration. *Mail*, 5 June 2016.

Duverger, M. 1954. *Political Parties: Their Organization and Activity in the Modern State*. London, UK: Methuen & Company.

Evans, D. 1996. *An Introductory Dictionary of Lacanian Psychoanalysis*. Hove, UK: Routledge.

Evans, G. & Mellon, J. 2016. Working Class Votes and Conservative Losses: Solving the UKIP Puzzle. *Parliamentary Affairs*, 69(2), 464–479.

Evans, G. & Menon, A. 2017. *Brexit and British Politics*. London, UK: John Wiley & Sons.

Evans, G. & Prosser, C. 2016. Was it always a done deal? The relative impact of short and long term influences on referendum voting. *EPOP Annual Meeting*. University of Kent, UK.

Farage, N. 2016. 'Reject this pathetic deal' Nigel Farage slams PM for 'utter surrender' to EU dictatorship. *Express*, 2 February 2016.

Farage, N. 2016. It costs £55 MILLION a day to be an EU member - and for what? *Express*, 7 February 2016.

Farage, N. 2016. Britain must leave the EU and control own borders. *Express*, 11 February 2016.

Farage, N. 2016. The Dutch referendum shows how the internet is taking back power from our Europhile elites. *Telegraph*, 6 April 2016.

Farage, N. 2016. The EU's green ambitions have cost thousands of jobs in the UK. *Express*, 27 April 2016.

Farage, N. 2016. Even lifelong Labour families are committed to leaving the EU. *Express*, 4 May 2016.

Farage, N. 2016. Nigel Farage's EU diary: 'Leave campaign MUST woo Labour voters to win referendum.' *Express*, 11 May 2016.

Farage, N. 2016. Nigel Farage's EU diary: Time to Liven Up the Debate. *Express*, 18 May 2016.

Farage, N. 2016. Nigel Farage's EU diary: We're on a roll to finally quitting Brussels. *Express*, 25 May 2016.

Farage, N. 2016. Don't let David Cameron and George Osborne fool you: here's what my vision of Britain really looks like. *Telegraph*, 10 June 2016.

Farage, N. 2016. UKIP advertising campaign sends a message that we are better OUT. *Express*, 15 June 2016.

Farage, N. 2016. Britain should be a proper democracy and the only way that can happen is Brexit. *Mirror*, 20 June 2016.

Farage, N. 2016. On Thursday Vote for Independence. *Express*, 21 June 2016.

Farage, N., Pursglove, T. & Hoey, K. 2016. We're putting country before party to win. *Telegraph*, 7 January 2016.

Fink, B. 1995. *The Lacanian Subject: Between Language and Jouissance*. Princeton, NJ, USA: Princeton University Press.

Flood, C. 2002. Euroscepticism: A Problematic Concept. *32nd Annual UACES Conference*. Belfast, UK.

Ford, R. & Goodwin, M. 2014. *Revolt on the Right: Explaining Support for the Radical Right in Britain*. Abingdon, UK: Routledge.

Forster, A. 2002. *Euroscepticism in Contemporary British Politics: Opposition to Europe in the Conservative and Labour Parties since 1945*. London, UK: Routledge.

Foucault, M. 1972. *The Archaeology of Knowledge*. London, UK: Tavistock.

Fox, L. 2016. Fear Won't Stop Brits. *The Sun*, 14 February 2016.

Fox, L. 2016. Bullying Bojo will backfire on Tories. *Mail*, 12 June 2016.

Frosini, J. O. & Gilbert, M. F. 2020. The Brexit Car Crash: Using E.H. Carr to Explain Britain's Choice to Leave the European Union in 2016. *Journal of European Public Policy*, 27(5), 761–778.

Gavin, N. T. 2000. Imagining Europe: Political Identity and British Television Coverage of the European Economy. *The British Journal of Politics and International Relations*, 2(3), 352–373.

Geddes, A. 2003. *The European Union and British Politics*. Basingstoke, UK: Palgrave Macmillan.

George, S. 1998. *An Awkward Partner. Britain in the European Community*. Oxford, UK: Oxford University Press.

Gifford, C. 2006. The Rise of Post-imperial Populism: The Case of Right-wing Euroscepticism in Britain. *European Journal of Political Research*, 45(5), 851–869.

Gifford, C. 2010. The UK and the European Union: Dimensions of Sovereignty and the Problem of Eurosceptic Britishness. *Parliamentary Affairs*, 63(2), 321–338.

Gifford, C. 2014. The People Against Europe: The Eurosceptic Challenge to the United Kingdom's Coalition Government. *JCMS: Journal of Common Market Studies*, 52(3), 512–528.

Gifford, C. 2016. The United Kingdom's Eurosceptic Political Economy. *The British Journal of Politics and International Relations*, 18(4), 779–794.

Gifford, C. & Tournier-Sol, K. 2015. Introduction: The Structure of British Euroscepticism. In: Tournier-Sol, K. & Gifford, C. (eds.) *The UK Challenge to Europeanization*. London, UK: Palgrave Macmillan.

Glynos, J. & Howarth, D. 2007. *Logics of Critical Explanation in Social and Political Theory* (1st ed.). Oxford, UK: Routledge.

Goodwin, M. & Heath, O. 2016. Brexit vote explained: poverty, low skills and lack of opportunities.

Goodwin, M. J. & Heath, O. 2016. The 2016 Referendum, Brexit and the Left Behind: An Aggregate-level Analysis of the Result. *The Political Quarterly*, 87(3), 323–332.

Goodwin, M. & Milazzo, C. 2016. *UKIP: Inside the Campaign to Redraw the Map of British Politics*. Oxford, UK: Oxford University Press.

Gove, M. 2016. It pains me to say it, but too often the EU has left Britain with no control when it matters. *Telegraph*, 21 February 2016.

Gove, M. 2016. A united Tory party will make Britain better. *Telegraph*, 20 March 2016.

Gove, M. 2016. Think the EU's bad now? Wait until Albania joins. *Mail*, 30 April 2016.

Gove, M. 2016. Would you now vote to join? If not, then why opt to stay in? *The Times*, 16 June 2016.

Gramsci, A. 1971. *Prison Notebooks*. London, UK: Lawrence & Wishart.

Haesly, R. 2001. Euroskeptics, Europhiles and Instrumental Europeans: European Attachment in Scotland and Wales. *European Union Politics*, 2(1), 81–102.

Hainsworth, P. 2008. *The Extreme Right in Western Europe*. London, UK: Routledge.

Halikiopoulou, D., Nanou, K. & Vasilopoulou, S. 2012. The Paradox of Nationalism: The Common Denominator of Radical Right and Radical Left Euroscepticism. *European Journal of Political Research*, 51(4), 504–539.

Hannan, D. 2004. 'Now I Can Get Back to the Business of Ignoring You.' *Telegraph*, 13 June 2004.

Hannan, D. 2005. Genocide Argument is the Last Resort of the Euro-Zealots. *Telegraph*, 14 May 2005.

Hansen, L. 2006. *Security as Practice: Discourse Analysis and the Bosnian War*. London, UK: Routledge.

Hansson, S. 2019. Brexit and blame avoidance: Officeholders' discursive strategies of self-preservation. In: Koller, V., Kopf, S. & Miglbauer, M. (eds.) *Discourses of Brexit*. London, UK: Routledge.

Harmsen, R. & Spiering, M. 2004. Introduction: Euroscepticism and the Evolution of European Political Debate. In: Harmsen, R. & Spiering, M. (eds.) *Euroscepticism: Party Politics, National Identity and European Integration*. Amsterdam, the Netherlands: Rodopi.

Harris, R. & Charlton, M. 2016. Voting out of the European Union: Exploring the geography of Leave. *Environment and Planning A: Economy and Space*, 48(11), 2116–2128.

Hawkins, B. 2012. Nation, Separation and Threat: An Analysis of British Media Discourses on the European Union Treaty Reform Process. *JCMS: Journal of Common Market Studies*, 50(4), 561–577.

Hawkins, B. 2015. Fantasies of Subjugation: A Discourse Theoretical Account of British Policy on the European Union. *Critical Policy Studies*, 9(2), 139–157.

Hearne, D., Semmens-Wheeler, R. & Hill, K. 2019. Explaining the Brexit Vote: A Socioeconomic and Psychological Exploration of the Referendum Vote. In: Ruyter, A. & Nielson, B. (eds.) *Brexit Negotiations after article 50: Assessing Process, Progress and Impact. 1 edn, vol. 1, Brexit Negotiations After Article 50: Assessing Process, Progress and Impact*. London, UK: Emerald Publishing.

Heffer, S. 2005. Europe and a Conspiracy of Silence. *Mail*, 13 May 2005.

Helm, T. 2007. Tories Commit to Binding Referendums on EU. *Telegraph*, 2 October 2007.

Helm, T. & Evans-Pritchard, A. 2004. EU 'triple axis' gangs up on Blair. *Telegraph*, 7 November 2004.

Henderson, M. 2007. Middle England has Lots of Time for Europe. *Telegraph*, 27 October 2007.

Hennessy, P. 2005. No Comment, No Opinion, and No Advice, Because People are Obviously Not Interested in My Advice. *Telegraph*, 19 June 2005.

Hitchens, P. 2005. Just Say Non! *Mail*, 15 May 2005.

Hobolt, S. B. 2016. The Brexit Vote: A Divided Nation, a Divided Continent. *Journal of European Public Policy*, 23(19), 1259–1277.

Hobolt, S. B. & De Vries, C. E. 2016. Public Support for European Integration. *Annual Review of Political Science*, 19(1), 413–432.

Hobolt, S. B., Van Der Brug, W., De Vreese, C. H., Boomgaarden, H. G. & Hinrichsen, M. C. 2011. Religious Intolerance and Euroscepticism. *European Union Politics*, 12(3), 359–379.

Hooghe, L. 2007. What Drives Euroskepticism?: Party-Public Cueing, Ideology and Strategic Opportunity. *European Union Politics*, 8(1), 5–12.

Hooghe, L. & Marks, G. 2005. Calculation, Community and Cues: Public Opinion on European Integration. *European Union Politics*, 6(4), 419–443.

Hooghe, L. & Marks, G. 2007. Sources of Euroscepticism. *Acta Politica*, 42(2), 119–127.

Hooghe, L. & Marks, G. 2009. A Postfunctionalist Theory of European Integration: From Permissive Consensus to Constraining Dissensus. *British Journal of Political Science*, 39(1), 1–23.

Howard, M., Duncan Smith, I., Lamont, N. & Lawson, N. 2016. Former Tory Leaders and Chancellors Accuse George Osborne of 'Ludicrous Scaremongering.' *Telegraph*, 15 June 2016.

Howarth, D. 2000. *Discourse*. Buckingham, UK: Open University Press.

Howarth, D. & Stavrakakis, Y. 2000. Introducing discourse theory and political analysis. In: Howarth, D., Norval, A. & Stavrakakis, Y. (eds.) *Discourse Theory and Political Analysis: Identities, Hegemonies and Social Change*. Manchester, UK: Manchester University Press.

Howe, M. 2007. How Britain can negotiate a New Relationship with the EU. *Telegraph*, 19 October 2007.

Hughes, D. 2004. Our Ball and Chain. *Mail*, 29 October 2004.

Hutchings, P. B. & Sullivan, K. E. 2019. Prejudice and the Brexit Vote: A Tangled Web. *Palgrave Communications*, 5(1), 5.

Iakhnis, E., Rathbun, B., Reifler, J. & Scotto, T. J. 2018. Populist Referendum: Was 'Brexit' An Expression of Nativist and Anti-elitist Sentiment? *Research & Politics*, 5, 1–7, https://doi.org/10.1177/2053168018773964

Ichijo, A. 2002. Nation and Europe in the British Public Discourse. The cases of Media and Political Elite Debates. *EURONAT Project: Representations of Europe and the Nation in Current and Prospective Member-States: Media, Elites and Civil Society*.

Ignazi, P. 2006. *Extreme Right Parties in Western Europe*. Oxford: Oxford University Press.

Jenkins, B. & Sofos, S. 1996. National and Nationalism in Contemporary Europe: A Theoretical Perspective. In: Jenkins, B. & Sofos, S. (eds.) *Nation and Identity in Contemporary Europe*. London, UK: Routledge.

Johnson, B. 2016. There is only one way to get the change we want – Vote Go. *Telegraph*, 22 February 2016.

Johnson, B. 2016. Erdogan is now silencing his critics in Germany – don't joke about it. *Telegraph*, 18 April 2016.

Johnson, B. 2016. Do Bremainers really think voters will be cowed by the likes of Obama? *Telegraph*, 25 April 2016.

Johnson, B. 2016. Of course our City fat cats love the EU – it's why they earn so much. *Telegraph*, 15 May 2016.

Johnson, B. 2016. 'The future is bright, the future is Brexit – it's history in the making.' *Telegraph*, 23 May 2016.

Johnson, B. 2016. The only continent with lower growth than Europe is Antarctica. *Telegraph*, 30 May 2016.

Johnson, B. 2016. You must vote to Leave, or wake up with the worst hangover in history. *Telegraph*, 6 June 2016.

Johnson, B. 2016. When it comes to the single market, you don't have to be in it to win it. *Telegraph*, 12 June 2016.

Johnson, B. 2016. It's time for us to leave the EU and to go global. *The Independent*, 16 June 2016.

Johnson, B. 2016. Please Vote to Leave on Thursday - we'll never get this chance again. *Telegraph*, 20 June 2016.

Johnson, B. 2016. "A Brexit vote is a vote to reclaim your democracy and decisions that affect your life." *Mirror*, 21 June 2016.

Johnson, B. 2016. UK was 'sick man of Europe'. Now we're racing ahead – we must LEAVE. *Express*, 22 June 2016.

Johnson, B. 2016. I cannot stress too much that Britain is part of Europe – and always will be. *Telegraph*, 27 June 2016.

Johnson, B. & Gove, M. 2016. Getting the facts clear on the economic risks of remaining in the EU – Vote Leave's letter to David Cameron. *Telegraph*, 5 June 2016.

Johnston, R., Pattie, C. & Hartman, T. 2020. Who Follows the Leader? Leadership Heuristics and Valence Voting at the UK's 2016 Brexit Referendum. *Innovation: The European Journal of Social Science Research*, 34, 28–43, DOI: 10.1080/13511610.2020.1746905

Jørgensen, M. & Phillips, L. 2002. *Discourse Analysis as Theory and Method*. London, UK: SAGE.

Kaufmann, E. 2016. It's NOT the economy, stupid: Brexit as a story of personal values. Available from: https://blogs.lse.ac.uk/politicsandpolicy/personal-values-brexit-vote/.

Kavanagh, T. 2005. France will say Non. *Sun*, 26 May 2005.

Koller, V., Kopf, S. & Miglbauer, M. 2019. *Discourses of Brexit*. Abingdon, UK: Routledge.

Kopf, S. 2019. 'Get your shyte together Britain': Wikipedians' treatment of Brexit. In: Koller, V., Kopf, S. & Miglbauer, M. (eds.) *Discourses of Brexit*. London, UK: Routledge.

Lacan, J. 1977. *Ecrits: A Selection*. London, UK: Tavistock.

Laclau, E. 1990. *New Reflections on the Revolution of Our Time*. London, UK: Verso.

Laclau, E. 1996. *Emancipation(s)*. London, UK: Verso.

Laclau, E. 1995. Subject of Politics, Politics of the Subject. *Differences*, 7, 145–164.

Laclau, E. 2000. Identity and Hegemony: The Role of Universality in the Constitution of Political Logics. In: Butler, J., Laclau, E. and Zizek, S. (eds). *Contingency, Hegemony and Universality: Contemporary Discourses on the Left*. London: Verso.

Laclau, E. 2005. *On Populist Reason*. London, UK: Verso.

Laclau, E. & Mouffe, C. 1985. *Hegemony and Socialist Strategy*. London, UK: Verso.

Laclau, E. & Zac, L. 1994. Minding the gap: the subject of politics. In: Laclau, E. (ed.) *The Making of Political Identities*. London, UK: Verso.

Lalić-Krstin, G. & Silaški, N. 2019. 'Don't go brexin' my heart': The ludic aspects of Brexit-induced neologisms. In: Koller, V., Kopf, S. & Miglbauer, M. (eds.) *Discourses of Brexit*. London, UK: Routledge.

Lamont, N. 2007. Looser EU Ties Can Only Help British Economy. *Telegraph*, 17 October 2007.

Lea, R. 2007. How Britain Can Get the Best Out of Europe. *Telegraph*, 16 October 2007.

Lefort, C. 1988. *Democracy and Political Theory*. Cambridge, UK: Polity.

Lutzky, U. & Kehoe, A. 2019. 'Friends don't let friends go Brexiting without a mandate': Changing discourses of Brexit in The Guardian. In: Koller, V., Kopf, S. & Miglbauer, M. (eds.) *Discourses of Brexit*. London, UK: Routledge.

Macshane, D. 2016. *Brexit: How Britain left Europe*. London, UK: Bloomsbury.

Mail. 2003. Blair "Doomed to Fail" Over Europe. *Mail*, 22 June 2003.

Mail. 2005. Brown's swipe at the EU economic failures. *Mail*, 17 May 2005.

References

Manley, D., Jones, K. & Johnston, R. 2017. The Geography of Brexit – What Geography? Modelling and Predicting the Outcome Across 380 Local Authorities. *Local Economy*, 32(3), 183–203.

Mclaren, L. M. 2002. Public Support for the European Union: Cost/Benefit Analysis or Perceived Cultural Threat? *The Journal of Politics*, 64(2), 551–566.

Mclaren, L. 2006. *Identity, Interests and Attitudes to European Integration*: London, UK: Palgrave Macmillan.

Moore, C. 2004. Blair has Signed Us Up to the Sharia of Euro-Enthusiasts. *Telegraph*, 30 October 2004.

Moore, M. & Ramsay, G. 2017. UK media coverage of the 2016 EU Referendum campaign.

Mudde, C. 2004. The Populist Zeitgeist. *Government and Opposition*, 39(4), 541–563.

Mudde, C. 2007. *Populist Radical Right Parties in Europe*: Cambridge, UK: Cambridge University Press.

Mudde, C. 2010. The Populist Radical Right: A Pathological Normalcy. *West European Politics*, 33(6), 1167–1186.

Mudde, C. 2018. *The Far Right Today*. Cambridge, UK: John Wiley & Sons.

Musolff, A. 2019. Brexit as 'having your cake and eating it': the discourse career of a proverb. In: Koller, V., Kopf, S. & Miglbauer, M. (eds.) *Discourses of Brexit*. London, UK: Routledge.

Myers, T. 2003. *Slavoj Zizek (Routledge Critical Thinkers)*. Abingdon, UK: Routledge.

Oliver, S. 2003. She is the new Joan of Arc. But this time the English are her friends. *Mail*, 15 June 2003.

Park, Y. & Kim, Y. 2018. Explaining the Brexit Referendum: The Role of Worker Skill Level in Voter Decisions. *The Political Quarterly*, 89(4), 640–648.

Pascoe-Watson, G. 2003. Sting in the Tail. *The Sun*, 20 June 2003.

Patel, P. 2016. This poster is insulting, offensive and plumbs new depths in scaremongering. *Mail*, 27 May 2016.

Patel, P. 2016. The wealthy leaders of Remain will never know the devestating effect EU immigration has on ordinary people. *Telegraph*, 28 May 2016.

Patel, P. 2016. Aussie migrants points system is a corking idea. *The Sun*, 1 June 2016.

Pelinka, A. 2013. Right-Wing Populism: concept and typology. In: Wodak, R., Khosravinik, M. & Mral, B. (eds.) *Right-Wing Populism in Europe: Politics and Discourse*. London, UK: Bloomsbury.

Phillips, M. 2003. Going, Going GONE! Or how Labour is selling off 1,000 years of British history. *Mail*, 12 May 2003.

Phillips, M. 2004. Unlike you, Mr Blair, we can distinguish myth from reality. The only delusions are yours. *Mail*, 21 June 2004.

Phillips, M. 2005. This Vote Reveals the Lies at the Heart of the European Project. *Mail*, 30 May 2005.

Rees Mogg, J. 2016. Barack Obama's unwanted intervention should spur on the Brexit campaign. *Mirror*, 27 March 2016.

Rees Mogg, J. 2016. Yes, victory may be bloody…but it will be final. *Mail*, 29 May 2016.

Rennie, D. 2005. Eurosceptics are unlikely source of sympathy for lofty Giscard. *Telegraph*, 26 May 2005.

Rennie, D. 2005. Schroder and Chirac ponder years of decline. *Telegraph*, 3 June 2005.

Richardson, J. 2006. *Analysing Newspapers: An Approach from Critical Discourse Analysis*. Basingstoke, UK: Palgrave Macmillan.
Rudolph, L. 2020. Turning Out to Turn Down the EU: The Mobilisation of Occasional Voters and Brexit. *Journal of European Public Policy*, 27(12), 1858–1878.
Ruzza, C. & Pejovic, M. 2019. Populism at Work: The Language of the Brexiteers and the European Union. *Critical Discourse Studies*, 16(4), 432–448.
Shipman, T. 2016 *All Out War: The Full Story of How Brexit Sank Britain's Political Class*. London, UK: Harper Collins.
Sobolewska, M. & Ford, R. 2020. *Brexitland: Identity, Diversity and the Reshaping of British Politics*. Cambridge, UK: Cambridge University Press.
Spiering, M. 2004. British Euroscepticism. In: Harmsen, R. & Spiering, M. (eds.) *Euroscepticism: Party Politics, National Identity and European Integration*. Amsterdam, the Netherlands: Rodopi.
Stares, J. 2005. EU bosses told: no "reckless competition" in the sauna. *Telegraph*, 1 May 2005.
Startin, N. 2015. Have We Reached a Tipping Point? The Mainstreaming of Euroscepticism in the UK. *International Political Science Review*, 36(3), 311–323.
Stavrakakis, Y. 1999. *Lacan and the Political*. London, UK: Routledge.
Stavrakakis, Y. 2005. Passions of Identification: Discourse, Enjoyment, and European Identity. In: Howarth, D. & Torfing, J. (eds.) *Discourse Theory in European Politics*. London, UK: Palgrave Macmillan.
Taggart, P. 1998. A Touchstone of Dissent: Euroscepticism in Contemporary Western European Party Systems. *European Journal of Political Research*, 33(3), 363–388.
Taggart, P. & Szczerbiak, A. 2001. *Parties, Positions and Europe: Euroscepticism in the EU Candidate States of Central and Eastern Europe*. Brighton, UK: Sussex European Institute.
Taggart, P. & Szczerbiak, A. 2004. Contemporary Euroscepticism in the Party Systems of the European Union Candidate States of Central and Eastern Europe. *European Journal of Political Research*, 43(1), 1–27.
Taggart, P. & Szczerbiak, A. 2013. Coming in from the Cold? Euroscepticism, Government Participation and Party Positions on Europe. *JCMS: Journal of Common Market Studies*, 51(1), 17–37.
Taylor, S. 2001. Locating and conducting discourse analytic research. In: Wetherell, M., Taylor, S. & Yates, S. (eds.) *Discourse as Data: A Guide for Analysis*. London, UK: SAGE.
Telegraph. 2004. After Europe, it's time to face some home truths. *Telegraph*, 15 June 2004.
Telegraph. 2004. Draft changes basic contract between us and Brussels. *Telegraph*, 21 June 2004.
Telegraph. 2004. Save us from an EU army. *Telegraph*, 22 November 2004.
Telegraph. 2006. Tories warn of EU constitution revival. *Telegraph*, 25 June 2006.
The Sun. 2005. Sun says: It's our future. *The Sun*, 26 May 2005.
Torfing, J. 1999. *New Theories of Discourse: Laclau, Mouffe and Zizek*: Oxford, UK: Blackwell.
Trimble, D. 2007. Time for some fresh thinking on Europe. *Telegraph*, 20 October 2007.
Usherwood, S. 2002. Opposition to the European Union in the UK: The Dilemma of Public Opinion and Party Management. *Government and Opposition*, 37(2), 211–230.

Usherwood, S. 2018. The Third Era of British Euroscepticism: Brexit as a Paradigm Shift. *The Political Quarterly*, 89(4), 553–559.
Usherwood, S. & Startin, N. 2013. Euroscepticism as a Persistent Phenomenon. *JCMS: Journal of Common Market Studies*, 51(1), 1–16.
Utley, T. 2005. We keep on mentioning the war because we treasure our freedom. *Telegraph*, 13 May 2005.
Vasilopoulou, S. 2013. Continuity and Change in the Study of Euroscepticism: Plus ça Change? *JCMS: Journal of Common Market Studies*, 51(1), 153–168.
Vasilopoulou, S. 2018. *Far Right Parties and Euroscepticism: Patterns of Opposition*. USA: Rowman & Littlefield Publishers.
Vines, E. 2014. Reframing English Nationalism and Euroscepticism: From populism to the British Political Tradition. *British Politics*, 9(3), 255–274.
Watson, M. 2018. Brexit, the Left Behind and the Let Down: The Political Abstraction of 'the Economy' and the UK's EU Referendum. *British Politics*, 13(1), 17–30.
Wellings, B. 2002. Empire-Nation: National and Imperial Discourses in England. *Nations and Nationalism*, 8(1), 95–109.
Wellings, B. 2008. English Nationalism and Euroscepticism. *Identity and Governance in England Seminar Series*. Edinburgh, Scotland: University of Edinburgh.
Wellings, B. 2010. Losing the Peace: Euroscepticism and the Foundations of Contemporary English Nationalism. *Nations and Nationalism*, 16(3), 488–505.
Wellings, B. 2012. *English Nationalism and Euroscepticism: Losing the Peace*. Bern, Switzerland: Peter Lang.
Wellings, B. 2019. *English Nationalism, Brexit and the Anglosphere: Wider Still and Wider*. Manchester, UK: Manchester University Press.
Wellings, B. & Baxendale, H. 2015. Euroscepticism and the Anglosphere: Traditions and Dilemmas in Contemporary English Nationalism. *JCMS: Journal of Common Market Studies*, 53(1), 123–139.
Wenzl, N. 2019. 'This is about the kind of Britain we are': National identities as constructed in parliamentary debates about EU membership. In: Koller, V., Kopf, S. & Miglbauer, M. (eds.) *Discourses of Brexit*. London, UK: Routledge.
Wodak, R. 2013. 'Anything Goes' – The Haiderization of Europe. In: Wodak, R., Khosravinik, M. & Mral, B. (eds.) *Rightwing Populism in Europe: Politics and Discourse*. London, UK: Bloomsbury.
Wodak, R. 2020. *The Politics of Fear: The Shameless Normalization of Far-Right Discourse*. London, UK: SAGE.
Wodak, R., Khosravinik, M. & Mral, B. (eds.) 2013. *Right-Wing Populism in Europe: Politics and Discourse*. London, UK: Bloomsbury.
Wolfson, S. 2004. Vote No to the Constitution, and Save Europe from Itself (Again). *Telegraph*, 29 October 2004.
Zappavigna, M. 2019. Ambient affiliation and #Brexit: Negotiating values about experts through censure and ridicule. In: Koller, V., Kopf, S. & Miglbauer, M. (eds.) *Discourses of Brexit*. London, UK: Routledge.
Zappettini, F. 2019. The official vision for 'global Britain': Brexit as rupture and continuity between free trade, liberal internationalism and 'values'. In: Koller, V., Kopf, S. & Miglbauer, M. (eds.) *Discourses of Brexit*. London, UK: Routledge.
Zizek, S. 1989. *The Sublime Object of Ideology*. London, UK: Verso.
Zizek, S. 1993. *Tarrying with the Negative*. Durham, NC: Duke University Press.

Index

A
Abu Hamza 98
Act of Union, 1707 27
'Anglo-Britain' 9
Anglo-British identity 163–164
  See also English national identity; identity groups, positive affirmation of; national identity; social logics, EU identity
Anglo-centric concept of Britishess 157, 160
Anglosphere 27, 90, 163
(Anti-)democracy 80–84, 99, 162
anti-elitist sentiments 13
anti-EU sentiment, hostility toward other cultures 28
anti-immigrant sentiments 111
Association Agreement, Article 217 TFEU 170
asylum seekers 95–97

B
Bamford, Anthony 87
Banks, Arron 6
Barking and Dagenham 12, 144–146
Barnier, Michael 170
Battle of Plassey, 1757 80
'beatific and horrific' dimensions of fantasy 55
beatific dimension, taking back control 129–131, 137; Brexit, as national renewal 131–135
Becker, S. 16–17
Beecham, R. 12, 15
Benn, Tony 158
Berlaymont Building 72
'Better Together' campaign 29
Bexley 12

big business 106–107
'big Other' 47
Billig, Michael 44
Blair, Tony 22, 62, 64, 91, 114, 140
'Blairite,' Labour Party 22
Blunkett, David 150
Bootle, Roger 69
'bosses club' EU as 157–158
Brexit: beyond 169–172; as conceptual challenge 161–165; discourse 119; as fantasy object 165–167; as hegemonic project 157–160; as keyword, Lexis-Nexis 58; as populist insurgency 160–161; resasons for 157; studies of 4
  See also pro-Brexit discourse; war and legacy, Brexit veterans
Brexit, as national renewal 131–135
Britain, France and EU 64
Britain, Germany and the EU 64–65
Britain and 'Europe,' positioning 67
Britain as Europe's savior 73–74
Britain's European 'other': EU as a colonial power 67–68; positioning Britain and 'Europe' 67
Britain Stronger in Europe 1
British constitutional tradition 27
British exceptionalism 2–3, 73
Britishness, English conception of 4–5
'British way of life' 76
'Britons' 80
Brown, Gordon 22, 68, 114
Brussels *See* EU
Bush, George 140
Butler, Judith 54

C
Cameron, David 5, 13, 104, 114, 126, 137–138, 154, 169
Carey, Sean 28

Carl, Noah 15, 17
Carswell, Douglas 4
Cash, Bill 6, 19
Charter of Fundamental Rights 70–71
'*che vuoi*?' ('what do you want?') 49
China 70
Christin, T. 28
Churchill, Winston 79–80
citizens' rights 19
Clarke, Harold 13–14
Clegg, Nick 153
coded messages 147–149
Communist Manifesto 47
conceptual framework: equivalence, difference, and limits of discourse 36; hegemony 36–38
Conservative Brexiters 123
Conservative Party 3–6, 29, 102, 113–114, 120, 146, 158, 169; and Euroscepticism 22
Conservative Party voter preferences 15–16
Constitutional Treaty 74
control, ever closer 84–85
Corbyn, Jeremy 13, 29, 102, 114, 151
Corbynite, Labour Party 22
COREPER, member-state Permanent Representations to the EU 170
Council of Ministers 68
Court of Justice of the European Union (CJEU) 24, 84
Covid-19 pandemic 172
Cox, Geoffrey 82
critical explanation, logics of 51–56
critical logics approach 7–8
cultural 'othering' 72

D
Dagenham 151
The Daily Express 7, 58
The Daily Mail 2, 57–58
The Daily Mirror 24, 57–58
The Daily Star 58
The Daily Telegraph 7, 57–58
Davis, David 57, 59, 114–116, 169
debate parameters 2
De jure /de facto sovereignty, understanding differences 84, 171
'Democrat Revolution' 44
demographic and socioeconomic factors (voters preferences) 16–17
demographics, referendum voters 12–14
deprivation, voting preferences 12

Derrida, Jacques 34
de Saussure, Ferdinand 34–35
Diez-Medrano, Juan 29–30
discourses 35–36
discourse theory, deploying: logics of critical explanation 51–56; media coverage of EU treaty reform process 56–60
discourse theory, Lacan and the subject, Laclaue and Mouffe's concept of the subject 39–42
discourse theory and nationalism: construction of political enemies 47–50; power of nationalist discourses 45–47
discursive strategies 4
dislocation and lack of structure 42
Djukanovic, Milo 127–128
'the don't know, don't care' capital (UK as) 23
Dorling, Danny 14–16, 159
Duncan Smith, Iain 22, 57, 59–60, 92, 95–96, 111, 120, 126, 135–136
Dyson, James 87

E
Eastern expansion, EU 127
Economic and Monetary Union (EMU) 19
education level, voting preferences 12
Electoral Commission 6
elite, definition of 120
embedded Euroscepticism: Britain as Europe's saviour 73–74; Britain's European 'other' 66–68; critical logics of Eurosceptic discourse 75–77; EU as economic other 68–71; EU politics as zero-sum game 63–66; Europe as cultural 'other' 71–72; hegemony of the Eurosceptic discourse 74–75; leaving the European Union 72–73; nationalist logic, European politics 62–63
emotional/fantasmatic investment 141
England 11
English (Anglo-British) nationalism 27
English national identity 157
Erdogan, Recep Tayyip 99
EU: affect on UK 2–3; as alien political entity 163–164; or 'Brussels' elite 103–107; as colonial power 67–68; as foreign, colonial power 85–86; as polity 162; regulatory standards 23, 63, 68, 72, 74, 87, 89, 91, 107, 123, 129,

135, 165, 171; and UK values, contrast between 25
EU (COREPER, member-state Permanent Representations to the EU) 170
EU as economic 'other': euro as economic catasrophe 91–92; eurozone as disciplinary control 92–94; international trade 89–91; single market 88–89
EU as economic other 68–71
EU as political 'other': (Anti-)democracy 80–84; control, ever closer 84–85; EU as foreign, colonial power 85–86
EU as source of unlimited migration: freedom of movement and asylum seekers 95–97; immigration as security threat 97–99; migration and European economy 95
'the EU juggernaut' 124
Euro 68–69, 100, 125
Eurobarometer surveys 29
Eurocentric model 87
'Euro-crisis' 91
'Europe' (European Union) 5
'EUropean' 9
European Army 144–145
European Commission 24, 84
European Council, 2005 63
European Economic Area 73
European economic model 68–69, 87, 95, 100, 165, 168–169
European Parliament (EP) 20, 163
European Union, leaving 72–73
"Europhiles'/'EU dreamers'/'true believers'/Euro-fanatics' 62
Eurosceptic discourse 9, 34, 56, 119, 122, 161, 163, 172; critical logics of 75–77; hegemony of 74–75
Euroscepticism: and (Anglo-British) national identity 25–27, 32–33; wider research context 18–23
Euroscepticsim 3–5, 11
Eurosceptic tropes 2, 78, 158
Eurozone 68, 87, 92, 125–126, 133; debt crisis of 17; as disciplinary control 92–94; ongoing crisis in 95
EU single market 171 *See also* single market
EU treaty reform process 4, 58, 61; European reform 132
Evans-Pritchard, A. 65
exhcange rate mechanism, withdrawal of UK 17

The Express 23, 60, 160
'extraction' society 106–107

F
Facebook 2
fantasmatic logics 8, 25, 53–56, 76–77, 120, 137, 140–141, 157, 161, 174
fantasmatic logics, horrific dimension 35, 76, 121–129, 141, 166
fantasmatic logics: the national is personal 153–155
fantasmatic model 169–170
Farage, Nigel 5–7, 13, 25, 31, 58–60, 141, 159–160
Farage, Nigel and *Leave.EU*: fantasmatic logics: national is personal 153–155; *political logics* 144–153; social logics 142–144
'Faragist' 9
Field, Frank 29, 114
Financial Times 57
Fontainebleau European Council meeting, 1948 126
Ford, Robert 13, 158
Foucault, Michel 34
Fox, Liam 57, 59, 89, 96, 123–124, 129, 136, 138
Franco-German alliance 65
freedom of movement 95–97
free-market principles 169
Frost, David 169–170

G
Geddes, Andrew 23
Ger-exit 21
Germany 64–65
Gifford, Chris 22, 31
global financial elite 105–106
'global variable' 12
Glynos, Jason 34, 51–56
Goldman Sachs 106, 113
Good Friday Agreement, 1998 170
Goodwin, Matthew 12, 14, 158
Gove, Michael 25, 57, 59–60, 80–81, 84–85, 87, 92, 97–98, 105–106, 114, 117, 124, 127–130, 133, 138–139, 160
Gramsci, Antonio 34, 37
The Guardian 60
The Guardian/Observer 57–58

H
Hackney 12
Hague, William 22

Halikiopoulou, Daphne 20
Hannan, Daniel 19, 62, 89
'hard remain' 161, 170
Haringey 12
Havering 12
Heath, Oliver 12, 14
Heffer, Simon 69
hegemony 36–38
Hegemony and Socialist Strategy (1985: 115 ff) 39, 42
Helm, Toby 65
Henderson, Michael 74
Hennessy, Patrick 63
Hillingdon 12
Hitchens, Peter 64, 70
Hoey, Kate 29, 60, 146
home control (leaving the EU) 134
  See also pro-Brexit discourse
Hooghe, Lisbet 28
horrific dimension 35, 76, 141, 166
horrific dimension: 'hard' remain: the Eurozone 125–126; opening the floodgates 126–128
House of Commons 163
Howard, Michael 60
Howarth, David 34–35, 51–56
Howe, Martin 66, 72–73
Hughes, David 70
humiliation, EU membership as 136–140

I
The I 58, 117
identity groups, positive affirmation of 156
immigration 116–117, 144
immigration, not talking about 149–153
immigration as class politics 111–118; interpellating the Lexit vote 113–116; platitudes of reasonableness 116–118
immigration as security threat 97–99
immigration debate, reframing 116–118
The Independent 58
Iraq 140
Ireland 170
Islam, influence of 21
'Islamist sympathisers' 97

J
Jenkin, Bernard 6
Johnson, Boris 7, 13, 57, 59–60, 79–80, 83–84, 86–92, 94–95, 98, 103–107, 116–118, 122–127, 129–133, 135, 137–138, 147–149, 160, 169–170
jouissance 39, 49–51, 54, 76
JP Morgan 106
Juncker, Jean-Claude 147
Justus Lipsius Building 63

K
Kaufman, Eric 13
The Know 6

L
Labour 7, 13
Labour Party 29, 102, 113–114, 150–151, 158
Labour voters 15, 159
Lacan, Jacques *See* conceptual framework; discourse theory, Lacan and the subject; discourse theory and nationalism
Lacanian idea of fantasy 141
Laclau, E. 8, 31–32, 53–55, 67
  See also conceptual framework; discourse theory, Lacan and the subject; discourse theory and nationalism
Lambeth 12
Lamont, Norman 60, 72
Lawson, Nigel 60
Lea, Ruth 72
leave areas 161
leave elite, actions of 4
Leave.EU (2016 referendum) 6–7, 9, 31, 60, 142, 159–160
(Leave) people, constructing: old fashion common sense 108; standing up to remain bullies 108–110; voting 'Leave' as heroic act 110–111
Leeds 11
Lefort, Claude 44
'left behind' voters 12, 160
Lexis-Nexis database, keyword search 57–58
Lexit vote, interpellating 113–116
Lexit voters 102
Liberal Democrats 29, 153
'liberal leavers' 89
Liverpool 11
logic of difference 53, 76
logic of equivalence 53, 75–76
logic of nationalism 77
Logics of Critical Explanation in the

Index

Social Sciences (Glynos and Howarth) 51
logics of equivalence and difference 102
London 11–12, 14

M

Maastricht era 3–4, 6, 158
  See also Treaty on European Union (Maastricht Treaty) (TEU)
MacShane, Dennis 3
The Mail 23, 57–58, 64
Mail on Sunday 57
Major, John 3–4, 19, 21, 126
Manchester 11
man of the people 147–149
Marks, Gary 28
Marxist concept of ideology, Gramsci 34
May, Theresa 82, 169–170
McShane, Demmis 62
media 2, 23–25
media, importance of 32
Mellon, Jim 6
Merkel, Angela 99, 136
Middle England (referendum votes) 11
migration and European economy 95
Milosevic, Slobodan 127–128
minimum wage 95
The Mirror 23, 58, 60, 117–118
Mogg, Jacob Rees 57, 59, 80, 83, 89–90, 105, 123, 132, 138–140, 148
'mono-lingualism' 162
Montenegro 127–128
Moore, Charles 71
Mouffe, Chantal 8, 31, 53, 55
  See also conceptual framework; discourse theory, Lacan and the subject; discourse theory and nationalism

N

nation, function of 44
national identity 26, 32
nationalist discourses, construction of political enemies 47–50
nationalist logic, European politics 62–63
national 'mission' 76
'national Thing' 72
'nation-state' 62
NATO 123
Newcastle 11
'New' Labour Home Secretary 150
newpapers 56–58, 60

News of the World 57
nodal point 36
'no demos' theory 80
non-democratic past, EU countries 174
North Atlantic Treaty Organization (NATO) 97
Northern Ireland 4, 9, 11, 83, 157, 169, 171

O

Obama, Barack 138, 140
objectivities 37
The Observer 57, 60
older, white, male, voters 154
Oliver, Sarah 70
'ontical/ontological distinction' 55
opinion poll data 3
opinion polls data 160–161
ordinary, decent (leave) people 146, 150
Osborne, George 104, 114, 154

P

Page Hall 150–151
'paleosceptics' 6
parallel (remain elite) economy 113
Patel, Priti 57, 59, 112–113, 115, 118, 127, 130–131
PEGIDA (transl. Patriotic Europeans Against the Islamaification of the West) 21
Phillips, Melanie 65, 71
platitudes of reasonableness 116–118
po-faced and dull, elite as 148
political enemies, construction of 47–50
political logics 8, 52–53, 55–56, 102, 141, 157, 174; of all parties and none 145–146; man of the people 147–149; not talking about immigration 149–153; ordinary decent people 144–145; war and legacy for Brexit veterans 146–147
'political subjectivity' 39, 41
post-structuralism, Derrida 34
post-structuralist discourse theory (DT) 2–5, 7–8, 31, 33, 141
  See also conceptual framework; discourse theory, Lacan and the subject; discourse theory and nationalism
post-structuralist psychoanalytic theory, Lacan 34
'£350 million a week' 105

Powell, Enoch 158
pre-symbolic enjoyment 39
print media 56–58, 60
pro-Brexit discourse 9, 61, 78, 131, 133–135, 156, 172
'Project Fear' 91, 136
public opinion 28–30
public persona 147–149
punitive reforms, immigration 151
Pursglove, Tom 60, 146

Q
Qualified Majority Voting (QMV) 68

R
Real, Lacan 39, 54
Reckless, Mark 4, 19
'red-tops' 23
'red wall' 15
referendum, 23 June 2016 18–23; critical logics approach 7–8; delivering 5–7; Euroscepticism and (Anglo-British) national identity 25–28; Eurosepticism and vote results 1–5; *Leave.EU* 6; long-term factors 16–18; media, importance of 2–3, 23–25; public opinion 28–30; results of, explained 11–17; right-wing populism 30–32; social class, voting preferences 15–16; turnout 14–15; voter demographics 7
referendum, contradictions and choices 167–169
'Remain' 104
'remain elite' 120
remain elite, constructing: big business 106–107; global financial elite 105–106; national elite 104–105
Rennie, David 65
right-wing media 24
right-wing populism 30–32
Robbins, Oliver (Olly) 169–170
Rudolph, Lukas 14
'the rule of law mechanism' 124

S
Scotland 11, 14
Scottish nationalists 27–28
sedimented 37
self-transparent consciousness/cogito 38
single market 88–89
Sobolewska, Marie 13
social class, voting preferences 12, 15–16

'social Europe' 3–4
social logics 8, 52, 56, 102, 111, 119–120, 141–144, 157, 174
social logics, EU identity 122
social logics, *Vote Leave* discourse: EU as economic 'other' 86–94; EU as political 'other' 79–86; EU as source of unlimited migration 94–99
'society effects' 35
South East region, voter turnout 14
South vs. North of England, voter preferences 15
specific vector 54
split ego 38
Stability and Growth Pact 92
The Star 23
Stares, James 72
Startin, Nicholas 61
status quo See Brexit, beyond; Brexit voters; Conservative Party; Eurosceptic discourse; Farage, Nigel; Johnson, Boris; media, importance of; *Vote Leave* discourse
Stavrakakis, Yannis 47
Stringer, Graham 6
structuralist linguistics 34
Stuart, Gisela 6
subject positions 39
subjects 38–41
The Sun 2, 23–24, 74
The Sunday People 58, 60
The Sun/News of the World 57–58
The Sun/NOTW 58
surfaces of inscription 37, 44
Sutton 12
Syria and Iraq wars 127
Szczerbiak, Aleks 20

T
tabloid sector, media 23
Taggart, Paul 20
'take back control' 105
Tarrying with the Negative (Zizek) 48
The Telegraph 23, 58, 60, 64, 71–72, 74, 118, 160
TEU (Treaty on European Union) *See* Treaty on European Union (Maastricht Treaty) (TEU)
Thatcher, Margaret 3, 88–89, 126, 158
theory of discourse, Foucault 34
Thing (national) 49

Tice, Richard 6
Times 23, 58
Tomlinson, S. 14–16, 159
Torfing, Jacob 43–44
Tory heartlands 102
Tory voter preferences 16
Trade and Cooperation Agreement (TCA) 170
Trades Union Congress 6
Treaty of Lisbon (ToL) 61, 64, 72, 94, 100, 124
Treaty on European Union (Maastricht Treaty) (TEU) 3–4, 19, 66, 70, 126, 157
Trechsel, Alexander 28
Trimble, David 66, 70, 73
'triple axis' (France, Spain and Germany) 65
turnout, referendum voters 14–15

U
UK-EU relationship 171
UKIP (United Kingdom Independence Party) 13–14, 16, 19, 22, 31, 158–159, 163
UK Prime Ministers 5
UK's special treatment 65–66
UK Statistics Authority 1
UK vs EU incompatibility 24
unitary political actor, EU as 66
United Kingdom Independence Party (UKIP 5–6
United States of America (USA) 70
Usherwood, Simon 19, 61
Utley, Tom 64–65

V
Vasilopoulou, Sofia 19
Vote Leave 118, 131, 135
Vote Leave campaign 6–7, 9, 29, 57, 60, 115–116, 119–120, 159–160
Vote Leave discourse 155–156
Vote Leave discourse, fantasmatic logics: beatific dimension: taking back control 129–135; EU membership as humiliation 136–140; horrific dimension: 'hard' remain 121–129; the lyin' and the unicorns: all the benefits and none of the costs 135–136
Vote Leave discourse, poliical logic of: constructing the (Leave) people 107–111; constructing the remain elite 103–107; immigration as class politics 107–111
voting preferences 12–14

W
Wales 4, 11, 31
war and legacy, Brexit veterans 146–147
Watson, Matthew 12
Wellings, Ben 26, 44, 163
Welsh nationalists 28
we vs. they 79
Wodak, Ruth 30
Wolfson, Simon 74
World Trade Organization (WTO) 71
WW1 65, 74
WW2 27, 64, 124, 162

Y
Yugoslav conflict 97

Z
Zappavigna, Marie 25
zero-sum game, EU politics as 90; Britain, France and EU 64; Britain, Germany and the EU 64–65; the Franco-german alliance 65; UK's special treatment 65–66
Zizek, Slavoj 48–50, 54, 72, 85, 163, 165